American
Temperance
Movements

Cycles of Reform

SOCIAL MOVEMENTS PAST AND PRESENT

Irwin T. Sanders, Editor

American
Temperance
Movements

Cycles of Reform

Jack S. Blocker Jr.

Twayne Publishers • Boston
A Division of G. K. Hall & Co.

American Temperance Movements: Cycles of Reform
Jack S. Blocker Jr.

Copyright © 1989 by Jack S. Blocker Jr.
All rights reserved.
Published by Twayne Publishers
A Division of G. K. Hall & Co.
70 Lincoln Street, Boston, Massachusetts 02111

Copyediting supervised by Barbara Sutton.
Book Production by Gabrielle B. McDonald.
Typeset by Compset, Inc., of Beverly, Massachusetts.

Printed on permanent/durable acid-free paper
and bound in the United States of America

First Printing 1989

Library of Congress Cataloging in Publication Data

Blocker, Jack S.
    American temperance movements : cycles of reform / Jack S.
Blocker, Jr.
        p. cm. — (Social movements past and present)
    Bibliography: p.
    Includes index.
    ISBN 0-8057-9727-0 (alk. paper). ISBN 0-8057-9728-9 (pbk. : alk.
paper)
        1. Temperance—United States—Societies, etc.—History.
    2. Prohibition—United States—Societies, etc.—History.   I. Title.
    II. Series.
    HV5229.B55 1988
    178′ 1′06073—dc19   88-16554
                                                         CIP

To David and his grandparents

Contents

About the Author

Jack S. Blocker Jr. received an undergraduate degree from the University of Florida and the Ph.D. from the University of Wisconsin. His previous books include *Retreat from Reform: The Prohibition Movement in the United States, 1890–1913* (1976) and *"Give to the Winds Thy Fears": The Women's Temperance Crusade, 1873–1874* (1985). He edited a volume of essays, *Alcohol, Reform and Society: The Liquor Issue in Social Context* (1979), and has published articles on American social and political history in *The Historian, Canadian Review of American Studies, Ohio History,* and *Signs: Journal of Women in Culture and Society.* In 1984–86 he served as president of the Alcohol and Temperance History Group. He is professor of history at Huron College, London, Ontario.

Preface

This book has two objectives. The first is to provide for the general reader a synthesis of the historical research on drinking and temperance in the United States published during the past century and especially during the last quarter century. This literature has simultaneously demonstrated the complexity and importance of its subject and made possible a clearer understanding of many issues involved; among others, the topics of drink and temperance among women, in the working class, and in the South can now be addressed with more confidence than was possible a short time ago.

Many authors have contributed to this research, but two deserve special mention: Joseph Gusfield and Norman Clark. Gusfield's *Symbolic Crusade* played a large part in defining the issues of modern temperance research; although I disagree with Gusfield on many points, this book enters a debate that he more than anyone else began. Where Gusfield described temperance reform as an indirect response to drinking through conflicts over values and life-styles, Norman Clark's *Deliver Us from Evil* argued eloquently that temperance reformers' case against drinking often was not overstated or misdirected. This insight provides the starting point for my attempt to determine when and where temperance reform can be explained by patterns of drinking and alcoholic damage and when it cannot.

The link between drinking and temperance reform is only one issue, although it is a central one, raised by recent research. This research has made possible a dialogue on many issues implicit in the study of those who drink and those who attempt to control drinking. To advance that dialogue is the second purpose of this book.

Besides the many scholars whose work has made this book both possible and necessary, I have incurred numerous debts to friends and colleagues in the course of its preparation. Bob Hohner not only read and commented incisively on most of the draft chapters, but he also was most helpful in introducing me to the *Nota Bene* word-processing package and in arranging extended access to an indispensable microfilm reader. Craig Simpson took time from a busy schedule to give a thoughtful critique to early formulations of two chapters. George Emery and Ian Tyrrell read the entire manuscript; one could not ask for more gracious, knowledgeable, and insightful critics. Others who read and commented on various portions of the manuscript include Don Alcock, Athenaide Dallett, Des Dutrizac, David Flaherty, Dick Fuke, Jean Matthews, Bruce Mellett, Ron Roizen, and Ian Steele. The help I have received has made this a better book than it would otherwise have been. Responsibility for errors that remain is, unfortunately, mine alone.

Such a project as this would not have been possible without the courteous and efficient work of the staff in the Interlibrary Loan Department of the D. B. Weldon Library at the University of Western Ontario.

This book is dedicated to my son, David Gordon Blocker, whose presence has animated this project—and the rest of his parents' lives as well—in ways even he cannot imagine. I hope his time with his father has not been unduly restricted by the requirements of composition. The dedication also recognizes four other people who have encouraged me in important though different ways. My wife's parents, Gordon and Diane Smith, have provided affection and occasionally crucial child care. My own parents, Jack and Bonnie Blocker, have given love, high expectations, and personal examples of accomplishment. To speak of recompense in such matters is inappropriate; besides, none was expected in the giving.

Jack S. Blocker Jr.

Huron College

Introduction

This is a story about the efforts of millions of Americans during a period of roughly two hundred years to control drinking—sometimes their own, but mostly that of other people. Referring to the *idea* motivating temperance reformers, historians customarily refer to the sum of their actions as "the temperance movement." Such a unitary label proves useful in directing attention to a basic agreement underlying the disparate activities of generations of reformers over a long period of time: they all felt that too much drinking was going on, and they all wanted drinking brought under control. But because both drinking and efforts to control drinking have flourished in so many different historical settings—so many different Americas—the various contexts may have given rise to not one but several movements, united in their goal but different in other ways. Exploring this possibility requires a preliminary look at two of the central concerns of this book: who temperance reformers were and what they did.

During the years of national Prohibition (1920–33) a stereotype grew up that has dogged temperance reformers ever since. Given classic expression in the cartoons of Rollin Kirby for the *New York World,* the stereotypical prohibitionist was a dour, cadaverous, puritanical fellow who was obviously not enjoying life very much because of his single-minded devotion to preventing other people from enjoying theirs. Misanthropy, not altruism, drove him; to his fellow human beings he offered a police club, not a helping hand. From his misguided efforts flowed violence and crime. The repeal of national Prohibition added to this stereotype the label of losers, a sour minority who tried but inevitably failed to deflect Americans from full enjoyment of the fruits of their abundant economy. For many years popular stereotype and historical perception coincided, as historians found inconceivable the notion that alcoholic damage could have any place in the causal chains they constructed to explain reform and reformers. Loss of status, loss of deference, loss of the certainty of sin, loss of traditional work habits, loss of order, virtually any lack but the lack of sobriety in the world around them was imaginable as motivation for reformers.

In truth, temperance folk have been such a varied lot that any attempt to put them into a single suit of clothes necessarily makes an awkward fit. Let us begin with the most basic of social distinctions. Although men led the reform in its early days, from the beginning women saw temperance as a woman's issue, one that allowed them to address important problems in their daily lives. In 1873 temperance crusaders launched the largest mass movement of women to that point in American history, and for the next quarter century women provided the reform's most creative and dynamic leadership. From Quaker women in the eighteenth century through the Woman's Christian Temperance Union (WCTU) of the nineteenth century to Mothers Against Drunk Driving (MADD) today, women have entered temperance reform for their own reasons and pursued temperance reform in their own ways.

Temperance was clearly a middle-class reform. Perhaps it was even the quintessential middle-class reform, since it articulated most forcefully and forced upon the public most articulately the theme of self-control that lay at the core of middle-class identity in the nineteenth century. Even so, temperance reform has never been solely a mirror for the middle class. During much of the reform's long history, most notably during the Washingtonian period in the early 1840s, it received substantial infusions of support from working-class men and women. From an early point in temperance history manufacturers' desires for sober and therefore (they thought) productive workers brought powerful recruits to the cause, and during the Progressive period of the early twentieth century a segment of the corporate elite provided crucial backing. To be sure, such supporters represented the classic American bourgeoisie, owners of the means of production, profit maximizers to the core. But their argument that poverty was caused by intemperance never wholly persuaded other temperance folk of both the working and middle classes, who continued to organize and support strikes and to seek alliances with other dissenters from bourgeois orthodoxy.

Like other early–nineteenth-century reforms, the temperance ethos and organization originated in the Northeast. But unlike antislavery and women's rights, the temperance center of gravity shifted elsewhere. By the late nineteenth century the Midwest became the prohibitionist heartland. Even during the years of northeastern hegemony a significant number of southerners gave their support to the cause, and the final wave of enthusiasm for statewide prohibition before the Eighteenth Amendment began in 1907 in Oklahoma and Alabama. That wave finally spread from the South through the West and Midwest to isolate the Northeast, which had changed in a hundred years from a temperance stronghold to the last redoubt of the antiprohibition forces.

Because rural states led the final march to national Prohibition, temperance has long been considered essentially an expression of rural values. We now know better. In the late eighteenth century the new ideology of temperance appeared first in Philadelphia, the metropolis of the infant Republic. When voluntary associations appeared to promote the temperance ideology, they found ready support in burgeoning industrial cities such as Worcester, Massachusetts, and Rochester, New York. Women's mass action against saloons later in the century sprang from small towns. Today, although the United States has become an urban nation, the temperance cause still flourishes in new forms in its cities and suburbs.

In the pages of the *Dictionary of American Temperance Biography* one finds few names that suggest other than English origins, and in this respect the leadership seems to have reflected faithfully the backgrounds of most temperance folk. Nevertheless, other groups have embraced temperance reform to control drinking within or outside their own group. During the antebellum period some blacks organized their own temperance societies while others joined white-dominated associations. Scandinavian-Americans during the late nineteenth and early twentieth centuries were overrepresented in the temperance ranks. Hibernian Total Abstinence Societies were not unknown, and Irish-Americans took the lead in organizing the Catholic Total Abstinence Union in 1872. During a triumphant American tour in the 1850s the Irish temperance priest Theobald Mathew persuaded thousands of his transplanted countrymen to take the total abstinence pledge. The presence of recruits such as these has served as a constant reminder that temperance reform must shape its strategies to the reality of a multicultural nation.

A similar point might be made about religion. Evangelical Protestant lay people and clergy have usually provided the bulk of temperance leadership and grass-roots support. At times, however, nonevangelical Protestants have played key roles, and the existence of the Catholic Total Abstinence Union and other Roman Catholic temperance associations indicates the persistent presence of non-Protestant temperance folk. From the earliest formulation of the temperance ethos reformers learned that they would have to deploy more than biblical arguments if they were to succeed in a materialistic and pluralistic society. Accordingly, they pictured their reform as indispensable to individual health and social welfare as well as necessary to salvation and attainment of the millennium. By framing their arguments in secular terms temperance reformers helped to undermine the churches' claims for divine sanction as the basis for social action. Recognizing the threat, most churches maintained arm's-length distance between themselves and the zealous drys. That temperance reformers were evangelical Protestants does not mean that their relations with their churches were either simple or stable.

Time, of course, changed the composition of temperance support along most of the dimensions we have considered. New generations of men and women came to the reform, bringing with them new experiences and ideas. Within a single generation the turnover in some organizations was massive, even more than one would expect of such a geographically mobile population as that of the United States. Changes in movement policy, such as the shift to the teetotal pledge in the 1830s and the WCTU's alliance with the Prohibition party in the 1880s, drove out many. Experience, policy, and membership danced an intricate dance, to a tune called by none of the dancers alone, but improvised by all three together.

In pursuit of their reform, temperance reformers argued, pleaded, cajoled, confessed, denounced, and declaimed; they produced articles, stories, poetry, plays, songs, and novels; published books and pamphlets; and posted advertisements. They conducted surveys, prayed and sang, marched on saloons, marched in parades, marched in demonstrations, and attended meetings and conventions. They destroyed the contents of saloons with axes, hatchets, hammers, rocks, and metal bars. They formed associations at every level from the neighborhood to the nation; they appeared in courts as prosecutors, plaintiffs, informers, and defendants; they created pressure groups and political parties, petitioned, circularized candidates, canvassed, voted, and watched the polls. They served in lawmaking bodies from village councils to the U.S. Congress. They were harassed, mocked, beaten, hosed down, hung in effigy, shot at, and shot down.

To make sense of this multifarious activity we need an index. The scale most commonly employed by historians of temperance reform—and that will be used in this book—is a spectrum between persuasion and coercion. At one end lies the tactic known in the nineteenth century as "moral suasion," which assumes a symmetrical relationship between individuals of equal power and presumed rationality. Its essence is dialogue, in which the reformer appeals to the intellect and emotions of his or her listener in an attempt to convince the person of the rightness and goodness of the reformer's position. In contrast, coercion requires an asymmetrical relationship between individuals or groups of unequal power, involves only the crudest form of communication, and considers intellect and emotions peripheral to the outcome. The rightness and goodness of the reformer's position are not at issue; the only question is whether the reformer can mobilize enough force to compel acquiescence. Between these polar extremes lie many gradations encompassing many combinations of moral suasion and coercion, and in practice one rarely finds, in temperance reform at least, a pure example of either. Nevertheless, the spectrum is useful in comparing the strategies of different groups or movements, or of the same reform at different times.

Temperance reform began, as we shall see, with methods more suasionist than coercive, but its history reveals no simple progression toward coercion. Alongside the Prohibition party in the late nineteenth century flourished a "reform club" movement, led by reformed drinkers and based on personal evangelism and pledge signing. Later the Anti-Saloon League, among the most coercive of temperance organizations, made a strong commitment to "education," turning out from its presses at Westerville, Ohio, millions of pages of propaganda. Even after the passage of national Prohibition, the most coercive of temperance measures, a significant faction within the Anti-Saloon League argued for renewal of an educational campaign. Time and again frustration pushed temperance reformers toward coercion, but again and again moral suasion found ways to assert its claims.

Attempts to control drinking, then, have been long-lasting and diverse in both constituency and strategy. In light of these facts I find it more useful to conceive of temperance as a series of movements than as a single movement. Although the various movements are united by the goal of control over drinking, they are distinguished by the specific constellations of historical forces that impelled men and women at different times to choose temperance as a solution to what they perceived as problems in their own lives or in the lives of others. Each movement was different as well because of the lessons temperance reformers drew from the remembered experience of their predecessors.

In the chapters that follow I identify five American temperance movements appearing in succession during the past two centuries. Although each movement was characterized by a distinct combination of constituency and strategy, I will argue that each followed a progression that led it toward a more coercive policy than that with which the movement began. The reasons for this shift are rooted both in each movement's historical circumstances and in the reformers who tried to deal with those circumstances. The best metaphor to describe the history of temperance reform is therefore neither a straight line nor the often-used tragic curve—ascent to triumph followed by descent to ruin—but rather a series of cycles. In each generation some Americans have confronted the problem of drinking; again and again they have begun by trying to persuade their fellow citizens to act in ways calculated to solve the problem; again and again the intractability of the problem has led them to entertain more coercive approaches. In proposing a cyclical metaphor I intend to put forward a guide to discovery, not a mechanical scheme of explanation. Different periodization could easily produce other cycles and a different progression within some cycles. Alternative periodizations, however, will not do justice to *both* the changes and the continuities in the experience of temperance reformers.

One element of continuity may be found in the fact that American society today has by no means arrived at widely accepted answers to the questions that impelled Americans in the past to become temperance reformers. Besides the questions they asked, temperance reform lives on in America of the 1980s in at least two other ways. As social action it is far from dead, as I hope my discussion of the fifth movement will make clear. In both the new guise of academic expertise and the old vehicle of voluntary associations men and women still attempt to control drinking, their own and that of others. Furthermore, the movements of the past have helped to shape the world of today. Certainly the experience of national Prohibition, however it is interpreted, looms extremely large over contemporary discussion of social policy toward alcohol use. Nor can today's citizens be unaffected by the hundred years of argument over alcohol and alcohol policy that preceded national Prohibition. Despite promises of new research and new approaches, contemporary debate over alcohol policy continually returns to the terms of that discussion. Reforms having such long-lasting effects should be well understood.

Chapter One

The First Temperance
Movement (1784–1840)

The Reverend Charles Nisbet had had enough. For more than ten years he had sought to keep secret the fact that his son Thomas was a drunkard. Nisbet had more than ordinary reason for reticence since, as president of Dickinson College in Carlisle, Pennsylvania, he occupied a prominent and delicate position. But now, in August 1797, he had decided on a desperate course of action—he was going to send Tom away, to the home of a family friend in western Pennsylvania. "It may seem astonishing," Nisbet wrote his friend, "that a young Man, of good Understanding and Education, should fall into a State of Insanity without any bodily Disorder and continue in it for ten or twelve years without Intermission;— But alas! so it is, to my unspeakable Sorrow and Loss."[1] Tom could not take a drink without going on to become totally intoxicated; for him there was no middle ground between total abstinence and drunkenness, and he refused to try abstinence. Perhaps in a different environment, Nisbet hoped, Tom could change his life.

Tom's background gave his father cause for hope. The family were devout Presbyterians, and the Reverend Nisbet had been a prominent minister in the Scottish church before emigrating to America to 1785 to take the helm of the new Pennsylvania college. In an age when few men attended institutions of higher learning, Tom had distinguished himself academically while earning an M.A. at the University of Edinburgh. After his family's arrival in the United States, he completed a course of study in the law. Tom had not always shown a fascination for liquor, according to his father. But in turning out for militia drill in Carlisle, he gained a set of drinking companions; Tom "was initiated in Intemperance before we were aware of it." Tom tried to establish a law practice in Harrisburg and then in Lewistown, Pennsylvania, but failed in both places and returned to his parents' home. There he continued to drink to drunkenness while his presence constantly reinforced his father's shame. So now he was being sent away in hope of reform.

The hope turned out to be illusory. Tom's father and his friend tried various schemes. The friend, a lawyer and judge, appealed to Tom's reason. "Represent to him," the father urged, "how mean a Thing it is, for one who was born a Man, to chuse rather to be a Brute, & an Object of Scorn and Contempt to every Creature, as he has been by his own Choice for some Years past. Labor to excite in him a lively Idea of the Baseness of Drunkenness and the Destruction it brings to a Man's Health, Life, Character, and Circumstances."[2] The friend publicly announced that Tom had adopted abstinence, but Tom shrugged off embarrassment and proved the announcement wrong. A contrived appeal by a young woman of Tom's acquaintance met with the same result. By November Tom made himself sufficiently obnoxious that he was asked to quit the friend's home; after another year he returned to Carlisle leaving a string of drinking debts behind.

After his return home Tom's conduct improved. He "abstained from all spiritous Liquors, taking only two Glasses of Wine, & sometimes Cyder only, at Meals." During this temperate interlude he even participated as an advocate in several court cases. But this was only a prelude to a disastrous new adventure. Conceiving a desire to undertake a naval career, Tom set out for the British base at Halifax bearing letters of recommendation. Along the way, however, he became drunk and fell through a ship's hatch into the hold, severely injuring himself. Presenting his letters while probably drunk as well as injured, he was refused. When he returned home after more wanderings his father was aghast: "He is worn to a Shadow by a frequent Bleeding at the Nose. His Limbs quiver as if in a Palsy & Sleep has in a great Measure fled from him. I fear he may become insane." Within a few years his father's fears were apparently confirmed, for Tom was placed in the Pennsylvania Hospital, where he died in 1804 at the age of thirty-six or thirty-seven.[3]

Tom Nisbet lived and died at a time when there was no temperance movement in the United States. The central tenets of what was to become a powerful temperance ideology were formulated and published in the year before the Nisbets' arrival by Benjamin Rush, a Philadelphia physician, signer of the Declaration of Independence, and former surgeon general of the Continental Army during the American Revolution. Indeed, Rush, a founder of Dickinson College, was among the first to welcome the Nisbets to America. But no movement had yet appeared to disseminate Rush's ideas, to warn men and women against the dangers of strong drink, to offer them a means of succor, to provide a model of a life without alcohol, or to bolster their resolve when they tried, as Tom Nisbet briefly tried, to lead a sober life. To the Reverend Charles Nisbet his son's uncontrollable drinking was not a social problem but an individual one, brought on by Tom's own choice. Although he railed in private at the liquor dealers who dunned Tom for unpaid debts, Charles Nisbet apparently did not think of them as agents of his son's downfall. In the America of the 1790s alcohol was omnipresent, and no one conceived of beer, wine, or cider as intoxicating beverages in the same class as distilled liquors; the Nisbets saw nothing amiss in Tom's consuming cider and wine as he struggled to subdue his thirst for alcohol. Within two generations all of this was to change. In the colonial experience with alcohol may be found some clues to both the dimensions and the roots of that change.

Drinking and Social Change

Colonial America contained such a diverse set of societies, economies, and populations that generalizations about social customs and behavior are risky. One fact that seems clear is that throughout the American colonies, as in their European parent societies, alcoholic beverages were a staple of daily diet and represented the principal form of liquid nourishment. Virtually everyone drank virtually all the time. When the *Arabella* arrived in 1630 with the main contingent of settlers for Massachusetts Bay it carried 10,000 gallons of beer, 120 hogsheads of malt for brewing more, and 12 gallons of distilled spirits. This was only the community stores; in addition each family transported its own supply of liquor and many brought home-brewing equipment. In Virginia during the early seventeenth century the ships that sailed up the great rivers each year to collect the tobacco harvest seem to have carried liquor as their main cargo; dropping anchor off the plantations, they became floating saloons for the thirsty planters. Estimates for 1790, at the end of the colonial period, place per capita consumption of absolute alcohol (the alcohol content of alcoholic beverages) at three gallons, about half again as much as per capita consumption in the United States today.[4]

This relatively high level of per capita consumption must be placed in its proper context if we are to understand why it failed to produce widespread concern about drinking. Alcohol researchers classify societies according to the degree to which drinking is integrated with social norms and practices. Where drinking takes place in situations controlled by family or community norms, it may be said to be highly integrated into its society. Indeed, most primitive societies deal with drinking by embedding it within a dense network of socially controlled activities such as religious rituals and public ceremonies. In this sense the drinking pattern of colonial America should be considered primitive. Most alcohol consumption probably took place within the family, as did much production of alcoholic beverages. Connecticut probate inventories from the early eighteenth century suggest that at least half of all households produced their own, with beer by far the most common drink, although cider was becoming increasingly popular. Since domestically brewed beer kept for only a few days, brewing was a regularly recurring responsibility of housewives, at least in the northern colonies where beer could be kept at all. Cider was made at home in the apple-growing belt from Virginia northward. Both beer and cider were drunk with meals as well as on community social occasions; heavy drinking to the point of drunkenness seems to have been expected, or at least tolerated, on such occasions. Weddings, funerals, ordinations, church raisings, court days, the militia training days on which Tom Nisbet began his drinking career, as well as haying, cornhusking, barn raising, and fence building—all required ample supplies of alcohol. For those farmers linked to the market economy and for the small population of city dwellers rum was available cheaply after the development of extensive trade ties with the West Indies in the early eighteenth century. Indeed, by the time of the Revolution distilling of West Indian molasses into rum had become a leading industry. The rum produced by colonial distillers flowed down American throats as well as into the export trade.[5]

Because of its high level of per capita consumption, colonial society probably contained a substantial number of habitual drunkards, but no one perceived their behavior as a social problem, for several reasons. In the first place, most chronic drunkards were probably able to function adequately in a rural society in which tasks and roles were traditionally defined and in which considerable interpenetration existed between work and leisure. Lack of control over one's drinking, which constitutes the essence of modern definitions of alcoholism, was less likely to be perceived as an issue in such a society. But even if persistent heavy drinking to intoxication became problematic for individual drinkers, to see their drinking as a social problem was difficult since the drunkards were distributed in isolated farm families, not concentrated visibly on the streets of cities and towns.[6]

With so much drinking either contained within the family or channeled within community activity, solo and small-group binges were probably rare, as was the social disorder such drinking events might have involved. Colonial cities were turbulent places periodically swept by riotous mobs, but crowd action, like drinking, took place according to generally understood rules. Mobs appeared either to protect the community against perceived threats or intruders such as bawdy houses and naval press gangs or to express the hostility of the unenfranchised toward some specific action by the city's leaders.[7]

The very omnipresence of drinking among all ages and all social groups is another reason why the high colonial level of per capita consumption was not regarded as problematic. When women were as likely as men to be drinkers—although not to consume the same quantities—and children were routinely fed alcoholic beverages from an early age, average consumption per drinker was lower than if adulthood and maleness had defined the drinking population.

As the evidence presented thus far suggests, the benign and wholesome nature of alcoholic beverages formed a principal theme in colonial thought about alcohol. Drink was indeed "the good creature of God." The sermon that best expressed this benign view, however, was entitled "Wo to Drunkards"; that conjunction of messages suggests correctly that the colonial view of alcohol included another side, a side that stressed the threat posed by drinking to social order. English colonists brought both views with them from the mother country.

In 1606, just as English settlement of North America was beginning, Parliament passed a law making both drunkenness and "excess and unmeasurable drinking" crimes punishable by fine. As the American colonies were founded Parliament's antidrunkenness law was duplicated, even to the exact amount of the fine, by colonial legislatures. Colonial officials used the law to maintain public order: in seventeenth-century Massachusetts and Virginia offenders were rarely punished merely for drunkenness but rather for disorderly conduct accompanying drunkenness. Officials were concerned to maintain public order, but they probably did not believe they could eliminate the sources of disorder, which were located in the sinful nature of humankind. In thinking about drinking, officials generally did not blame alcohol itself for the various undesirable actions committed by those who had been drinking, and therefore did not entertain the notion that such undesirable actions could be eliminated by removing alcohol from society. That is, they lacked a concept of addiction, the belief that alcohol is a substance of irresistible attraction and powerful effect, capable of overcoming human will. Therefore the most that society could do was to control drinking and attempt to mitigate its effects.[8]

The dual nature of colonial thought about alcohol is well illustrated by the web of regulations woven about the tavern. As in placing legislative controls on individual drinking, colonial lawmakers followed English example. In some respects, such as setting prices and fixing measures, both English and colonial laws treated retailing of liquor as a business like any other. Recognizing that taverns fulfilled an essential public purpose in the lodging and feeding of travelers, legislatures encouraged them as they did other local businesses. But at the same time legislators saw in the retail sale of liquor a unique threat to public order; from at least the sixteenth century laws were enacted that clearly placed the business in a class of its own. This was evident in the first English licensing law, passed in 1552, which justified creation of a uniform system of licensing by the belief that "intolerable hurts and troubles to the commonwealth of this realm doth daily grow and increase through such abuses and disorders as are had and used in common ale-houses and other places called tippling houses." The English licensing system was re-created in the colonies, and colonial officials used it to regulate the number, type, and character of dealers. Dealers were enjoined to restrict or eliminate sales to specified classes of persons, and they were held responsible for actions committed by their customers. The licensing system established the necessary legal basis for prohibition, since the power to license implies the power to destroy.[9]

Colonial governments did in fact sometimes attempt to destroy significant parts of the retail liquor business. When Georgia was founded in the 1730s its fundamental law included a prohibition of the use of hard liquor, although the prohibitory clause was repealed after seven years. During Bacon's Rebellion in Virginia all "ordinaries, ale houses, or tippling houses" were prohibited save two, and those were permitted to sell only beer and cider. In 1637 the General Court of Massachusetts Bay forbade the keepers of ordinaries from selling distilled spirits, wine, and strong beer. Although those who enacted such laws may have regarded sinful human nature as the ultimate source of threats to public order, they clearly felt that human readiness to sin could be curbed by removing temptation in the form of strong drink. Similarly, strict laws in Massachusetts Bay against excessive drinking—prescribing, for example, how long and how much one could drink at a single tavern sitting—were designed to make it difficult for a potential sinner to fall. Finally, at least three colonies—Plymouth, Massachusetts Bay, and Connecticut—prohibited the sale of liquor to habitual drunkards. Such laws, as historian Carol Steinsapir points out, seem to have reflected a "belief that habitual drunkards were not capable of drinking in moderation, or at least that they could not be trusted to do so." Although this belief falls short of the modern concept of addiction, it contained the seed of that concept insofar as it held that some forms of alcohol were addictive for some people.[10]

By 1830 that seed produced a plant so fruitful that it scattered temperance societies across the American landscape like apples after a windstorm. During the early period of its growth the most assiduous gardener was Dr. Benjamin Rush, who contributed the argument that *one* form of alcohol was addictive for *everyone* and who also spread a good deal of moral suasion in strategic places. Although others in both England and America were reaching the same conclusions, Rush was the one who presented the new ideology in its most influential form, in his pamphlet *An Inquiry into the Effects of Ardent Spirits Upon the Human Body and Mind* (1784). Rush resolved the contradiction between the two views of alcoholic beverages as dangerous and beneficial by assigning alcohol's dangerous qualities to distilled spirits and its beneficial effects to the fermented beverages. His argument rested almost entirely upon the deleterious physiological effects of distilled spirits, mentioning damage to the "moral faculties" only in passing and alluding not at all to possible spiritual erosion. He described both acute and chronic effects of alcohol consumption and pointed out that the latter could undermine a drinker's constitution even if he or she never drank to intoxication. "Thus," he concluded, "we see poverty and misery, crimes and infamy, diseases and death, are all the natural and usual consequences of the intemperate use of ardent spirits," and he provided an estimate—"not less than 4000"— of deaths caused annually in the United States from the use of distilled liquor. He argued that spirits were not necessary, as was commonly believed, either to help the body endure extremes of weather or to sustain it during hard labor. He recommended substitutes: water, cider, malt liquors, wines, molasses or vinegar and water, coffee, tea, and, under

certain circumstances, opium. In Rush's view total abstinence from distilled spirits was the only means of avoiding the dangers he described,
and he suggested that governments take what actions they could to foster this end. Until his death in 1813 he worked to promote his views,
primarily by trying to persuade other physicians and ministers.[11]

Despite the efforts of Rush and other individuals the new temperance
ideology made little headway during the forty years following publication
of Rush's pamphlet. During that period the situation that had alarmed
Rush and others—the high level of per capita consumption of distilled
liquor—became even worse. Rising consumption played an important
role in stimulating the powerful temperance movement that eventually
arose in the 1820s. Both phenomena—drinking and antidrink—were produced in turn by significant economic and social changes that affected
primarily citizens of the northern states.

The American Revolution and the subsequent severance of the thirteen colonies from the British Empire set these changes in motion. Excluded from imperial markets, merchants in northern cities began to
expand their own domestic markets, which had been far less important
than international trading networks during the colonial period. Expansion
of the domestic market involved extension and growth of trade links with
rural communities whose previous extralocal trading had been restricted,
as well as assertion of greater control over the production process so
that larger volumes of goods could be produced more cheaply. Increased
volumes of domestic trade implied urban growth and greater specialization of work in both commerce and manufacturing as well as more attention by farmers to production for the market. In the years after the
Revolution market growth and regional specialization were greatly facilitated by the movement of masses of people into frontier areas of the
former colonies and into the new western lands acquired under the
Treaty of Paris.

With the spread of the market came market discipline. Meeting the
needs of the market required new, more regular work habits of those
who produced both agricultural and manufactured products and those
who transported them. Learning to live with the market meant somehow
coming to terms with uncontrollable fluctuations in supply and demand.
Taking part in a widening market also taught that, just as the conditions
of one's own life could be unpredictably affected by the actions of distant
others, so one's own ability to affect distant outcomes could be increased. The market brought both a new sense of power and new fears,

and both were grounded in the experiences of ordinary men and women.

Other developments reinforced the changes brought by expansion of the market. Attacks on imperial elites during the revolutionary process together with gradual expansion of the male electorate through elimination of property requirements reduced the deferential attitudes that once characterized interclass social contacts. Disestablishment of formerly established churches opened the field of competition to new sects and helped to establish revivalism as the dominant mode of winning converts. At the same time the basic lines of class structure remained firm, even though some individuals moved up and others down. In addition, new lines of division formed in cities as men's work moved out of the home while women's remained there and an ideology of separate male and female spheres appeared to explain and justify the change.

Drinking changed too in important ways. Rum declined from its former position as Americans' favorite liquor with the reduction of dependence on the West Indies trade and was replaced by various whiskeys distilled from domestic grains. As settlers moved into the new lands of the Ohio Valley they found them well suited to growing grain, especially corn, but poorly situated for marketing their crops in their natural state because of the Appalachian mountain barrier. Before construction of the Erie Canal was completed in 1825, western farmers discovered that the most profitable way to market their corn was to distill it into whiskey. This was because the mountain barrier created two grain markets. West of the mountains grain was plentiful; it was also cheap since farmers, prevented by high transport costs from carrying their grain overland, were dependent on the New Orleans market. East of the Appalachians grain sold in a seller's market at up to three times the western rate because of low yields and a large nonfarming population. Western whiskey, however, could be transported across the mountains and sold for less than whiskey distilled from expensive eastern grain. This situation created a national whiskey glut by the early 1820s, with prices at twenty-five cents to fifty cents per gallon. When a poorly paid farm laborer earned a dollar a day, that price was cheap.[12]

During the first quarter of the nineteenth century the whiskey glut combined with existing conditions and traditional attitudes to send per capita consumption soaring. In cities, water supplies were often polluted, and water in general was considered to lack nourishment. Milk was inconsistently available and expensive; tea and coffee were consistently more expensive than whiskey. Most Americans continued to regard alcohol as a necessary companion to every mood and season. In 1814, a temperance reformer summed up the common view. "Strong drink in some form," he said,

is the remedy for every sickness, the cordial for every sorrow. It must grace the festivity of the wedding; it must enliven the gloom of the funeral. It must cheer the intercourse of friends and enlighten the fatigues of labor. Success *deserves* a treat and disappointment *needs* it. The busy drink because they are busy; the idle because they have nothing else to do. The farmer must drink because his work is hard; the mechanic because his employment is sedentary and dull. It is warm, men drink to be cool; it is cool, they drink to be warm.[13]

By 1830 annual per capita consumption reached nearly four gallons of absolute alcohol.[14]

Expansion of the market economy affected drinking in other ways besides bringing cheap western whiskey to eastern drinkers. Not only were Americans drinking more on a per capita basis, but some of them were drinking in new contexts. Movement to urban places limited home production and thereby drove drinkers to new drinking places outside the home. Formation of new work groups gave workers new companions with whom to drink in commercial establishments. Proliferation of such places multiplied the number of persons whose own living depended upon encouraging others to drink. For an increasing number of people a commercial drinking context replaced the domestic or community setting, and drinking as an informal individual or small-group activity took the place of drinking as a domestic, formal, or ceremonial activity. As more and more people had to purchase alcoholic beverages rather than produce them at home, liquor became a competitor for the family cash that was increasingly necessary for survival in a commodity economy. Meanwhile, geographic mobility diminished the likelihood that family or neighborhood resources would be available for families in need.[15]

The drinking population was probably shrinking relative to total population, so that the effects of increased consumption were shared by a smaller proportion of the population, but with correspondingly greater impact upon drinkers. As the ideology of separate public and private spheres for men and women spread among urban women it set forth new norms for the behavior of those who aspired to "true womanhood." The refinement and delicacy, piety and purity, prescribed by the cult of domesticity may well have reduced both the number of women who drank and the amounts consumed by those who continued to drink, thereby widening existing differences between the drinking patterns of men and women.

A Campaign Begins

Organized action against intemperance appeared on the local level during the first decade of the nineteenth century, but not until 1813 did societies active on more than a local scale emerge. In Connecticut and New York, reformers attacked a range of social problems including crime, dueling, and Sabbath breaking as well as intemperance. But the Massachusetts Society for the Suppression of Intemperance (MSSI) devoted its efforts primarily to the temperance issue. Founded in Boston in 1813, the MSSI reached its peak in 1818 with more than forty local auxiliaries enrolling an average of a hundred members each. The number of members is a misleading standard by which to measure the work of the MSSI, however, because the organization was self-consciously elitist, enrolling in its ranks only men from the top ranks of society.[16]

The MSSI was selective in its choice of tactics as well as in its recruitment. Eschewing the mass appeal represented by publication of literature, hiring of organizers, or sponsorship of rallies, the society attempted to influence only those whose social standing resembled that of its members. Employers were enjoined to promote temperance by denying ardent spirits to those they employed. Members of the MSSI also appealed to local officials to arrest drunkards, restrict the number of licenses to sell liquor, and grant licenses only to men of character and standing. Some proposed appointment of special officers in each town to oversee the sale and use of liquor. The MSSI did not seek to eliminate the liquor business, only to place it once again under the sort of control by a local elite that they believed had existed previously. Beyond this the society sought to reestablish an elite standing and influence that had been eroded by disestablishment, the decline of deference, and the rise of mass political participation. Still politically powerful within their communities, these men, most of them Federalists, saw political influence slipping away from them in both state and nation. Economic dislocation and poverty resulting from Republican policies at the federal level appeared in their communities despite their local influence. Therefore MSSI means and ends were closely related: their object was to control the behavior of their social inferiors, but to adopt a mass appeal to reach that goal would have been self-defeating. A good index to their feelings is afforded by the fact that the MSSI advocated only moderation in the use of ardent spirits, not the abstinence that had been urged by Benjamin Rush nearly thirty years before. To promote abstinence was to attack the preferences and practices of the social elite and to threaten vested interests in the liquor industry. Such a course was too radical for the conservative men of the MSSI.[17]

The cautious approach of the first temperance reformers, however, was no match for the social forces encouraging drinking; the tide of consumption rolled over the MSSI and its companion societies. By the early 1820s these societies had declined and were soon replaced by more militant and more radical successors.

The founding in 1826 of the American Society for the Promotion of Temperance, better known as the American Temperance Society (ATS), marked the beginning of a new and far more important phase of America's first temperance movement. Like the MSSI, the ATS was organized in Boston, but it shared little else in common with its failed predecessor. In its goals, strategy, ideology, motivation, and sources of support, as well as in the degree of opposition it provoked, the ATS represented a new departure in temperance reform. To complete the contrast, the crusade launched by the ATS became one of the most successful reform movements in American history, whether measured by the decline of drinking in the near term or by the inculcation of temperance values in the long term.

The ATS was founded by a group of ambitious evangelical clergymen whose previous leadership in organizing nationwide distribution of religious tracts had been superseded by a more strategically placed rival group in New York. The movement led by the ATS spread so far and so quickly beyond its local origins because it tapped powerful forces in American life. Its ability to do so stemmed from the vigor of its organizing and, more important, the breadth of its appeal. The ATS placed only a single limitation on its constituency: it aimed to persuade the already temperate to undertake total abstinence from distilled spirits—Benjamin Rush's program—rather than to reclaim drunkards. Its leaders believed that this approach represented the most direct route to a sober society since, when the current generation of drunkards died, none would appear to replace them. Nevertheless, and despite their initial intentions, ATS workers found themselves attempting to save drunkards and that experience, as we shall see, helped to force the entire movement in a new and traumatic direction by the end of its first decade.[18]

Unlike the MSSI, then, the ATS appealed to the masses, as did their contemporaries and coworkers, the revivalists and the tract society workers. Itinerant agents were hired and sent out, like revivalists, to bring into being state, county, and local auxiliaries within an organizational structure imitating that of the tract and missionary societies. The New York State Temperance Society (NYSTS), founded in 1829, provided impetus for rapid growth in its state by undertaking to organize a central society in each county that was in turn to spur creation of local organizations. The Schenectady County society, founded in 1830 in response to circulars sent out by the NYSTS, enrolled 663 members during its first year, approximately one-quarter of the adult population of the city of Schenectady; in addition, it saw to the establishment in the surrounding countryside of more than thirteen auxiliaries totaling over 600 additional members. Later bursts of activity by the county society were usually provoked by injunctions emanating from the NYSTS. After a year's work by the NYSTS, twenty-nine county societies had been created claiming three hundred local auxiliaries and 40,000 members. By 1833 the ATS proudly reported nineteen state societies, six thousand local and county auxiliaries, and a million members. These results were achieved through vigorous organizing from the top down that elicited an enthusiastic response from the grass roots.[19]

The ATS followed the example of the tract societies in relying on the written word as well as in their use of itinerant agents. Cheap tracts presenting the total abstinence message in succinct form flooded the country. The ATS paid the salary of the editor of a weekly newspaper and circulated it both by subscription and at ATS expense. Circulars were aimed at special groups such as women and young people. Special occasions, too, brought forth temperance propaganda. During the cholera epidemic of 1832, temperance workers surveyed the backgrounds of those who died from the disease in Albany, New York, and publicized their finding that abstainers were underrepresented among them. Such publicity was claimed to have added fifty thousand new members to temperance societies.[20]

Although the temperance movement during the ATS years attracted many capable propagandists, few careers matched the scope of that of Edward C. Delavan. Delavan was a cosmopolitan businessman from Albany who amassed a fortune, first through a local hardware business that he represented in London for seven years, and then as a wine merchant in New York City. In 1827, at the age of thirty-four, he permanently retired from business and devoted his abundant energies to temperance reform. He helped found the NYSTS and became its secretary. Delavan established and directed two Albany-based temperance journals and arranged the publication and distribution of a set of lithographs showing in graphic detail the progressive effects of liquor on the stomach. In a pioneering piece of investigative reporting, Delavan reported in 1835 that Albany brewers made their beer from water polluted by offal from nearby slaughterhouses. The brewers sued, but Delavan was acquitted. Through both his own publications and his subsidies of other temperance propaganda, Delavan was responsible for the distribution of over 13.6 million documents and graphic works.[21]

The extensive propaganda efforts of the ATS were made possible by a well-organized system of finances. The itinerant agents played an important part in this system by gathering contributions from the local groups and congregations they addressed. In addition, the ATS encouraged large donors by appointing them honorary members or directors according to the size of their contribution. Although about two-thirds of total donations during its first years came from those who gave more than thirty dollars, two-thirds of all donors gave less than five dollars each. Together, large and small donors enabled the ATS to mount more dynamic and wide-ranging campaigns than its predecessor, the MSSI, and to enjoy an operating surplus each year until the mid-1830s.[22]

By 1835 the ATS had reached the peak of its organizing success, claiming over 1.5 million members in more than eight thousand auxiliaries. This represented about 12 percent of the free population of the United States and possibly as many as one in five free adults. The bulk of these were enrolled in open-membership local auxiliaries, but one key to the ATS appeal was its readiness to abandon the MSSI practice of limiting its membership to a single society in each community. Instead the ATS accepted as auxiliaries associations restricted to specific groups whose members felt more comfortable pursuing the common cause in the company of their peers. In Schenectady, New York, for example, the Schenectady County Temperance Society in 1832 remained the largest society with 915 members, but other local temperance groups included an "African" society (65 members), a society at the cotton factory (93 members), one at Plank's tavern (30 members)—the pledge proscribed only distilled, not fermented beverages—one for young men (50 members), and the oldest special interest group, the Union College Temperance Society (292 members). In Providence, Rhode Island, special societies were organized by blacks, sailors, youth, and reclaimed drunkards. Albany, New York, contained a Hibernian Temperance Society, whose members all survived the cholera epidemic. Sometimes this diversity of membership resulted from specific appeals. No group, in fact, was excluded by the ATS approach, which embraced even drunkards (despite some leaders' original intentions) and liquor manufacturers and retailers. Its reliance on the written word broadcast across the country and its vigorous organizing of previously neglected groups made the temperance movement under the ATS, like its English counterpart at the same time, one of the agencies undermining traditional hierarchies and deferential attitudes.[23]

The growth of their young organization reinforced an optimistic outlook that seems to have been common among the ATS leadership. As they contemplated the steam presses that churned out millions of pages of instructive or inspirational material, or the canals and turnpikes that sped their words to readers across the country, they could see unprecedented material progress. As they counted the converts brought to the churches by revivals or the pledges signed and societies founded as a result of their own work, they could find evidence of what seemed to be moral progress as well.

This side of the temperance outlook has been well described by historian Ian Tyrrell. After a careful study of temperance reformers' backgrounds, rhetoric, and actions, Tyrrell labeled them "improvers." If they were clergymen, as most of the founders of the ATS were, they were men who welcomed revivals, promoted tract, missionary, and other benevolent societies bent on evangelizing the world, and had little patience with predestinarian theology. If they were businessmen, they were likely to be employers of labor, identified with the emerging industrial economy rather than with mercantile pursuits, and to be innovators in technology or business organization. If they were farmers, they were employers and innovators deeply involved in commercial agriculture. In short, they were men who welcomed change and looked forward to a world of tomorrow that would be better than today's. For such men, personal achievement and success prefigured social progress, and the sense of power they gained from participation in a dynamic market economy whetted their appetite for further change.[24]

Tyrrell's argument provides a necessary rebuttal to an earlier view that portrayed temperance and other reformers as fearful conservatives disoriented by the rapid pace of social change in nineteenth-century America. Men and women, however, do not usually become reformers out of a sense of unalloyed optimism. As Tyrrell points out, temperance leaders sought to remove the human misery they attributed to intemperance, which they perceived as a removable evil in a progressive society. But temperance reformers' pessimism seems to have gone even deeper. Consider the idea of total abstinence. Often described as evidence of reformers' belief in human perfectibility, the total abstinence pledge was actually adopted both in recognition of, and as protection against, human fallibility. The earlier ideal of moderation promoted by the MSSI in fact required a greater degree of moral fortitude, since it allowed consumption of ardent spirits while failing to draw any line beyond which consumption became immoderate. The emptying of each successive glass confronted the drinker with a portentous choice, but the ideal of moderation provided no clear guidance in making that choice. For drinkers like Tom Nisbet injunctions to moderation, no matter how persuasively worded or attractively presented, were of no help at all. The failure of the ideal of moderation, a fact apparent during the 1820s to anyone who had eyes to see, carried a message that the forces of American society presented fallible human beings with temptations they were unable to resist, with often disastrous results.[25]

Temperance reformers during the 1820s therefore modified the basic idea of control that always formed the heart of temperance doctrine. Individuals were to exercise self-control, to be sure. But since they could not be consistently trusted to do so, the public commitment symbolized by the pledge and the watchful fellowship of the temperance society must be mobilized to support their resolution. Given human frailty in the face of temptation, the clear line between moderation and intemperance represented by total abstinence from ardent spirits became indispensable in achieving self-control.[26]

This heightened distrust of human ability took temperance reformers a long step toward a concept of addiction. By the late 1820s some were following the lead of Benjamin Rush in explicitly labeling drunkenness a "disease." Experience with drinkers who wished to stop drinking but could not do so underlay this development, and for some reformers that experience occurred at home through close contact with fathers, brothers, and sons who could not control their own drinking. But while they came to acknowledge drink's addictive power, temperance reformers refused to force this insight to a thoroughly environmentalist conclusion. Human beings were weak, they felt, but individuals were still morally responsible for their actions. Drink held a power to enslave men and women, but men and women still made the decision to drink. As one reformer put it, drunkards were "voluntary slaves."[27]

Such talk reflected a heightened concern for autonomy that gave added resonance to the temperance appeal of the 1820s and 1830s. Temperance literature and orations resounded with warnings of the loss of independence.

> We can all call to mind the case of some individual, whom we have known for years . . . who is now a poor miserable drunkard. . . . His family was respectable and he received all those advantages which are necessary and which are calculated to make him a useful and respectable member of society. . . . He entered into business and for a time did well. . . . He accumulated property, and, in a few years, with ordinary prudence and industry, would have become independent. . . . [But] he grew fond of ardent spirits . . . [and] by degrees he became intemperate. He neglected his business. . . . He is now a drunkard, his property wasted.[28]

Personal autonomy now appeared problematic to many people; consequently discussions of how to gain control over one's own life received a sympathetic hearing. Habitual drinking to intoxication took on a new meaning and brought new effects when both personal success and personal failure could be achieved on a larger scale than before. Wider changes in society made control both more difficult to acquire and more portentous for one's future, and so the temperance movement, promising means for the achievement of self-control and self-advancement, reached a larger, and probably more diverse, audience than any other antebellum reform.[29]

Support

The improvers—from the ranks of the evangelical clergy, manufacturers, and farmers—may have founded temperance societies, but men from all ranks and conditions joined them. Established elites varied in their responses to the movement, leading in some communities and becoming conspicuous by their absence in others. The more innovative employers adopted abstinence themselves and preached its virtues to their workers. Many workers responded to these and other appeals by taking the pledge and joining a temperance society. For some workers, taking the pledge was no doubt the result of simple coercion by a boss determined to create a sober work force. But for others the temperance movement's direct approach, democratic organization, and emphasis on control over an increasingly uncertain world touched responsive chords in their own experience and outlook.[30]

As with social class, so with religion. Ministers and converts of the evangelical churches led the way into the temperance societies, but non-evangelicals and the unchurched followed. In Schenectady, Presbyterians and members of the Dutch church created the county society, but by the end of its first year the society contained three who were not church members for every member; those who were church members represented a virtual cross-section of Schenectady's denominational mixture. In Providence, and probably in other communities as well, temperance provided a unifying force for Protestants disputing with each other over theological and social differences.[31]

Although social elites divided over temperance, the intellectual elite seems to have moved virtually as a unit into the temperance camp. Temperance reform found widespread and vigorous support among the presidents and faculties of colleges across the nation. Faculty support in turn stimulated student commitment to the cause, as did the revivals that frequently swept antebellum campuses. Neither faculty encouragement nor the impact of revivalism, however, provides a full explanation for student temperance activity. Students also felt a need of their own, rooted in the dilemmas of dependence among young men capable of economic independence, which they seem to have met through conversions to both Christianity and total abstinence. As a result, American colleges became nerve centers for temperance reform, providing leadership, intellectual justification, and a dedicated, energetic, and strategically placed cadre of supporters.[32]

Partly as a result of colleges' conversion to temperance and partly because of the work of the temperance movement in general, the more formally educated members of the medical profession also contributed strong support to the cause. Alcohol had never held a primary place in the pharmacopeia of regular physicians, and its use declined under the impact of arguments following the lines laid down by Benjamin Rush. Medicine in the early nineteenth century was a profession in turmoil, as "regular" physicians struggled to distinguish themselves from folk practitioners; one means of doing so was to adopt the new view of alcohol. Medical improvers therefore joined their kindred spirits in other fields of endeavor by decrying the use of alcohol as medicine or beverage. The result was a substantial body of expert opinion mobilized behind the temperance movement.[33]

At the grass roots, the ATS became one of the first American voluntary associations to attract large numbers of women. In all regions women joined ATS-affiliated societies, and, in the northeastern states at least, they often outnumbered men. Twenty-four women's societies were reported in 1831, although women more often joined open-membership organizations led by men. The typical society of this type contained a women's membership of between 35 and 60 percent. In Schenectady, where the movement enjoyed more success among men than among women, the county society still claimed the support of one in seven adult women. In Elizabethtown, New Jersey, five hundred women signed a petition in 1834 requesting that local officials suppress superfluous liquor shops, and their action was duplicated by six hundred women in Wilmington, Delaware, three years later. Twelve hundred women in Portland, Maine, petitioned the state legislature in 1838 for legal assistance to the temperance cause. Even if we discount the membership claims of the ATS, the temperance cause clearly attracted hundreds of thousands of women. [34]

A striking characteristic of women's temperance work was its ability to attract activist women of diverse backgrounds. This has been shown by a recent study of women's organizations in Rochester, New York, which demonstrated that, contrary to a conventional view, individual women did not progress from benevolent work to temperance to antislavery to women's rights. Instead, Rochester contained three separate groups of women activists, distinguished both by the radicalism of their goals and by the militance of their methods. Women belonging to the three clusters were also divided by social class, religious affiliation, and length of residence in Rochester. The only cause that transcended these divisions was temperance. Although their representatives advocated different approaches to the problem of intemperance, all three networks contributed leaders to the temperance society. [35]

Male leaders of the ATS welcomed women into the movement on the basis of separate-spheres ideology, citing the need for women's moral influence upon the coming generation; such spokesmen restricted women's temperance work to those activities consistent with a domestic role. Nor did women assume leadership positions in any of the open-membership societies whose records are extant. Nevertheless, this view did not find universal agreement in temperance literature, as other writers used women's victimization by male intemperance to justify women's participation and supported actions more militant than exerting influence by the fireside. As the Elizabethtown, Wilmington, and Portland examples suggest, women did take a more active role than the ATS leadership was willing to allow them. They mobilized for petition campaigns, and in 1835 in Montpelier, Vermont, they organized and conducted the first women's temperance convention. At least one women's temperance society was among the first local associations to adopt the teetotal pledge prohibiting use of wine, ale, or strong beer as well as distilled spirits. Although such activities fell short of the militance shown by women antislavery reformers in the 1830s, they indicate that some women at least were not prepared to accept confinement to a domestic role or a position as followers in the reform.[36]

Although the ATS organized an unprecedented number of women, its efforts did not represent women's initial appearance in temperance reform. The first temperance tract written by a woman was published by the Pennsylvania Quaker minister Elizabeth Levis in 1761, and at about the same time other Quaker women ministers were beginning in their writings to question the use of strong drink. By 1818 women's names began to appear on petitions in Chester County, Pennsylvania, opposing the granting of tavern licenses. These early actions suggest that differences between the drinking patterns of men and women—differences like those found in all known societies—led to differing perceptions of the problem of intemperance. For men the problem was first of all self-control; for women the principal problem was controlling the behavior of men. Men's drinking became a problem for women because within families the welfare and happiness of individual men and women were linked so tightly. The common-law placement of property rights in the hands of husbands compounded the problem for wives, and inheritance practices that transmitted the bulk of family wealth to sons made widows vulnerable. Legal divorce was available only in some colonies and states, and then on restricted grounds. Prospects for life outside the family were dimmed by the scarcity of remunerative occupations for propertyless women. As the market economy expanded, population shifted to towns and cities, and the spheres of urban men and women diverged, families in general and women in particular became more dependent upon regular male income and therefore more vulnerable to its disruption or diversion because of drink. Together with the inclusive organizing drives of the ATS and the widening differences in men's and women's drinking patterns, these forces turned a women's concern in the eighteenth century into a women's campaign in the nineteenth.[37]

Women were able to participate extensively in the work of the temperance movement during the ATS years because so little of the work of the movement involved formal political activity, from which women were excluded. Instead, ATS strategy emphasized informal persuasion, public speaking, distribution of propaganda, creation of alternative institutions such as temperance hotels, and, most of all, organization, the classic vehicles of moral suasion. In Providence, for example, the public meeting in 1827 that launched the local movement declared its members' faith in "the concentration of public opinion" while disclaiming any intention "to impose the slightest restraint or dictation upon any individual." Coercive measures, however, were mixed with moral suasion elsewhere in the early history of the new movement. Two years after its founding, the NYSTS advocated total abstinence from ardent spirits as a condition of employment for teachers. Meanwhile its auxiliary, the (Erie) Canal Temperance Society, worked to persuade canal transportation companies not to provide liquor to either passengers or crews and to require total abstinence of drivers on pain of loss of a month's pay and possible dismissal. In 1834 temperance men convinced insurance underwriters to permit a 5 percent reduction of premiums for ships that operated entirely without the use of spirits; within a few years the crews on more than a thousand ships were deprived of their liquor ration. Temperance pressure brought about elimination of the army's liquor ration and halving of the navy grog ration. Although the effect of these measures on the persons concerned was coercive, that was not their primary purpose. In the case of teachers, the aim was educational; in those of drivers, crews, and military men, the goal was public safety. Moral suasion remained the basic strategy of temperance reform. [38]

Teetotalism

While they remained committed to suasionist means, temperance reformers came to envision a new goal. Beginning in the early 1830s, local societies began to debate and then to adopt a new pledge that proscribed the use of wine, cider, and beer as well as distilled spirits, which became known as the "long" or "teetotal" pledge. By 1835 several state temperance societies endorsed the new pledge, and spurred on by Delavan, a national convention at Saratoga, New York, in 1836 formally recommended teetotalism. That convention also changed the name of the national organization to the American Temperance Union (ATU). This wave of support for teetotalism rode on the experience of the temperance movement, but it was to outrace the commitments given by significant bodies of supporters.

One reason for teetotalism's attraction was the progress of the reform. The movement had enjoyed great success in pledging moderate drinkers to temperance. Now that hundreds of thousands had committed themselves to abstinence from ardent spirits, a thoroughgoing reform of

American drinking habits that included heavy drinkers and drunkards as well as moderate drinkers began to seem possible. Contributing to this hope was the perfectionist impulse that emerged from the revivals of the Second Great Awakening (1800–35), a belief that, with God's grace, human beings could speed the coming of the millennium by improving themselves and their society on earth. The perfectionist vision appeared to be confirmed by the success of the temperance movement in mobilizing its army of reform.

Despite its considerable success, however, the temperance movement did encounter opposition. Ostracism and ridicule often greeted arguments for total abstinence and attempts to form temperance societies; where local elites opposed the cause such measures sometimes carried considerable force. Temperance activists were regularly called upon to answer charges that they were seeking to unite church and state or to destroy individual liberty. Among opposition arguments, attempts to rebut the claim that intemperance was a serious social problem seem to have been rare; instead, opponents focused on the means proposed to overcome a problem whose existence all acknowledged. Where argument ended harassment began, as shaving of horse tails, girdling of trees, and defacing of house fronts became standard responses to temperance campaigns and campaigners.[39]

More troubling to temperance reformers were charges of hypocrisy and inconsistency made by their opponents. Temperance workers arraigned drunkenness, yet their antagonists pointed out that those who took the pledge could become just as drunk on wine, cider, and beer as they had on distilled liquors. This argument included an important class dimension, since the old pledge had the effect of proscribing poor people's cheap liquor while allowing the rich to continue drinking their expensive wines. Responding to this point, temperance speakers were forced to concede that "drunkenness in silver slippers is not a whit better than drunkenness in rags." The temperance appeal to moderate drinkers had always emphasized the power of their example for others; now this argument was turned against the reformers.[40]

Although the ATS crusade initially was not directed toward reform of drunkards, temperance workers were gratified when drunkards came to their meetings, took the pledge, and joined their societies. Those who attempted to help drunkards stay sober soon discovered that the old pledge gave little help in this difficult endeavor, since the use of fermented beverages often put former drunkards back on the slippery slope to uncontrolled drinking. The power of example also contributed to the problem since the old pledge not only permitted a redeemed drunkard access to alcohol but also left him or her surrounded by a world of alcohol. In 1830, Gerrit Smith told the NYSTS that "formerly . . . the state of society was against [the drunkard] . . . now the drunkard, when he quits his cups and attempts the reformation of himself is sustained and cheered onward." Experience with drunkards by reformers using the old pledge threatened to make this claim a mockery.[41]

New information about alcohol also played a part in the shift to teetotalism. Before the 1820s many people, including temperance reformers, conceived of alcohol as an ingredient of distilled spirits but not of fermented liquors. Alcohol, they thought, was created by distillation. Although one could obviously become drunk on fermented liquors, wine, cider, and beer were believed to contain only the constituent elements of alcohol, not alcohol itself. During the 1820s the findings of chemist William Brande that alcohol was present in fermented liquors were disseminated in the United States, and that discovery gradually caused a change in the popular perception of wine, cider, and beer.[42]

Although the shift to teetotalism seemed a logical step to the men who controlled many state societies and the national society, others refused to accept their arguments, and the issue proved a fertile source of conflict within the movement. Some groups, such as the New York City Temperance Society, agreed that the teetotal pledge was correct in principle, but they believed that it should not become the only tool of reformers, since some drinkers needed to be weaned gradually from alcohol. Among the latter, the New Yorkers claimed, were members of the city's black and Irish populations. Therefore the New York City society continued to circulate both pledges even after the state association adopted teetotalism.[43]

Other reformers found teetotalism itself too radical for their taste. Among these were many wealthy and prestigious supporters of the ATS, who resisted teetotalism for one or both of two reasons. In the first place, the proscription of wine struck at their own drinking practices as the prohibition of distilled spirits had never done. In high social circles wine served as a common social lubricant; wealthy men and women saw no need to give it up in order to set an example for those whom they considered irresponsible and improvident. Since teetotalism required sacrifice by the upper classes, it seemed subversive of the principle of social hierarchy the wealthy held so dear. Conversion to the teetotal pledge therefore resulted in stripping temperance reform of some of its wealthy supporters, a process that was to accelerate with the emergence of the Washingtonians in the 1840s.[44]

The shift to teetotalism also cost the movement the support of a significant component of clergy and Christian lay people. Some of these were no doubt responsive to the expediency argument or charges of teetotal radicalism, but the principal reason for their disaffection was the impact of teetotalism on the liturgy, an impact that produced a lasting controversy over the use of wine in Communion services and ramified into a dispute over the use and interpretation of the Bible. The churches, of course, provided leading elements of the temperance army; to many temperance activists the rationale for their crusade was ultimately religious. Intemperance, they felt, constituted a principal obstacle to dissemination and reception of the gospel message. Ironically, the means reformers were forced to adopt in order to appeal to a diverse public undercut both the institutions and the belief system they intended to benefit by the spread of temperance. By assuming human control over human fate, justifying temperance in terms of individual and social welfare rather than on the basis of biblical injunctions, and creating secular agencies—the temperance societies—for social regeneration, reformers advanced the process of secularization that had provoked some of them to become reformers in the first place. In this they were not alone, as their English counterparts followed the same course and with the same result. In both countries, the Communion wine controversy played a key role.[45]

During the 1830s wine was used in every Communion service, so the teetotal pledge threatened widespread disruption. Teetotal advocates addressed the problem in two ways, neither of which was likely to induce comfort among the devout. Gerrit Smith spoke for one teetotal position when he argued that, although the Bible did indeed condone wine drinking, new conditions and new knowledge in the nineteenth century rendered this biblical view obsolete. For the churches, this argument represented the nose of the camel appearing under the edge of the tent. If modern wisdom were allowed to supersede Scripture on this point a precedent would be established for denying scriptural authority on others as well. Unwilling to disclaim the continuing authority of the gospel, other teetotalers, led by Delavan and the distinguished biblical scholar Moses Stuart, argued that the Bible, in its favorable references to wine, did not refer to fermented wine at all but rather to the unfermented juice of the grape. Such a patent attempt to reinterpret Scripture according to the needs of the temperance movement convinced few. By 1840, five years after the NYSTS endorsed teetotalism, only 7 percent of the congregations in New York State used unfermented wine. The Methodist Episcopal church, in other ways a leading temperance denomination, refused to endorse the use of unfermented wine in Communion until 1880. During the 1830s many temperance supporters in the churches broke ranks with the movement over this issue. As in the case of the wealthy, the loss of Christian supporters during the teetotalism controversy began a process that was to accelerate with the appearance of the Washingtonians a few years later.[46]

Disputes over teetotalism slowed or even stopped the progress of the temperance movement by the late 1830s. Temperance reformers were affected, too, by the economic depression beginning in 1837, which diminished the financial support available to all reform movements. The double impact of division and depression clouded optimistic visions of a sober society and gave further impetus to a tactical transition already under way: a shift to more coercive measures.[47]

Toward Coercion

When temperance reformers began to seek the aid of law they acted not primarily to compel changes in behavior but rather to effect a symbolic change in the communal stance toward liquor selling. When the community licensed liquor sellers, they argued, it covered them with a mantle of respectability. To remove that mantle was therefore a necessary part of the task of persuading citizens that drinking was both a sin for the individual and a blow against community welfare. Beginning in the early 1830s, temperance folk in Massachusetts began to seek from their town selectmen a policy of recommending to the appointed county commissioners, who granted liquor licenses, no names of would-be sellers at all. Initially this makeshift local option was aimed only against sellers of distilled liquors, but as the temperance movement shifted to teetotalism the targets of temperance people in the towns were broadened to include sales of all alcoholic beverages. In 1835 the office of county commissioner was made elective and thereafter commissioner elections became tests of temperance and antitemperance strength. Several counties, most of them in southeastern Massachusetts, became legally dry by these means. The mantle of respectability was thereby lifted from the trade, but unlicensed sellers rushed in where respectable former licensees feared to tread. In order to make a means of persuasion work, therefore, reformers began to advocate deploying the coercive power of law to suppress the illegal trade.[48]

After establishing no-license in several counties, the Massachusetts temperance movement turned to its legislature, the General Court, in order to win statewide prohibition. By organizing effectively rather than providing clear evidence of majority support, they succeeded in 1838 in gaining enactment of what was in effect a partial statewide prohibition act, the Fifteen-Gallon Law. Under this law, sales of distilled spirits in quantities less than fifteen gallons were prohibited in Massachusetts, except for medicinal and mechanical purposes. The law provoked bitter opposition and produced an escalation of the harassment that had previously been visited upon temperance folk. Physical assaults and mob violence now became more common. In addition, opponents mobilized politically, turned out temperance-minded officials in the next state election, and secured the repeal of the hated Fifteen-Gallon Law only two years after its enactment.[49]

Temperance reformers in other states also moved at the same time in the direction of coercion. Tennessee made the retail sale of ardent spirits an offense punishable by fine, and Rhode Island, New Hampshire, Connecticut, and Illinois passed new state laws allowing local option on liquor licensing. Mississippi enacted a One-Gallon Law forbidding the sale of distilled liquor or wine in quantities less than a single gallon. In New York, Pennsylvania, South Carolina, and Georgia, temperance reformers organized petition campaigns for statewide prohibition. Antitemperance violence escalated. During the 1838 no-license referendum in Providence, Rhode Island, one prohibitionist found his trees cut down, another's house was blown up, and a third was shot at. In Georgia, much bitterness was caused by entry into the 1839 state campaign of a slate of no-license candidates, led by a prosperous Methodist planter named Josiah Flournoy. Flournoy was denounced by representatives of both major parties, his buggy was destroyed, his mule was shaved and painted, and his meetings were disrupted.[50]

The no-license campaigns in the South followed a history of temperance organization in that region that paralleled that in the North. Southerners organized local temperance societies beginning in the 1820s, and by 1831 such societies could be found in every southern state but Louisiana. State societies were established in Virginia, Georgia, Mississippi, North Carolina, Alabama, and South Carolina. In 1831 there were 339 local organizations in the South, 15 percent of the national total, and Virginia and Georgia ranked eighth and ninth among all states, respectively, in total membership. As in the North, evangelical Protestants, particularly Baptists and Methodists, took the lead in organizing and spreading the movement. Despite the many ways in which the South constituted a distinct region, in their arguments for temperance southern reformers presented little that differed from what their northern counterparts were saying at the same time. Themes such as slave control, while present and seemingly attractive in a slaveholding society, received little emphasis. Southern paternalism did not prevent women from joining temperance societies, sometimes in equal numbers to men, and the argument that women were the chief sufferers from male intemperance appeared in the South as well as in the North. Southern reformers built their movement around the pledge of total abstinence from distilled spirits, began to adopt the long pledge at least as early as 1829, and then suffered disputes and division in the mid-1830s. In the late 1830s those temperance folk who remained in the movement after the teetotal controversies shifted their efforts to no-license campaigns.

Although the history of the southern temperance movement ran parallel to its northern counterpart and temperance was the only antebellum reform to receive substantial support in the South, nevertheless southern temperance was only a movement in miniature compared to the North. In 1831, for example, when the southern states contained 44 percent of the nation's population, their temperance societies could report only 8.5 percent of the pledges. Nor did the southern movement wield power or influence. The enactment of Mississippi's One-Gallon Law was a fluke, and the law was repealed shortly after its passage. Flournoy's movement in Georgia, for all it cost him and his fellow reformers, elected only four state legislators and failed to achieve its goal, a state no-license law. The weakness of southern temperance forces reflected the retardation by the South's slave system of many of the economic and social changes that had energized temperance reform in the North.[51]

By 1840 American temperance reform had completed its first cycle. Had Tom Nisbet been alive in that year he would have found that much had changed since the turn of the century. Drinking was now a focus of public debate and political action. Antidrink societies existed in most communities and enrolled many, such as women, who had previously taken only a small part in public activity. Most of the members of these societies no longer regarded wine, cider, and beer as acceptable substitutes for ardent spirits, and their generally negative view of alcohol was shared by an increasing number of physicians. Antialcohol views were now especially strong within academic settings such as that over which his father had presided. Within society as a whole, drinking had been reduced. Nevertheless temperance reformers continued their crusade, now commonly directing their efforts toward eliminating the source of temptation created by the sale of liquor.

Beginning as a suasionist crusade, the first temperance movement spread through effective organizing as its message spoke to the experience of large numbers of citizens of both sexes from every region, class, religion, and ethnic group. Through teetotalism the movement became more radical and through no-license it became more coercive. Both teetotalism and no-license required modification of the temperance view of the relationship between human beings and alcohol. Benjamin Rush had postulated that one class of substances—distilled spirits—was addictive for some people. The temperance movement under the ATS, accepting this view, argued that all should abstain from distilled spirits in order to help some avoid addiction. The teetotalism controversy resulted in enlarging the class of substances deemed to be addictive to include fermented as well as distilled liquors. In the no-license campaigns temperance reformers put forward the view that all members of a community must be denied access to this larger class of substances in order, again, to help some avoid addiction. Contrary to the claims of some scholars, temperance reformers did not thereupon adopt the belief that drink was inherently addictive. Although reformers believed that alcohol was a poison and drinking was a sin, they did not also believe that this substance was addictive for everyone. Instead, the danger in drinking arose from the combination of a hazardous substance and a weakness that human beings shared in varying degrees. For the weaker members of society drinking was a sin because it exposed them to a substance capable of destroying their lives, endangering their souls, damaging the lives of those who depended upon them, and entailing significant costs to society. For stronger persons drinking was a sin because it made alcohol respectable and available, thereby heightening the temptation facing their weaker fellows. Even in the latter phase of the temperance reform's first cycle, its concept of alcohol represented an evolutionary development from the view held by Americans during the colonial period, not a radically different image. The principal force behind that development was not a new, more optimistic belief in human ability but rather the often disconcerting experiences of temperance workers as they came to grips with the difficulties involved in converting a society of drinkers into a society of abstainers.[52]

As the 1830s ended, the work of temperance reformers seemed to have been rewarded with success. Per capita consumption of absolute alcohol suffered its most precipitous decline in American history, from nearly four gallons in 1830 to about two gallons by 1840. Temperance reformers could rightly claim credit for at least a part of this decline. Spirits consumption, which accounted for about three-fifths of total alcohol consumption in 1830, dropped by almost a gallon by 1840. Cider consumption is estimated to have fallen even more, but here the temperance case seems to be on weaker ground, since much of the decline in cider drinking appears to have taken place before 1835, at a time when the teetotal pledge had not yet come into widespread use. But even if temperance activity was responsible for only the decline in spirits consumption, its achievement was considerable. Within a single generation it played a leading part in bringing about a significant change in patterns of mass behavior.

The work of temperance reformers was assisted by larger changes in values, to be sure, as during these years the theme of control that occupied such a prominent place in temperance ideology became a central element in the culture of at least the American middle class. This new desire for control flowed from the same economic changes that stimulated temperance reformers. Prodded by temperance propaganda, many Americans came to believe that drinking was incompatible with a standard of conduct suited to the emerging possibilities and uncertainties of their society. Products of historical change, temperance reformers also served as agents of change. The reduction of drinking they helped bring about was a significant achievement, and in the next cycle of temperance reform they were to extend their influence even further.[53]

Chapter Two

Washingtonians, Fraternal Societies, and Maine Laws (1840–60)

To many eyes the situation in which Neal Dow found himself on the evening of 2 June 1855 must have seemed a strange one for a temperance advocate. With two dozen armed militiamen and a squad of police at his back, the mayor of Portland, Maine, stood on the ground floor of his city hall, defending a stock of liquor from an angry mob. The police had already fired their pistols at the mob, but failed to disperse them, and the room through which Dow peered was filled with smoke and the smell of gunpowder. Sighting several members of the mob through the opposite door, Dow ordered the militiamen to level their rifles and take aim. The three volleys that followed his next command carried temperance reform into a world of coercion undreamt of by the early temperance reformers, a world unrecognizable as well to millions of Americans who were drawn to the vision of peace and plenty that enthusiastic prohibitionists such as Dow himself set before them.

After many years of trying, temperance reformers had finally enlisted the help of the state in creating their dry utopia, and prohibition became the principal instrument by which the new world was to be shaped. The shift to prohibition, however, was not a simple evolution from the no-license campaigns of the late 1830s. The reform that Neal Dow led into the country of prohibition was simultaneously revitalized and reshaped in the early 1840s by Washingtonianism, a remarkable popular upsurge partly working-class in composition and entirely devoted to moral suasion. But by the time Dow and his militiamen faced the Portland mob, temperance reform had traversed another cycle. Dow himself played a leading role in these events, and his story provides a good introduction to them.

Neal Dow was born in 1804, the second son of Josiah Dow, a Maine pioneer and Portland tannery owner, and Dorcas Allen Dow, the daughter of a prosperous Quaker family. American Quakers were early advocates of sobriety, as they were of the other nineteenth-century middle-class virtues, and Neal's upbringing anticipated that of many other young men of his century. He grew up industrious, thrifty, and sober, but self-control in some aspects of his life appears to have been bought at some psychological price, as he was also self-willed, hot-tempered, and outspoken. Although much of his wealth and position was inherited, he easily accepted an equation between personal virtue and public success. At the same time Neal learned from his mother's benevolent activity a sense of responsibility toward those less fortunate than he.

In both his business and his civic affairs Neal Dow was a relentless improver. He welcomed the age of steam and installed in his family's tannery the first stationary engine made in Portland. He supported Bible, tract, and missionary societies, and in 1827 he was converted to total abstinence from ardent spirits. He joined the Maine Charitable Mechanic Association, an organization of employers, and played a leading role in the group's decision to abolish the traditional rum ration provided to workers during the workday. Like other reformers active during the heyday of the American Temperance Society, Dow at first considered the use of wine acceptable, until in 1829 reflection upon the inconsistency of wine for the rich and abstinence for the poor led him to become the first of his social circle to entertain without the juice of the grape. When he spoke in public he chose to derive his arguments for temperance from the correlation he perceived between abstinence and economic success. This concern pervaded his personal life, too, as he punctuated family drives through the countryside by pointing out rundown houses and farms and telling his children, "Rum there," or "Rum did that." Meanwhile, capital begat by the family tannery provided funds for investment in real estate as well as in canal, cotton mill, and bank stock. The income from these investments allowed Dow to turn his industry more and more to reform and in particular to the cause of making others sober. During the late 1830s he worked assiduously, but without much success, to commit both the Maine temperance forces and the voters of Portland and Maine to some form of prohibition.

Temperance reform in the state, as elsewhere, received a fresh jolt of energy in the early 1840s from a new source: reformed drunkards. The Washingtonian movement spread across the nation from its original locus in Baltimore, using as its most dramatic tool the public confessions of former drinkers. Although the Washingtonians arose in Baltimore and in other places on the initiative of heavy drinkers, in Portland the movement was manipulated into existence by Neal Dow. Working behind the scenes, Dow arranged a meeting to which temperate workingmen brought their heavy-drinking friends. At the meeting Dow kept his prohibitionist loyalties in the background as he sang the praises of abstinence and moral suasion. Twenty-five of his hearers signed the total abstinence pledge, and the Washingtonian movement in Portland was under way. By the end of the first year Portland Washingtonians claimed to have pledged over fourteen hundred men, Dow had organized a companion Young Men's Total Abstinence Society, and his wife, Cornelia, helped lead the Martha Washington Society for women. When a Congregational minister protested that the Washingtonians envisioned a reformation without salvation, Dow—a Congregationalist though not a church member—characteristically went on the attack, charging that clergymen sought to exert sectarian control over the movement.

Dow then sought to convince the reformed men that they had been victimized by the rum seller and that prohibition was the only weapon that could prevent his further depredations. Dow's efforts produced a solid victory in Portland's next no-license referendum and provoked his opponents to form a splinter organization of suasionists, aptly named the Peace Washingtonians. In Dow's view city officials failed to enforce no-license effectively, so he turned to the state legislature for help. After a winter spent stumping the state he brought to the legislature in 1846 petitions for prohibition containing forty thousand names and won from it a statewide prohibitory law. The law forbade the sale of spirits and wine in small quantities, but, contrary to Dow's advice, prescribed only light fines for violators. Once again Portland officials, fearing the effect of prohibition upon the city's commerce, failed to provide adequate enforcement.

In 1850 Neal Dow began a new prohibition offensive. As president of the Maine Temperance Union (MTU) he organized Maine temperance voters into a disciplined bloc which wielded the balance of power in close legislative districts. In Portland he ran successfully for mayor on the Whig ticket. Finally, he drafted a new statewide prohibition bill designed to remedy the defects of the 1846 law. Dow's bill, which became known as the Maine Law, marked a new phase in American temperance reform by its thoroughgoing use of state power. Manufacture of liquor was forbidden and its sale was permitted only by the bonded agent of a municipality for medicinal and industrial uses. Searches of suspected premises were authorized and any liquor found was to be seized, with the burden of proof of legality placed upon its owner. Heavy fines were prescribed, with jail sentences for repeated offenders. In tightening up the 1846 law, Dow "smoothed the path of the prosecution, multiplied difficulties for the defense and limited the discretion of often hostile judges."[1] With the passage of his bill in 1851 and the publicity given his efforts to enforce the law in Portland, Neal Dow became a national figure.

By 1855, when he won a second term as Portland's mayor, Dow the man had become identified with the issue of prohibition. His enemies in Portland must have taken much relish in contriving the trap that brought him face-to-face with the mob in June. After assuming the mayoralty Dow arranged for purchase of a supply for the city liquor agency, which was now the only legal outlet for liquor to be used for nonbeverage purposes. With his customary zeal, Dow made the purchase before appointment of a city agent. Under the stringent provisions of Dow's law, however, only an officially designated city agent was allowed to sell liquor. Conveyance of the liquor from Dow to the agent might therefore be construed as an illegal sale. If it were so construed the liquor might be seized and destroyed, leaving neither Dow nor the city able to recoup its cost. "Let the lash which Neal Dow has prepared for other's [*sic*] backs," cried an old enemy, "be applied to his own."[2] The mob formed when police went to city hall to investigate a complaint laid by Dow's political opponents; it refused to disperse when the police failed to seize the liquor. The goal of both complaint and mob was specific: to embarrass Neal Dow. Dow could not have cooperated more effectively had he been a conspirator in the scheme, although no one seems to have anticipated the eventual outcome. When the militia swept the liquor agency and the street outside with their volleys, one man was killed and seven wounded. In defending the city's liquor Dow was not really acting to enforce the Maine Law, although those who read an account of the affair in the next day's newspaper may have believed that he was. Many Americans did perceive accurately that enactment of a tough prohibition law and a thoroughgoing attempt to enforce it polarized the community and escalated the level of violence between prohibitionists and antiprohibitionists, thereby irretrievably tarnishing the prohibitionist dream of an orderly world of upwardly mobile abstainers. Although he lacked the insight of a tragic hero, Neal Dow's career was indeed the stuff of tragedy. He did more than anyone else to make prohibition the centerpiece of temperance reform; he more than anyone else was responsible for demonstrating the divisive effects of legal coercion.[3]

Dow's career illustrates the course of temperance reform's second cycle, but since it is the story of only a single person it cannot answer the questions that cycle provokes. Why did thousands of workingmen suddenly in the early 1840s begin to find temperance reform attractive? What was their impact on the reform? How and why did the Washingtonians come to abandon moral suasion for prohibition? More generally, why did the prohibitionist drive gain impetus in the absence of a general rise in liquor consumption? What was the relationship, if any, between the onsurge of the Maine Law forces and the realignment of the American party system ending with the rise of the Republican party? Finally, why did the prohibition drive suddenly lose momentum in the late 1850s? As in its first cycle, the course of temperance reform from 1840 to the Civil War involved the thoughts and actions of millions of men and women; to understand why they thought and acted as they did, we must begin again with drinking.

Drinking: Decline, Reinforcement, and Innovation

The drinking scene in 1840 was different from what it was only a generation before, as the lowered level of per capita consumption suggests. Modifications in social customs reflected the influence of the first temperance movement. Domestic hospitality no longer was considered to require an automatically proffered drink. Most doctors on house calls probably did not mind the change, since a combination of temperance persuasion and the new availability of alternative drugs such as quinine and opium made them less ready to view alcohol in a favorable light. The old custom of serving liquor to mourners at funerals went out of general usage; when in the 1840s Irish immigrants brought the practice with them it became cause for comment because of its rarity among the native-born. The number of families serving alcohol to New Year's Day visitors declined. New York governor William H. Seward gave public sanction to the new custom when he provided only lemonade and cold water for his New Year's callers in 1842. Agricultural laborers, soldiers, and other workers found their workday liquor rations cut off by their employers. Perhaps in reaction to this sort of intervention, young male workers in the cities claimed Christmas as a day for unrestrained public rowdyism, usually fueled by heavy drinking. Although middle-class moralists fumed as their holy day was filled with fireworks, fantastical parades, noise, and costumes portraying symbolic inversions of the social order, they failed to note that opportunities for working-class drinking were steadily contracting. Evangelical churches prayed, browbeat, and coerced their members into drinking less or not at all, although the pace of change varied from congregation to congregation.[4]

Institutional change produced alternatives to the ways of the old alcoholic society, although in the case of some institutions the pace of change was painfully slow. The major cities gradually made water centrally available to their citizens through the construction of public waterworks. In New York, temperance groups took a prominent part in celebrating completion of the Croton Aqueduct in 1842, but not all homes were immediately supplied with Croton water, and two decades later the city still contained very few publicly accessible sources of drinking water. Central water was not necessarily clean water; construction of filtration and sewage systems did not begin until much later in the century. The price of coffee, which had previously made the imported beverage too expensive to substitute for whiskey, began to drop in the late 1820s, and coffee consumption per capita more than tripled between 1820 and 1840; temperance reformers deliberately assisted the process by persuading Congress to eliminate the duty on coffee. From the early 1830s attempts were made to operate temperance hotels, and although some efforts failed, dry hostelries could still be found in the 1850s. In Pittsburgh, temperate developers built a suburb, Temperanceville, from which saloons were barred.[5]

Changes in customs and institutions ate into the fabric of traditional society, changing reciprocal relationships into impersonal ones mediated by the cash nexus. An example of this process can be found in Wethersfield, Connecticut, where the Congregational minister, Calvin Chapin, customarily served a potent derivative of apple cider to the parishioners who attended the annual woodcutting party that provided the minister with his winter firewood. When the temperance movement swept through Wethersfield, Chapin became a leading advocate of total abstinence, and suiting his practice to his new beliefs, he stopped serving alcoholic cider to the woodcutters. The congregation thenceforth ceased attending the woodcutting party, which came to an end. Thereafter the congregation presumably paid Chapin wholly in cash for his preaching, and Chapin in turn paid hired woodcutters for his winter's warmth.[6]

Larger social changes both reinforced and undermined the structure of popular behavior and belief constructed by the first temperance movement. Continuing migration to frontier regions throughout the mid-nineteenth century produced small societies made up largely of young males engaged in hard physical labor outdoors and containing few institutional alternatives to the omnipresent saloon. Drinking consequently flourished in such places. In frontier towns drinking probably took place as a voluntary and informal small-group activity rather than as a community ritual; it therefore shared more in common with drinking practices in eastern cities than with those in older rural areas whose population density was closer to that of the frontier. But if drinking practices in older cities and in frontier towns resembled one another, drinking places did not. In both settled rural areas and on the frontier, taverns were multifunctional institutions that provided a range of social services and a locus for community activities having little intrinsic connection with drinking. Saloons and taverns served as banks, message centers, concert halls, lodging places, hiring halls, post offices, courtrooms, and religious meetinghouses, among other functions. Although saloons in larger urban places maintained some of these social functions, most were performed by other, specialized institutions, leaving the commercial role of the saloon correspondingly enlarged in relation to its diminished social role.[7]

Urban migration concurrent with the westward movement brought an increasing proportion of the population into places where they could come into contact with saloons whose existence depended primarily on retailing large volumes of alcohol. In addition, community restraints on drinking behavior were weakened by the size and impersonality of the city. Rural migrants carried into such an environment the tolerant attitudes toward drinking that prevailed in the slower-paced world they left behind. Temperance reform represented an attempt to create a new set of inner controls and external institutions to replace the old community controls, thereby equipping individuals to cope with the new requirements and drinking patterns of urban society. Insofar as it succeeded, its success owed as much to the larger social forces that created the "problem" as to its own efforts, prodigious and creative though they were. In the new commercial world fostered by expansion of the market economy, self-discipline did matter for those who lacked a cushion of inherited wealth. The workers who listened to Neal Dow's equation of industry, thrift, and sobriety with material success had cause to feel that it made sense. In Philadelphia during the middle third of the century, for example, evangelical journeymen amassed more substantial property holdings and achieved greater upward occupational mobility than nonevangelical workers. The discipline imposed by the new factories reinforced the temperance message for those who worked in them, even if the factory owner did not. In the stormy seas of a market economy the bourgeois virtues could not guarantee an individual's safe arrival, but they could at least help him steer a steady course.[8]

By 1840 the drinking population, which was once coterminous with the population at large, had shrunk to a segment of the larger society defined by gender, class, age, and ethnicity. Further research is needed to define the size of the drinking population and to estimate its proportion of each subgroup in society, but its outlines can be crudely sketched. All women did not stop drinking altogether—indeed, through consumption of some patent medicines many women drank unknowingly, while otherwise abstemious families continued to use liquor in cooking—but so far as beverage alcohol was concerned most native-born women by mid-century were probably either cautious drinkers or abstainers. German women joined their husbands on Sundays in beer gardens whose celebrations of leisure scandalized native-born moralists; such family- and community-centered insobriety represented a traditional drinking pattern transplanted to American towns and cities. Irish women drank too, but their poverty, the gender segregation of Irish immigrant communities, and the domestic violence and desertion that marked their marriages made their drinking more an act of desperation than celebration, and they seem to have contributed more than their share of female drunkards.[9]

In their drinking habits elites divided along occupational lines, with merchants, planters, and many lawyers continuing to use wine or spirits, and manufacturers tending to adopt the same abstinent code they urged—and often forced—upon their workers. The middle class is usually pictured as the exemplar of temperance because a multitude of self-appointed spokesmen for the middle class wanted it that way; their voices speak clearly and persistently in the documentary record of the period. Certainly sobriety was a central element in the ideology of self-control employed by the middle class to distinguish itself from the "idle" above and the "vicious" below. Through that ideology the middle class identified itself with the "true" interests of society. Self-control aided middle-class men as well as working-class men to weather the recurrent storms of the market economy. But possession of the marginal financial security that helped distinguish middle class from working class also meant that middle-class men could afford to drink, up to a point, without exposing themselves and their families to economic disaster. As the advocates of teetotalism pointed out, "temperance" could be interpreted in a multitude of ways; the participation of middle-class women in temper-

ance activity in order to reform their men suggests that the latter's inter-
pretations were often very broad indeed. Among those who eventually
became abstainers the life-cycle experience of Neal Dow may well have
been representative in that it included a youthful period of wine drinking.
Other abstainers probably went through a similar time of experimentation
with liquor while young.

The drinking practices of working-class men were equally complex.
Apostles of abstinence appeared among articulate workers even before
the advent of the Washingtonians, the most eloquent of such apostles.
During the 1830s working-class radicals and union organizers (who were
usually the same people) urged temperance upon their fellow workers as
a necessary condition for both self-improvement and effective resistance
to bosses. Few seem to have listened, however, until the depression of
1837–43 and the Washingtonian crusade stimulated enthusiasm for temperance among hundreds of thousands of workingmen while the depression wiped out their fledgling unions. The segment of the working class
converted to temperance by Washingtonianism was overwhelmingly
native-born, as was the working class as a whole at that time. Massive
immigration from Ireland and the German states, which reached flood
tide in the late 1840s, changed the ethnic composition of the working
class to largely foreign-born by the early 1850s and set back the progress
of temperance among the working class by more than a decade. Immigrants brought with them indulgent attitudes toward drink; among young
Irishmen such attitudes had been intensified by the peculiar conditions of
land shortage and an introverted bachelor subculture. In America those
attitudes were reinforced by daily experience, as immigrant workers
often found themselves working hard but intermittently, outdoors and in
all-male work groups, while living as transients in preponderantly male
immigrant subcommunities hard by the commercial districts where city
saloons proliferated. Under such conditions drinking thrived.[10]

In addition to reinflating the size of the drinking population German
immigrants added a new ingredient to the American drinking scene: lager
beer. Before the 1840s, beer, much of which was home-brewed, contributed only a small proportion of total alcohol consumed. American
brewing derived from the British tradition, producing strong-flavored,
strong-smelling ale made with a top-fermenting yeast. German immigrants brought with them different techniques and a different product,
made from bottom-fermenting yeast, lighter, more effervescent, and
with a slightly lower alcohol content. Immigrants quickly established
breweries to serve local urban markets containing large numbers of their

countrymen, but their lager also found customers beyond the immigrant community.

Although the period of beer's greatest popularity was not to come until after the Civil War, four of today's largest brewing companies—Anheuser-Busch, Schlitz, Pabst, and Miller—originated during the antebellum years. Per capita beer production rose from 1.3 gallons in 1840 to 3.8 gallons by 1860; in the latter year beer contributed about one-sixth of total absolute alcohol consumed. During the same period per capita spirits consumption seems to have decreased by about one-quarter; as beer added one-tenth of a gallon of absolute alcohol per capita to American consumption, the decline in spirit-drinking reduced absolute alcohol consumed by about four-tenths of a gallon from its 1840 level of 1.8 gallons per capita. By the time of lager beer's arrival the leading sectors of temperance reform had long since condemned beer along with wine, cider, and spirits; in such company the brewers' depiction of beer as a temperance drink fell on deaf ears. Nevertheless, to the extent that lager beer replaced spirits in American preferences total alcohol consumption, drunkenness, and alcoholic damage declined.[11]

The Washingtonians

Before immigration complicated the drinking scene with new drinkers and a new drink, the first temperance movement was already fragmented. With total abstinence from distilled spirits as their goal, temperance forces led by the American Temperance Society were able to win widespread support through a suasionist approach. When the new goal of total abstinence from all that can intoxicate was adopted by temperance societies, the movement split, as a new set of temperance sympathizers apart from the organizations came into being alongside those whose temperance consisted of moderation in the use of all alcoholic beverages. When campaigns for no-license began, further complications arose. Some of those who upheld the goal of teetotalism found no-license too harsh and divisive; meanwhile some temperance folk who rejected total abstinence or teetotalism supported no-license as a means of eliminating others' public tippling, while they continued in private to enjoy their beverages imported from other jurisdictions. This process was to be repeated again and again during the life of the reform as each change in the temperance army's direction brought in new detachments while leaving its route strewn with stragglers and deserters. The first temperance movement made temperance a widely popular ideal and a continuing flood of literature helped keep the ideal bright; from that time to the 1980s few were to be found to contest it. The movement's leaders, however, were frustrated again and again as they strove to formulate policies capable of both building upon what they had learned from experience and uniting the scattered forces of temperance. Their dilemma, born of fragmentation, would never die.

The Washingtonians appeared in this context of fragmentation, and at first their approach appeared to be suited not only to revitalizing but also to unifying the divided reform. Traditional accounts of the movement's origins make its provenance seem almost whimsical. Six artisans drinking at Chase's tavern in Baltimore dispatched several of their number to hear a temperance lecturer; upon the emissaries' return the group decided to organize a new kind of society aimed at the reformation of drunkards through moral suasion. Because some of the original members turned out to possess considerable oratorical abilities, the movement spread across the nation rapidly. Recent research has corrected this eccentric image by revealing forerunners to the Washingtonians whose emergence in the late 1830s clearly links the movement to the distress experienced by workers in the economic depression of 1837–43.

The depression itself compressed and intensified a growing threat to artisans from the rise of large-scale production. Workers' principal weapon to combat the dangers facing them was their unions, but these crumbled as the depression shifted the balance of power decisively in favor of employers. Before the depression artisans had organized beneficial societies—in effect small-scale insurance cooperatives—and as the cold winds of hard times shriveled workers' resources, a temperance theme was added to the mutual-protection function of such societies, or new temperance-beneficial societies were created. The membership lists of two temperance-beneficial societies in Philadelphia in 1837–38 show that journeymen made up from one-half to three-fifths of the members, and unskilled workers contributed another one-fifth to one-quarter. Temperance was not the only course available to unemployed or underemployed workers at the time; radicals blamed the depression on the manipulations of bankers and pointed to political action as a remedy. Their listeners, however, apparently preferred first to attempt to ensure survival through means less momentous, less difficult, and closer at hand. Organizers of temperance-beneficial societies in the late 1830s pioneered what was to become a distinctive feature of Washingtonianism by featuring "experience speeches" of reformed drunkards at their frequent meetings. In Cincinnati at the same time women working under the "temperance-beneficial" rubric anticipated another theme of the Washingtonian phase by attempting to ameliorate the poverty of drunkards and their families. By these means the ground was prepared for the seeds of Washingtonian rhetoric.[12]

During its first year the new society in Baltimore organized its hometown, and by Christmas 1840 it had enrolled about three hundred members, two-thirds of them reformed drinkers. As winter came to an end the Baltimoreans sent out feelers to New York, inquiring whether the New York City Temperance Society was willing to pay the expenses for a visit by five lecturers. The New Yorkers welcomed the new approach; the resulting public meetings in March 1841 more than justified their enthusiasm, as thousands of new recruits slid into temperance societies on the teetotal pledge that only a few years earlier had proved such an obstacle to the reform's progress. On the morning after the first meeting a New York newspaper reported what transpired:

During the first speech a young man arose in the gallery and, though intoxicated, begged to know if there was any hope for him; declaring his readiness to bind himself, from that hour, to drink no more. He was invited to come down and sign the pledge, which he did forthwith, in the presence of the audience, under deep emotion, which seemed to be contagious, for others followed; and during each of the speeches they continued to come forward and sign, until more than a hundred pledges were obtained; a large proportion of which were intemperate persons, some of whom were old and gray headed.[13]

After their success in New York, Washingtonian speakers fanned out across the country, reaching Boston in June and Cincinnati in July; Virginia and North Carolina also welcomed Washingtonian speakers during 1841. In Pittsburgh in July, thirty-six hundred signed the pledge during a two-week period. Estimates vary, but historians agree that the Washingtonians brought large numbers into temperance societies at a pace heretofore unknown in the reform. A conservative estimate of enrollment in Baltimore in May 1842 gives the Washingtonian societies about 11 percent of the city's free population over ten years of age; a similar estimate for New York City shows 7 percent of the free population over ten enrolled in the societies. Once again temperance became a mass movement.[14]

Temperance also became for the first time a movement *of* the masses. The original six founders included a tailor, a carpenter, a coachmaker, a silversmith, a wheelwright, and a blacksmith. In New York City and

Worcester, Massachusetts, artisans made up between one-quarter and one-third of traceable Washingtonian activists, and laborers and other unskilled workers added another one-eighth, although historians' inability to trace a significant number of Washingtonian names suggests that many more belonged to the least-skilled, most transient occupations. In Taunton, Massachusetts, 355 Washingtonians paid an average property tax of $3.41, whereas their predecessors in temperance, 304 men who petitioned for no-license in 1834, were assessed an average of $7.64. Those arrested in Taunton for public drunkenness paid less tax, an average of fifty-one cents, which indicates that experience speeches picturing Washingtonians as the dregs of society were exaggerated, but the movement clearly appealed to a segment of society that had never before been aroused in such numbers by a call to temperance. "The Washingtonian movement," as Ian Tyrrell concludes, "was essentially a creation of the artisan classes."[15]

Still, other classes were represented in the Washingtonian societies, sometimes in substantial numbers; in New York City, for example, merchants and professionals together made up the largest occupational group among Washingtonian officers. The new movement drew from both middle and working classes; the only groups conspicuous by their absence were the Congregational, Presbyterian, and Unitarian clergymen and the wealthy capitalists who together had provided much of the leadership for temperance in the 1820s and 1830s. The churchgoers who became Washingtonians were as likely to represent the Methodists, Baptists, or even nonevangelical churches such as the Episcopalians as they were the older evangelical churches. The best explanation for the nature of the Washingtonian appeal is that the movement was what it appeared to be, an attempt to convince drinkers to become abstainers and to remain so. The existing temperance leadership were abstainers who had already decided that more than moral suasion was necessary to achieve their goals; while they wished, like Neal Dow, to manipulate the new movement, for the most part they attempted to do so—unlike Dow—from the outside. In addition, many temperance activists were repelled by Washingtonian methods.[16]

Not all were. In some communities existing temperance societies simply changed their name to "Washingtonian" following a visit from a lecturer for the new movement. Where this occurred the only effect of Washingtonianism might be to put an end to the teetotal controversy of the 1830s, uniting reformers behind the goal of total abstinence from all that can intoxicate. This appears to have been the situation in Virginia and North Carolina. Elsewhere in the South, however, the Washingtonian years brought thousands of fresh recruits, both whites and blacks, to the formerly moribund reform. In the North hundreds of thousands of former drinkers poured into both new and existing teetotal societies. Only a minority of these were chronic drunkards, although Washingtonianism clearly was more effective in recruiting drunkards than any previous approach had been. Most new members were simply working-class or middle-class drinkers who in the midst of hard times found the Washingtonian approach more congenial than those of previous temperance societies. Many were young men to whom the Washingtonian promise of assistance in achieving autonomy through self-control spoke directly. The greater receptivity of drinkers to the Washingtonian message should not be surprising. While the prohibitionists who dominated the older societies wrote them off as victims of the rum seller, Washingtonians addressed drinkers as agents capable of controlling their own lives even under difficult circumstances.[17]

The new message was carried by various means. The experience speech, a narrative of one's personal odyssey from debauchery to sobriety, remained the principal device for publicizing the movement and attracting new recruits. Its medium was probably at least as important as its message: in contrast to printed literature that unavoidably distanced writer from reader and consisted of learned biblical exegesis or arguments rising to higher and higher moral planes, the spectacle of a single man recounting events of his own life seemed authentic and direct. The pledge devised by the Baltimore founders required no commitment to "discountenance" the use of liquor by others. It simply read as follows:

We, whose names are annexed, desirous of forming a society for our mutual benefit, and to guard against a pernicious practice which is injurious to our health, standing, and families, do pledge ourselves as gentlemen that we will not drink any spirituous or malt liquors, wine or cider.[18]

Whereas older temperance societies convened infrequently and focused their meetings on a formal lecture by a visiting notable, Washingtonian societies met weekly or more often and filled their meetings with experience speeches made by their own members. Where older societies advertised through printed announcements, Washingtonians combed the streets, docks, vice districts, and gutters to find drunkards and personally bring them to meetings. Washingtonian missionaries to Skid Row grasped an insight that Alcoholics Anonymous was to rediscover much later. "By saving others," as Tyrrell notes, "they simultaneously saved themselves."[19] Their predecessors depended upon the power of reason and morality to keep members true to their commitment; Washingtonians sought to create alternatives to the sociability of the saloon. Both group singing at society meetings and concerts by professional temperance singers brought music to the aid of temperance reform for the first time. Washingtonians in the cities organized a round of picnics crowned by a cold-water Fourth of July celebration, as well as fairs, processions, concerts, and balls.[20]

Washingtonians understood another fact that escaped previous temperance reformers, namely that those whose lives were damaged by drink often needed material assistance as well as moral support and encouragement. Washingtonian societies paid court fines and put up bonds for drunkards in trouble with the law, found lodgings for them or rented or bought buildings to shelter them until they could find their own lodgings, and furnished food, clothing, loans, and other assistance to reformed drunkards and their families. Financial needs were met in two ways. First, Washingtonians turned to the wealthy members of the old societies for contributions to their work. Second, Washingtonian women, enrolled in their own Martha Washington societies, raised money in a variety of ways and provided countless woman-hours of benevolent work. Sometimes the societies were led by women whose husbands had long been active in temperance work; more often the initiative in forming and running a Martha Washington Society came from the same artisan class that provided the male Washingtonian leadership. Some Martha Washington leaders were the wives of artisans; others were single women who were self-supporting. In some communities, the Martha Washington Society outnumbered its male counterpart.[21]

Like their predecessors in temperance reform, the Washingtonians feared the power of alcohol to overcome frail human will power. But whereas the old temperance societies had come to see prohibition as a means to keep potential drinkers from temptation, the new reformers preferred to provide a network of support that could encourage those already ensnared by the habit to help themselves. A Washingtonian speaker in 1844 explicitly depicted this network as an alternative to legal means: "Show us the man . . . [,] that is all we want. Bring the inebriate to us, or tell us where we can find him; we have something to reach him more potent than legislation. We can place him where his old haunts will no longer have any temptation for him; where he will no longer require legal enactment for his protection."[22]

The Washingtonians began a new cycle of reform, but not because they convinced temperance veterans of the virtues of moral suasion. Those who had walked the road from moral suasion to coercion during the 1830s saw no need to retrace their steps on account of the surprising and gratifying, but no doubt transient, success of the new movement. Instead the Washingtonians brought into the reform thousands of new men and women who, while sharing the veterans' hard-won respect for teetotalism, prized their own autonomy too much to deprive others of their right to choose.

This perspective was reflected in the structure of the movement. A local society would spring up following a visit by one of the movement's traveling lecturers and thereafter functioned independent of any central control or assistance. Delegates from the local societies sometimes attended county and state conventions, but no central organization was formed to hire organizers, publish literature, or in any other way stimulate the formation or maintain the activity of local groups. Societies apparently made little effort to keep track of those who took the pledge under their auspices, relying instead on individual members to do so. The lecturers who initially energized and spread the movement lived on contributions solicited from each community they visited; they soon constructed independent careers that did not require the continued existence of the movement they had helped create.

Temperance activists in the older societies at first welcomed the Washingtonians as they witnessed the rejuvenation of their reform and its placement on a firm teetotal basis, but a power struggle soon began. Three issues became bones of contention: entertainment, religion, and moral suasion. Some of the resulting animosity derived from a predictable competition for control of the movement between different groups advocating different measures; some boiled up from the class differences between old and new reformers.

To male Washingtonians the only objectionable aspect of the grogshop was the fact that it sold liquor. Therefore they attempted to re-create in their societies the elements of its sociability—its songs, good humor, and fellowship—so as to keep the reformed drinker true to his pledge. To them temperance meant respectability, but that of the worker who practiced an honest trade and won a "competence," that is, a sufficient wage to support his family. To middle-class reformers, however, respectability implied not only temperance but also upward striving supported by a new model of family life. According to this ideal, after the workday was over respectable men separated themselves not only from drink but also from the raucous male world outside the home, placing themselves instead within a domestic sphere in which moral lessons were taught in calm, quiet voices at the fireside, not belted out in humorous verses ringing through a rented hall. When clergymen and middle-class moralists perceived "crude and coarse remarks," "uncouth expressions," and "disgusting recitals" as features of Washingtonian meetings, support often turned to criticism. To those whose principal aim was reclamation of the drunkard such criticism seemed gratuitous, irrelevant, and condescending.[23]

Middle-class critics also accused the Washingtonians of irreligion, but statistics of church membership on the surface show little basis for the charge. The only comparative case study reveals that in Taunton, Massachusetts, 18 percent of Washingtonians were church members compared to 21 percent of signers of an 1834 no-license petition. Washingtonian practices certainly differed in some ways from those found among older temperance societies. Prayer was excluded from their meetings so as to forestall evangelical recruitment attempts that might divert attention from the Washingtonians' primary purpose; in addition, Washingtonians showed themselves less willing than those who survived the doctrinal battles of the 1830s to make exceptions from their pledge for Communion wine. In other ways, Washingtonianism resembled its predecessors more than it differed from them. Washingtonians did not insist upon a religious conversion prior to or concurrent with a decision for sobriety. They stressed human agency in bringing about reform and put forward a secular institution, the Washingtonian society, as the means of reform. The churched and the unchurched met as equals in Washingtonian halls. As some churchmen pointed out at the time, temperance reformers before the coming of the Washingtonians inadvertently pushed along the process of secularization through many of the same means their spokesmen were later to criticize when employed by the Washingtonians. The readiness of established temperance leaders to magnify differences with the Washingtonians on this score suggests that displacement, or the fear of it, lay behind their complaints.[24]

For the Washingtonians the massive influx of new members into their societies testified to the efficacy of moral suasion, while the fact that intemperance survived the no-license campaigns of the late 1830s bore witness to the failure of prohibition. Faced by the demonstrable successes of the new movement, veteran reformers held their tongues, for a time. Still, despite all they saw of Washingtonianism's harvests of reformed drinkers, they could not help but view suasionist activity as ultimately futile: it was remedial, an effort to clean up a mess that was constantly augmented by the work of an untouched liquor industry. Prohibition, in contrast, meant prevention. Before long they mounted efforts to convince their new comrades of the insufficiency of moral suasion. They were opposed by those who supported moral suasion on principle, by those who wished to avoid the divisions inevitably caused by efforts to coerce, and by those former drinkers and former liquor sellers who had felt the law's lash personally or knew someone who had. All three groups drew sustenance from the artisan tradition of self-help and from a working-class distrust of reform applied from above. Some prohibitionists such as Neal Dow had sailed into Washingtonian societies under false colors and their attempts to lead the movement into the stormy waters of legal suasion split local societies. Some Washingtonians were driven by the conflict out of temperance reform altogether. Others left for reasons not directly caused by conflict over methods.[25]

As we have seen, the loose structure of the Washingtonian societies did not facilitate careful attention to the condition of every member. Energetic societies provided a round of social activities to distract former drinkers from the alcoholic world they left behind, but even the most enterprising groups were ill prepared for massive invasions from that world. Such an attack apparently took place during the presidential campaign of 1844, a contest marked by a high level of voter participation fueled by a enormous supply of free liquor to which voters were treated by candidates of both Whig and Democratic parties. The temperance press reported numerous Washingtonian casualties. To reinforce the attack, the return of prosperity in 1843 brought spare cash and, to some workers, renewed support for the belief that one could get by without the support of one's fellows. Other artisans rode the opposite belief out of their temperance societies with or without the impulsion provided by a prohibitionist takeover. As trade unions revived with prosperity many workers found them a better weapon than the temperance movement to combat poverty and exploitation. Such workers took with them organizational and oratorical skills learned in the Washingtonian societies and, as well, their appreciation for temperance; this explains why some of the new unions adopted a rule of total abstinence. Many Washingtonians sought to institutionalize the best of what they learned from Washingtonianism in new fraternal societies. Although its legacy was to linger on in a multitude of ways, by the mid-1840s Washingtonianism as a distinct movement was dead, its former adherents having scattered in several directions.[26]

Fraternal Societies

Former Washingtonians who remained active in the temperance movement joined or created fraternal societies which represented a new organizational form. The largest of these was an order founded in New York
City in September 1842, the Sons of Temperance. The Sons are best
thought of as an institutionalization of the Washingtonian impulse which
preserved some elements of its parent's approach while taking on other
features in response to perceived flaws. The practice of providing material support to reformed men and their families was elaborated into a
regular system of contributions and benefits. An initiation fee ranging
from two to ten dollars and weekly dues of six and one-quarter cents
provided a benefit fund that was expected to produce four dollars a week
in sickness benefits, thirty dollars in death benefits, and fifteen dollars in
case of a wife's death. Benefits were paid only to or for members in good
standing, which mainly implied adherence to the pledge of total abstinence from all that could intoxicate. The Sons also continued the Washingtonians' secularism and, in the beginning, their commitment to moral
suasion.

The Washingtonians were occasionally embarrassed by public backsliding on the part of those who signed their pledge. The Sons adopted a
policy of secrecy to remove the liability of public exposure from both the
organization and its individual members; in doing so they anticipated a
basic principle of Alcoholics Anonymous. A leader of the Sons articulated
the rationale for secrecy:

If a brother should unfortunately subject himself to animadversion by breaking
the pledge, the matter is kept a profound secret. The society cannot conceive
that amendment can be at all promoted by the promulgation of his shame, or that
a proceeding which has a tendency to harden the offender, can ever be successful
in winning him back. . . . In the distribution of their benefits, they prefer . . . to
lessen the weight of an obligation, by confining its knowledge to the recipient.[27]

Elaborate regalia, an idea copied from the Freemasons and Odd Fellows,
decorated both the meeting rooms and the officers and members of the
order. Offices and titles flowered. Members were admitted by vote of
the existing membership, using a blackball system in which five negative
votes meant refusal. A carefully prescribed ritual governed the conduct
of every meeting. This proliferation of functions and activities on top of

the social events pioneered by the Washingtonians created a dense organizational life designed to insulate former drinkers from the world of alcohol.[28]

Structure reflected a related preoccupation with organizational integrity: the order was built to be temperance reform's most centrally controlled organization. Grand Divisions—the state organizations—consisted only of past and present Worthy Patriarchs of the local divisions; they controlled the age of admission, the eligibility and number of officers, the music sung, and the punishments meted out to delinquent members in the divisions. Grand Divisions met four times annually so as to carry out their supervisory functions effectively. The leaders of state organizations made up the National Division, which exercised ultimate control over the affairs of the order.[29]

The Sons of Temperance spread rapidly from its origin in New York City. By 1844 Grand Divisions had been chartered in six states and the District of Columbia, and the National Division organized. Five years later, Grand Divisions were functioning in twenty-two other states; total membership was reported as 221,478. Membership peaked in 1851 at 238,902. Meanwhile a sister organization, the Daughters of Temperance, was created, reaching its peak membership in 1848 with thirty thousand women, although it continued to spread geographically after that date.[30]

Little is known of the backgrounds of the Daughters of Temperance, but their activities and those of other women temperance reformers of the 1840s suggest the emergence of a more woman-centered view of temperance activity than was evident during the 1820s and 1830s. The Daughters was an organization run by women. The society operated a mutual benefit scheme that insured wives and widows against the sickness or death of male breadwinners. In Cincinnati the two-hundred-strong Daughters of Temperance chapter established a house of employment that sought to provide work at decent wages for abstinent women. The *New York Olive Plant,* founded in 1842, became the first temperance newspaper edited by women; its emergence was followed four years later by inauguration of another women's temperance paper. Temperance men began to recognize the existence of a distinct women's point of view and provided for its expression through regular columns in their papers. Beginning in the 1840s, groups of young women began to enforce sexual embargoes against drinking men, a tactic that may well have succeeded in small towns. Finally, the 1840s witnessed the first examples of vigilante activity by women against saloons. During the same period a justification of such activities emphasizing women's suffering caused by male intemperance rather than woman's essentially benevolent nature gained wide currency within the temperance movement and beyond it as well.[31]

The membership of the Sons of Temperance reveals continuity with its Washingtonian parent. In Beverly and Salem, Massachusetts, a majority were artisans and they were younger, poorer, and less likely to hold church membership or town office than were prohibitionists in their communities. In Jasper County, Georgia, craftsmen—especially propertied ones—clerks, and proprietors were overrepresented among the Sons, and in Covington, Virginia, and Salisbury, North Carolina, artisans and proprietors of small manufacturing establishments predominated. Ian Tyrrell has woven these findings into an ingenious argument to explain the restricted support given to the temperance cause in the South compared to the North. To simplify a complex argument, the predominance of artisans and industrial entrepreneurs in temperance societies in both South and North suggests that the same forces were responsible for producing temperance support in both regions. In particular, a need to inculcate disciplined work habits motivated manufacturers; artisans responded to the ethic of self-respect and self-improvement implicit in the temperance message. The perspectives of both groups were shaped by their involvement in the process of industrialization. Since this process proceeded further in the North than the South during the antebellum period, artisans and entrepreneurs represented more numerous and powerful social groups north of the Mason-Dixon Line, and this fact explains the greater resonance of temperance there.[32]

Temperance reform during the ATS years was weaker in the South and only one slave state, Delaware, was to be among the thirteen states enacting prohibition laws during the 1850s, but southerners demonstrated a powerful affinity for temperance fraternal societies, first the Sons of Temperance and then its rival, the Independent Order of Good Templars (IOGT), founded in 1851. In 1850 the slave states contained 44 percent of the American membership of the Sons of Temperance compared to only 32 percent of the nation's white population (the Sons did not admit blacks). The Daughters of Temperance also made inroads in the South. The IOGT was even more successful than the Sons in organizing the South: by the early 1870s the region held 54 percent of the order's American membership. Unfortunately, establishing southerners' affinity for fraternal temperance is easier than explaining it. Neither the benefit feature nor the Sons' introverted organizational nature is helpful, since the Good Templars never adopted a benefit system and from their society's beginnings gave energetic support to prohibition. In training themselves to deal with the vicissitudes of the market economy and in maintaining their resolve to avoid the temptations of drink, southern artisans and entrepreneurs may well have found the secrecy and ritual of the fraternal societies to be effective supports, as did their counterparts in the north. Furthermore, in the repressive political climate of the South in the 1850s, secrecy was useful for any southern organization having links with northern reformers.[33]

To evangelical temperance leaders in the North, ritual was theologically unpalatable and secrecy was politically dangerous, since it tended to associate the movement with the unpopular Masons. Criticism of the fraternal orders was led by the Congregational minister John Marsh, editor of the *Journal of the American Temperance Union*. The Washingtonians would probably have ignored such attacks, but the Sons were led by men who were disturbed by criticism from middle-class sources, at least in part because they had themselves recently risen from the working class into the middle class. These leaders responded to criticism by dropping the fraternal grip and signs and resisting internal pressure to adopt a system of degrees. If Marsh and other prohibitionist leaders had had their way, they would have transformed the fraternal orders into political pressure groups. The Sons never went that far, but by the end of the order's first decade it had resolved the tension between fraternalism and temperance in favor of the latter by deemphasizing the benefit system and endorsing prohibition. A membership decline resulted that brought the Sons' enrollment to less than one hundred thousand by 1856. The founding of the IOGT did not compensate for the drop in Sons' membership during the 1850s. Admission of women as equal members chiefly distinguished the Good Templars from the Sons, and some of the 78,185 Templars enrolled at the order's pre–Civil War peak in 1860 were female. Losses were probably greatest among artisans; for the temperance movement as a whole the result was a narrowing of its base to the middle class and those workers who aspired to middle-class status.[34]

Toward Coercion

A renewed campaign for legal measures began in the mid-1840s and peaked in the mid-1850s. This campaign gained momentum in a context of economic prosperity, increasing immigration, declining worker support for temperance organizations, and a reduced level of per capita consumption of alcohol. Instead of celebrating the positive aspects of these changes, prohibitionists painted threatening pictures in which social disorder and disintegration took a prominent place beside the traditional images of sobriety and success. Instead of happily greeting the replacement of spirits by lager beer in American drinking, prohibitionists deplored the fact that lager beer was drunk in public on Sundays. Rather than perceive immigrants as hands and brains needed by the expanding economy and legitimate successors of those who arrived in previous times of prosperity, prohibitionists recoiled at unfamiliar speech and strange ways. Both German lager and Irish Catholic temperance societies represented possible grounds for hope that moral suasion might yet produce a temperate republic, but temperance reformers preferred to believe that suasion was futile and only prohibition could stave off impending civic ruin. They read the signs of their times as through a glass darkly, thereby revealing a deep-seated unease for a world they helped create.

Such unease was a reaction to specific economic and social changes that went beyond the numbers of new immigrants arriving at American ports. The improvers who took the lead in temperance reform welcomed industrial progress, but economic transformation was beginning to show an unexpected dark side. Growth placed larger and larger fortunes in the hands of a few. Industrialization promised further growth, but its progress increased class differences by undercutting the position of artisans and augmenting the ranks of factory workers. These changes were to become more evident after the Civil War, but already in the 1850s they were provoking doubts about the necessity and sufficiency of sobriety, thrift, and industry as guides for survival in a changing world. To doubt the potency of those values, however, was to question the moral legitimacy of the middle class, whose spokesmen justified its members' position in society by their exemplary pursuit of self-discipline. To middle-class spokesmen, of course, this argument represented not self-justification but rather a reason to regard their class as uniquely fitted to articulate and defend the interests of the community. Only the middle class both achieved its position and deserved its achievements. Support for prohibition fitted into the middle-class worldview by affirming the utility of sobriety for members of all classes; in addition, it demonstrated the prohibitionist's concern for community welfare. As well, prohibitionism placed the blame for social disorder upon the activities of only a single industry—the liquor business—not upon economic change in general.

Urban prohibitionists had even more specific reasons to feel alarmed at increasing disorder. With the decline of apprenticeship systems and before the coming of compulsory schooling, boys and young men in urban places were a severely underemployed group that included both native and foreign-born. The appearance of youth gangs on city streets frightened the middle class, since in the days of the "walking city" gang fights, rowdy Christmas parades, and brawls between rival fire companies could occur anywhere in the city. Since most such activity involved heavy drinking, prohibition represented both a direct response to disorder and a diversion of attention from its other possible causes.[35]

The shift to coercion first materialized after the Washingtonian period in a series of no-license campaigns during the late 1840s. Those who initiated and led such local campaigns were not necessarily part of the organized temperance movement, although their activity certainly placed them within temperance reform broadly defined. No-license campaigners may not even have accepted total abstinence as a personal rule, using the temperance issue as a means of protecting their communities from encroaching disorder. A variation of this scenario appeared in various local demands during the 1840s for "high-license," which meant that the annual license fee for retail liquor dealers was to be set so high—at five hundred or a thousand dollars—that only "respectable" men would be able to enter the trade. Such campaigns were mounted in order to protect upper-class or middle-class neighborhoods from the presence of working-class saloons. Leaders of the organized temperance movement denounced high-license as a fraud, since they knew that alcohol caused the same damage no matter who sold it. High-license campaigns would not have been possible, however, if the organized temperance movement had not succeeded in forging a link in the public consciousness between intemperance and disorder.[36]

Unlike high-license, no-license was an acceptable tactic within the temperance movement, as it aimed at precisely the opposite impact on the retail liquor trade. Once community sanction was removed from the liquor business, prohibitionists believed, respectable men and women would be convinced to leave it. The result would be educative for the community, as in the absence of public sanction the liquor business would be seen as the evil it truly was. No-license forces won their point at the Ohio constitutional convention of 1851, which submitted the following constitutional provision to the public: "No license to traffic in intoxicating liquors shall hereafter be granted in this State; but the General Assembly may, by law, provide against evils resulting therefrom." The no-license clause received majority support in the ensuing referendum and was duly incorporated into the state constitution. In Massachusetts no-license campaigns gradually elected sympathetic county commissioners in county after county until by 1851 licenses were granted nowhere in the state. Liquor control in Mississippi was centered in the state legislature; during the 1850s it responded favorably to a flood of petitions from localities seeking restrictions on the liquor trade in counties, in parts of counties, and in areas surrounding courthouses, schoolhouses, colleges, and churches. New York State held a no-license referendum in 1846 in every town except New York City; 728 of the 856 towns voted to grant no licenses.[37]

The no-license campaigns seem at first glance to confirm a view, advanced by sociologist Joseph Gusfield, that pictures temperance as a symbolic reform. According to this view, temperance reformers spoke for a middle class for whom total abstinence served as a potent symbol of their way of life. Adoption of no-license by the community provided symbolic affirmation that the middle-class life-style represented the community's desired norm. Whether total abstinence actually prevailed among all members of the community was less important to middle-class reformers than community endorsement for a value that middle-class people viewed as respectable. No-license advocates quickly showed, however, that they would not be content with the symbolic endorsement provided by community adoption of the no-license policy. As soon became clear after adoption of no-license, public officials generally lacked either the capacity or the will or both to pursue the unlicensed sellers who moved quickly into the vacuum created by departure of the respectable from the liquor business. Noncooperation by local officials reached an extreme in the case of the mayor of Albany, New York, who simply refused to recognize the voters' mandate for no-license and proceeded to issue more than two hundred licenses. Everywhere proof of illegal sale was difficult to obtain except through use of paid informers. Conviction usually brought only a fine too small to act as a deterrent. Prosecutors anxious to ease crowded dockets often dropped cases against sellers. Exemption of medical use of liquor left a large loophole through which unsympathetic doctors poured rivers of liquor into their "patients'" stomachs. In Ohio constitutional no-license simply permitted the uncontrolled proliferation of liquor dealers. Rather than accept the situation, no-license advocates searched for means to achieve an instrumental, not merely a symbolic result. In 1851 they discovered the Maine Law.[38]

Neal Dow's law was carefully designed to correct the defects of no-license. The provisions allowing police to search suspected premises and seize any liquor they found were intended to eliminate the need for informers; punishments were increased, the discretion of prosecutors and judges in liquor cases was restricted, and appeals were discouraged by a system of bonds and double fines; bonded agents, who were the exclusive legal dispensers of alcohol, were required to scrutinize closely requests for liquor to be used for medicinal and mechanical purposes. Across the nation temperance forces mobilized to demand enactment of the Maine Law in their states. In some states new parties appeared to advance the cause. But a more common technique was interrogation of candidates of existing parties followed by endorsement of those willing to pledge support for prohibition. In many states, temperance became a major political issue for the first time. [39]

In some respects support for the Maine Law was broader than that received by temperance reform in its previous phases, but in other ways it was more restricted. For the first time the states of the Ohio Valley provided substantial support for the reform. To a considerable extent this development reflected the increasing integration of the region into a national market. As transportation links multiplied, midwestern corn went more often into hogs and less often into whiskey stills; farmers began to feel the discipline of the market and to perceive self-control and management of their farmhands in a different light than before. Similarly, the increasing numbers of midwestern manufacturers were led by the lure of eastern markets and driven by the spur of production and shipping schedules to regard worker discipline as problematic and temperate behavior as a step toward a solution. Midwestern workers also began to grasp the imperatives of emergent capitalism, and some unions, including the German United Tanners of Cincinnati, adopted a total-abstinence rule for their organization. But although they found temperance personally useful, workers saw prohibition as a form of elite coercion, and even abstinent workers were reluctant to cast their ballots for Maine Law candidates. Midwestern prohibitionism therefore became a movement dominated by the middle class. [40]

Rural areas, where most Americans lived, provided most of the voting power for Maine Law campaigns but, as the midwestern example suggests, rural prohibitionism varied with linkage to the national market. Support for the Maine Law in urban areas is noteworthy in light of historians' tendency to portray temperance reform as rural-based. Economic change was most evident and most pronounced in cities and towns, and urban populations were most vulnerable to downswings in the business cycle. Consequently the themes of disorder and control that informed prohibitionist rhetoric were resonant there. As we have seen, although Maine Law campaigns were mounted in various southern states, only in Delaware was success achieved. In that state prohibition- ist support came primarily from the more urbanized northern section around Wilmington. In Virginia, where a substantial but ultimately unsuc- cessful campaign for local option was conducted in the early 1850s, pro- hibitionist support centered in the Shenandoah Valley, whose connections to Philadelphia and Baltimore markets supported a thriving commercial agriculture. In 1854 Pennsylvania voters narrowly defeated a prohibitory law in a statewide referendum, but both Pittsburgh and Philadelphia re- turned strong majorities for the law. Voters in New York State had their only opportunity to vote on prohibition in the no-license referenda of 1846; New York City was exempted from the referendum, but all eight of the state's other cities voted for no-license. Across the state the no- license vote increased with towns' population size, rate of growth, and location on a canal, railroad, or both.[41]

Not all of those who were affected by the spreading market economy responded in the same way, of course. Market discipline may have en- gendered respect for temperance among both workers and employers, but the shift to prohibition tended to organize support and opposition to the Maine Law along class lines. Working-class opposition to prohibition was further strengthened by the drinking habits of the German and Irish immigrants who came to compose such a large segment of the class and by the willingness of middle-class reformers and voters to use prohibition as a panacea for larger social problems. The Maine Law crusade made its way among contradictory social currents: as the spread of the market economy made its goal attractive to more and more citizens as a solution to conditions defined as both personal and social problems, the temper- ance movement's chosen means increasingly restricted its constituency to a fearful middle class.[42]

The prohibition cause profited from the volatility of American politics at the time of the Maine Law crusades. The Compromise of 1850, adop- tion of new constitutions in many states, and a period of prosperity re- moved or softened many of the issues that had divided the Whig and Democratic parties, but party leaders evinced little desire to take on another issue that would certainly prove divisive, and probably in unpre- dictable ways. Nevertheless, they were unable to exert party discipline strongly enough to keep the prohibition issue off the political agenda. Prohibition appealed most strongly to Whigs, but it also elicited sufficient support from Democrats to make the Maine Law a powerful solvent of party lines. Successful Maine Laws owed their enactment to various combinations of party support: in Massachusetts, a Free Soil–Democratic coalition, with Whig support; in Delaware, an American party majority; in New York, a Whig majority; in Maine, virtually equal percentages of Whig and Democratic legislators. When they had the choice, however, temperance men kept theirs a single-issue movement, thereby forgoing what opportunity existed to place prohibition at the center of a new coalition.

When nativism arose in the early 1850s in the form of the Know-Nothing movement and then the American party, some prohibitionists welcomed the promise of excluding the immigrant vote and thereby removing an obstacle to prohibition's triumph, and some Know-Nothings seized upon prohibition as a tool to discipline the immigrant hordes. In the short run the prohibition cause probably profited from its association with nativism. Before long, however, the differing priorities and constituencies of the two movements forced a parting of the ways. As the slavery issue split the nativists and destroyed their ability to reduce the immigrant vote, most prohibitionists turned to the oncoming Republicans to realize their political aspirations. By that time, however, prohibition's ability to compel the attention of party politicians had declined because of its own manifest failings, and the Republicans were able to sweep in much of the northern prohibitionist vote without making a single concession to its unique concerns.[43]

In the Maine Law crusades, prohibitionists organized effectively to exploit political flux, to mobilize middle-class fears of urban disorder, and to channel middle-class hopes for control of both self and society. They were also fortunate to confront very little organized opposition. Statewide prohibition campaigns swept to victory in thirteen states and territories between 1851 and 1855: Maine, Massachusetts, Minnesota Territory, Rhode Island, Vermont, Michigan, Connecticut, New York, Indiana, Delaware, Iowa, Nebraska Territory, and New Hampshire. In Pennsylvania the campaign fell just short of prohibition but won an anti-dramshop law that outlawed barrooms and sales in quantities less than one quart. Texas, too, banned sales of less than one quart. Ohio followed its no-license constitutional amendment in 1854 with a law forbidding the sale of spirits for on-premises consumption. The Mississippi legislature passed a new license law requiring applicants to present a petition signed by a majority of the legal voters in the district in which they wished to operate. These results represented the fruit of the educational campaigns conducted by temperance societies since the 1820s; they demonstrated that prohibition could command widespread support beyond the membership of the existing societies and fraternal orders.

The Maine Law campaigns changed American politics and society in several ways. The intrusion of prohibition into politics helped to loosen party ties in the massive realignment that scholars now describe as the death of one party system and the birth of its successor. Together with the antislavery movement, the temperance crusade "defined and disseminated the values around which the middle classes coalesced, pioneered new means of molding public opinion, and propagated a new social order resting on self-discipline rather than on deference to external authority."[44] Antislavery and temperance also brought into the public sphere of politics thousands of women, who were assigned by the conventional wisdom of the day to the private sphere of home and fireside. Although prohibitionists such as Neal Dow argued that prohibition would free business enterprise from the unnecessary costs entailed upon society by intemperance, his Maine Law in fact advanced the significant principle that property used contrary to the general welfare was subject to confiscation.[45]

The Maine Law crusades also changed the temperance movement. In addition to becoming more narrowly middle class in composition and orientation, the movement lost much of its sympathy for the drunkard, who was once again described as beyond redemption and fit only for the grave. In an atmosphere of coercion men like Neal Dow and Thomas Carson rose to the top. Carson organized a society, the Carson League, to aid in enforcing New York's no-license laws; he is reputed to have had his brother prosecuted for a liquor-law violation, and is said to have proclaimed, "The best temperance tracts I know of are rumsellers' tracks to jail." With such men in the vanguard, temperance reformers should not have been surprised to find society polarized by their movement's success. After the Maine Law, polarization was not long in coming.[46]

Although liquor dealers were known to join temperance societies during the days when total abstinence from ardent spirits was reformers' goal, and the Washingtonians were able to convert some sellers to total abstinence, advocacy of no-license or prohibition drove the liquor trade to organize in opposition. In 1855, Liquor leagues appeared in Philadelphia, New York, Boston, and Milwaukee to provide legal defense funds for prosecuted dealers and to support legal challenges to restrictive or prohibitory laws. Many such challenges were successful, as Maine Laws were struck down or crippled in Massachusetts, Minnesota Territory,

Michigan, New York, and Indiana. Liquor dealers also joined with other antiprohibitionists to mount political campaigns against the Maine Law. Such campaigns ignored intemperance, skirted the disorder issue, and instead raised the cry, "Prohibition does not prohibit!" disingenuously accompanying it with arguments that prohibition destroyed "personal liberty" along with private property and community prosperity.[47]

Where successful, antiprohibitionist campaigns won because prohibition achieved its specific aim while falling short of the grandiose claims made by Maine Law supporters. To a considerable extent prohibition did end the manufacture and sale of beverage alcohol within jurisdictions where public officials committed themselves to enforcing it. Portland under Neal Dow provides a good example. At the same time, however, prohibition mobilized resistance among both foreign-born and native-born drinkers which sometimes burst forth in violence. Restrictive legislation short of prohibition brought the same results in Chicago's Lager Beer Riots in 1855 and in New York City two years later. Such resistance amply disproved prohibitionists' claims that the Maine Law provided a solution to urban disorder; indeed, the Maine Law clearly produced disorder of its own. Disillusionment and disaffection by former supporters allowed repeal movements to triumph in Delaware and Nebraska Territory and left temperance forces in disarray within a short time after 1855, the year of their greatest victories. Some historians have claimed that the sectional crisis was responsible for prohibition's decline by diverting attention to more pressing matters, but this interpretation gives too much credit to sectional controversy. The Maine Law discredited itself, not by too little enforcement but by too much, before Bleeding Kansas and John Brown forced themselves onto the public stage. The sectional crisis merely brought to its conclusion a tragedy in which the Maine Law played the leading role.[48]

Temperance reform's second cycle was completed when temperance women in some northern communities turned to violence in the late 1850s. During the Maine Law crusades, women extended the active role they had taken on during the reform's earlier days. They petitioned for restrictive legislation in both northern and southern state prohibition campaigns and canvassed voters in electoral and referendum contests. Increasingly they justified their political activity by pointing to women's victimization by male intemperance. Unlike an argument based on women's benevolent nature, this claim supported autonomous and militant action toward goals that could be determined only by women themselves, based on their own distinct experience. Such arguments were familiar to a substantial component of women who joined the temperance crusade after participating in the bitter and divisive debate over women's place in the abolition crusade. When abolitionism turned to single-issue political action in the 1840s, antislavery women flocked to the temperance banner.

Women followed the male leadership of the temperance movement until the 1850s, when temperance men demonstrated that they were unwilling to allow rhetorical acknowledgement of women's claims to be translated into action specifically on women's behalf. The Sons of Temperance did not accept female members and in addition did not allow Daughters of Temperance to speak at their conventions. In New York State in 1852 the Sons' refusal to allow women to participate on an equal basis provoked a walkout from their convention and formation of the Woman's New York State Temperance Society (WNYSTS). Led by prominent women's rights activists such as Elizabeth Cady Stanton, Susan B. Anthony, and Amelia Bloomer, the WNYSTS advocated women's suffrage and legal equality as well as prohibition and enrolled about two thousand women. A similar movement appeared in Ohio in 1853. Male prohibitionists feared that the Maine Law crusade would lose respectability and momentum if it were associated with the cause of women's rights, and they stoutly resisted demands for equality within temperance societies. The women's societies lasted only a few years, as many of the women who were active in them shifted to the women's rights movement; the societies' disappearance left the sex-integrated Templars the only meaningful avenue for women's temperance activity. With the decline of the Maine Law women in dozens of communities scattered across the North began to take direct action on their own behalf, invading saloons and destroying their contents. In some places the raiders carried out their work unmolested, and where they were arrested and charged they escaped with fines, which were paid by sympathizers. Women's vigilantism was a short-lived and ineffectual phase of temperance history, but the forces that produced it continued to operate. In fact, they were to transform temperance reform during its next cycle.[49]

Chapter Three

Women Take the Lead (1860–92)

By the winter of 1873–74 the actions of drinkers and liquor sellers had once again provoked women to take direct action, although this time they marched on saloons armed with Bibles and hymnbooks rather than axes and iron bars. In contrast to the 1850s when only a few hundred women scattered in several dozen communities attacked liquor outlets, tens of thousands of women in nearly a thousand towns and cities now enlisted in the new crusade. One of them was Bethiah Yeoman Ogle, a middle-aged housewife in Washington Court House, Ohio. The story of Bethiah Ogle, who never held an official position in a temperance organization or pursued the temperance cause beyond her hometown, sheds light on the actions of the militant army of women who marched in so many communities across the nation in 1873–74.

During the 1870s Washington Court House was a prosperous market center and shipping point for the corn-and-hog farms dotted across the flat plains of southwestern Ohio; the town contained a growing population of about two thousand. Born in 1818 into one of the town's leading families, Bethiah married a prosperous dry-goods dealer and bore three sons and two daughters. By 1870 Bethiah was widowed and living off the income generated by her husband's share in the dry-goods store, which had been left in equal portions to her and the children. Her older sons, twenty-seven-year-old Gilbert and Marshall ("Marsh"), twenty-four, worked in the store.

From the perspective of many women of Washington Court House the town's very prosperity became its undoing, since it seemed to attract liquor dealers like flies to a hogpen. At the beginning of the Civil War the census taker found no retail liquor dealers in the town, but by late 1873 eleven saloons and three liquor-selling drugstores were competing briskly for the patronage of townsmen and the county's farmers. For the Ogle family the threat of liquor became personal as well as communal when Marsh showed an inordinate taste for drink. In 1871, the worst year, Marsh was arrested and jailed four times for drunkenness. The members of the Baptist church, to which Bethiah and her daughters, Alfretta ("Brightie") and Florence ("Flora"), belonged, offered sympathy but could do little more. Brightie joined the local lodge of the Good Templars, which tried to bring pressure on local politicians to control the burgeoning liquor trade, but such efforts were largely unsuccessful.

Efforts to abate the evils of drink had a long history in Washington Court House. The town council first voted for no-license in 1832, and similar action followed in 1852 and again three years later. State law had prohibited sale of hard liquor by the drink since 1854, and in 1869, in response to temperance pressure, the council passed an ordinance outlawing ale, beer, and porter shops. Except for wine—never a staple for most nineteenth-century drinkers—Washington Court House should have been virtually dry in the early 1870s as far as retail sale was concerned. That it was clearly not dry may be attributed mostly to a failure of law enforcement caused by the inability of the temperance issue to survive the cross-cutting effects of other issues in local politics. Again and again temperance men launched municipal slates only to see them wrecked on the shoals of partisan loyalty. When sympathetic officials sought to enforce the law, unsympathetic juries or uncooperative witnesses torpedoed their efforts. Unhelpful in so many ways, the law did offer suffering women one avenue of recourse, a civil-damage provision allowing those injured by the sale of liquor to a third party the right to sue the dealer who made the sale. The hope thus offered was slim since few married women possessed the means to hire lawyers or to pay court costs in the event their suit failed. Although seven women launched suits against liquor dealers between 1871 and 1873, few collected damages: either legal technicalities defeated them or long delays and interminable appeals wore them down.

By the winter of 1873 judicial and other official failures to control a burgeoning liquor trade and to protect women therefrom had become obvious to many women in Washington Court House. When a touring lecturer named Dio Lewis advised nonviolent mass marches they quickly organized, appointing Bethiah Ogle and three other women to draft an appeal to local liquor sellers that would explain to the community the reasons for their unusual action. For Bethiah Ogle the task must have been both poignant and unavoidable. The appeal read:

Knowing, as we do, the fearful effects of intoxicating drinks, we, the women of Washington, after earnest prayer and deliberation, have decided to appeal to you to desist from this ruinous traffic, that our husbands, brothers, and especially our sons, be no longer exposed to this terrible temptation, and that we may no longer see them led into those paths which go down to sin and bring both soul and body to destruction. We appeal to the better instincts of your hearts, in the name of desolated homes, blasted hopes, ruined lives, widowed hearts; for the honor of our community, for our prosperity, for our happiness, for our good name as a town; in the name of God, who will judge you as well as ourselves, for the sake of your own souls, which are to be saved or lost, we beg, we implore you, to cleanse yourselves from this heinous sin and place yourselves in the ranks of those who are striving to elevate and ennoble themselves and their fellow-men; and to this we ask you to pledge yourselves.[1]

Appeal in hand, Bethiah, Brightie, and Flora Ogle, in company with twoscore other women, marched from the Methodist church on 26 December 1873 to visit the liquor dealers of Washington Court House. They marched again on the twenty-seventh while male supporters prayed in the Presbyterian church for their success, ringing the church bell at the conclusion of each prayer. On Monday, 29 December, the marching women achieved their first success when two saloon-keeping partners "surrendered" and agreed to turn over their entire stock, four barrels and one cask. Amidst jubilant song and prayer "axes were placed in the hands of the women who had suffered the most, and, swinging through the air, they came down with ringing blows, bursting in the heads of the casks, and flooding the gutters of the street."[2] On 30 December curious farmers thronging the streets for stock-sale day were treated to the sight of marching women, a second surrender, and "whiskey, gin, port wine, and brandy" flowing "in one steady stream on their way to Paint Creek."[3] By Friday, 2 January 1874 all the saloon keepers and liquor-selling druggists within the municipal limits had given in to the women, and by the middle of February the marching women had conquered all the dealers in the immediate vicinity of Washington Court House.[4]

The actions of Bethiah Ogle, her daughters, and the other marching women of Washington Court House played a significant part in launching the Women's Temperance Crusade, the largest mass movement of women yet seen in the United States. Newspaper reports of the successes in Washington Court House, where the liquor traffic was first suppressed using the new method, encouraged other women to march on liquor dealers in their own towns; furthermore, the appeal Bethiah Ogle helped to draft was carried to the saloons by the women who marched in many other places. Their marches set off a chain reaction that culminated in the founding of the Woman's Christian Temperance Union (WCTU), the largest women's organization to that point in American history. Bethiah died a few years after the Crusade ended, but Brightie Ogle was still campaigning with the WCTU in the early 1890s.

Through the Crusade women seized the initiative from men, who had always led the temperance forces, and for the next two decades the WCTU made sure that women kept the initiative. Women's initiative set the third cycle of temperance reform apart from its predecessors; the emergence of new leadership helps explain why this cycle became the temperance reform's most innovative in institutions and methods. In addition to the Crusade and the WCTU, the period from the Civil War to the 1890s produced a durable political party committed to prohibition and a professional association of medical experts on pathological drinking. During the 1880s a series of campaigns for statewide prohibition gathered momentum behind a new demand: prohibitory constitutional amendments adopted by popular referendum. Furthermore, the WCTU under Frances E. Willard, its dynamic, inventive, and charismatic president, built a new kind of temperance organization that demanded a more diverse range of reforms and sought a wider social reconstruction than its predecessors had hoped to achieve. Temperance remained a principal aim, but many temperance reformers now envisaged universal abstinence accompanied by women's suffrage, the success of the labor movement, and the evangelization of American society in the day of their cause's triumph.

Drinking: The Long Plateau

In understanding these changes perhaps the best place to start is with drinking. During the latter half of the nineteenth century drinking practices experienced no change as drastic as the steep drop in per capita consumption that had occurred during the 1830s. For a few prosperous years in the early 1870s per capita consumption rose sharply, although only to a level far below the peak years of the antebellum period. This increase helped precipitate the Women's Crusade, and within a short time the Crusade and the long depression that began almost simultaneously forced per capita consumption down again. For the entire period between 1850 and 1900 per capita consumption of absolute alcohol fluctuated between one and one and a half gallons, showing no trend either up or down. After the momentous peaks and valleys of the early nineteenth century, per capita consumption reached a plateau where it remained for fifty years.

Although the level of per capita consumption remained relatively constant, its composition changed dramatically. The replacement of whiskey by beer in American preferences, which began in earnest during the 1850s, accelerated after the Civil War. In 1865 per capita consumption of beer totaled a little over three gallons, which represented double the level of 1850. By 1900 per capita beer consumption reached sixteen gallons. During the last third of the century absolute alcohol intake through whiskey drinking dropped by four-tenths of a gallon per capita, while the tremendous jump in beer consumption added only six-tenths of a gallon. Stability in per capita consumption of absolute alcohol masked a major shift in American drinking habits, which may have enlarged the drinking population while reducing the incidence of drunkenness and damage.[5]

Both the brewing industry and the retail liquor trade underwent significant changes during the late nineteenth century. The technological simplicity of brewing made the industry easy to enter, and widening markets tempted many new operators to try their luck. Competition in the major urban markets became fierce as a result; this situation was exacerbated by technological changes such as refrigeration and pasteurization, which made possible the shipment of a uniform product across the country from the main brewing centers in the Midwest and Northeast. The national market for beer expanded rapidly, interrupted only slightly by the business depressions of the period, but brewers' productive capacity increased even more rapidly.

The response of large brewers was similar to that made by other industrialists in the face of unrestrained competition: consolidation. Following the lead of the Pabst Brewing Company of Milwaukee, some large companies bought out rivals; the most thoroughgoing such attempt was made in the late 1880s and early 1890s when British investors financed large-scale purchases and consolidations of American breweries. Through takeovers the number of brewers declined by a third between 1876 and 1900. In addition, brewers sought control over retail outlets in order to guarantee a predictable level of sales. This process, beginning in the mid-1880s, eventually created a system of largely producer-controlled retail outlets like the "tied-house" system that had prevailed in

England for more than fifty years. In the beginning the brewers provided saloon fixtures, then they paid for the license, and finally they bought the premises and rented them out to prospective dealers. Movement toward the tied-house system was accelerated by the triumph of high-license advocates in many cities during the 1880s, which raised the price of a liquor license to levels few aspiring saloon keepers could afford. The number of retail liquor dealers in the United States continued to increase through the early twentieth century, but more slowly than the population, and in per capita terms the peak occurred in the fateful year of 1873, when 4.8 dealers per thousand population paid the required federal tax. By 1890 only three dealers per thousand population were in business, and by 1900 only 2.6.[6]

These broad changes added up to a shift from a pattern of alcoholic-beverage distribution characteristic of a rural society to one more suited to an increasingly urban population. Beer, more expensive to transport and store, was preeminently an urban beverage, and demand for it was heightened by the general lack of clean water in cities. The relatively concentrated populations of an urban society require a smaller number of retail outlets of all kinds than the more dispersed populations of a rural society. In this transition from a rural to an urban alcohol distribution system, the 1880s seems to have been a key decade.[7]

Temperance reformers took less notice of these structural changes than they did of the founding in 1862 of the brewing industry's first national organization, the U.S. Brewers' Association (USBA). Shortly before, the federal government imposed a system of taxes on the liquor industry for the first time since the War of 1812, and the USBA was organized as a direct response. Liquor taxes, originally intended as a war measure, outlasted the war and during the following half-century provided between one-half and two-thirds of federal internal revenue. The USBA remained an indispensable instrument of the larger brewers in negotiations with the government over the size of the beer excise and the manner of its assessment and collection. The brewing industry's trade association thus pioneered a style of business-government cooperation that was to become common in other industries during the Progressive Era after the turn of the twentieth century. Prohibitionists saw the USBA as a symbol of liquor-industry power, but as a channel of influence on matters beyond the excise the USBA was an excellent platform for brewer rhetoric and little more. Paid-up membership often sank to as few as one-third of the nation's brewers and never exceeded one-half. The liquor exise itself contributed to the brewers' political feebleness by giving them confidence in their industry's indispensability to federal finance.[8]

The basis of the brewing industry's prosperity was of course the drinking population, whose profile during the late nineteenth century probably changed little from the latter years of the antebellum period. In all classes and all ethnic groups except the Irish, men were far more likely to drink than women. Drinking patterns seem to have been shaped more by ethnic cultures than by religious values. Irish Catholics, for example, incurred far greater risk of dying from the effects of drink than their Italian coreligionists, while alcoholic death rates of English Protestants fell between those of the two Catholic groups. Massive immigration to America from societies where drinking was culturally prescribed generally augmented the drinking population. One of the notable exceptions was the pietist Norwegian farmers who colonized the Upper Midwest and Plains states, employed total abstinence to set themselves apart from their native-born neighbors, and furnished crucial support for both Populism and the successful prohibition campaign in North Dakota. In general ethnic cultures exerted greatest force on drinking behavior in places where immigrants maintained their own communities; elsewhere, immigrant drinking patterns blended with those of their neighbors.[9]

Historians tend to accept at face value self-descriptions provided by middle-class spokespersons that portray a temperate group standing between heavy-drinking extremes above and below. On balance, however, the available evidence does not support such descriptions. By the late nineteenth century segregated middle-class residential districts had evolved in large cities apart from the commercial and working-class residential areas where saloons clustered; the social distance thereby created gave an advantage to middle-class parents wishing to raise their children in a relatively drink-free environment. Where local or district option was available middle-class voters often solidified this advantage by voting their neighborhoods dry. Their votes, however, were not an accurate reflection of their drinking habits.

The suburbs were knit into the metropolis by the modern (for the time) transportation systems that made suburban life possible, so streetcars and omnibuses gave access to center-city saloons as well as to downtown offices and shops. Denver, for example, was surrounded by dry suburbs, but taverns clustered around the streetcar lines' downtown terminals, heavily used stops, and transfer points. Boston's dry suburbs poured forth a daily stream of thirsty suburbanites who flowed into the city, took on an admixture of alcohol, and then flowed back again. Dry

Cambridge stationed police on its side of the Charles River bridge to intercept the disorderly drunks. In 1887 two out of five drunks arrested by Boston police came from out of town; twenty years later, a more specific breakdown of origins showed that one out of three drunks arrested in Boston lived in other Massachusetts towns, most of them dry. In addition, suburbs were dry in only a legal sense, as drugstores and soda fountains managed to carry on illegal or quasi-legal liquor sales, and obliging delivery companies were eager to convey bottles to one's front (or back) door. While Mother was putting the children to bed with temperance tales Father may well have been imbibing at a well-appointed downtown "restaurant," indulging in a "cherry wink" at the corner soda shop, or even relaxing downstairs with a nightcap from a bottle delivered to the doorstep C.O.D.[10]

In a typical small town, where homes and businesses shared a smaller space, outlets for the retail sale of liquor were virtually omnipresent. Washington Court House during the early 1870s, for example, contained slightly over two thousand people and fourteen liquor dealers in an area six blocks long and four blocks wide. Those drinkers who came to the attention of local authorities closely matched the class profile of the entire adult male population. Drinkers were younger on average, which suggests that drinking served as an extended ritual of initiation into manhood. Some men of all classes never completed this rite of passage.[11]

For the urban working-class saloon the late nineteenth century was a golden age. Its prosperity depended upon the vitality of the all-male groups that gathered around its bar; their existence in turn flowed from historically specific changes in work life. With the spread of factory discipline, work became more routinized, more tightly scheduled, and more closely controlled, while its setting became larger, more hierarchical, and more impersonal. One casualty of the new pace and direction of work was workplace drinking, which threatened both the scheduling and the efficiency of machine production. The ejection of drinking from the workplace in some cases led directly to the establishment of leisure-time drinking institutions, such as the saloons that clustered around most factory gates. More generally, the elimination of workplace drinking created the necessary conditions for commercialization of a segregated sphere of leisure. In the saloon men found both a sense of group belonging and, within the group, egalitarianism and an opportunity for self-expression.[12]

Working-class men seem to have been more likely than middle-class men to do their drinking in public or at least semipublic places. In addition to camaraderie saloons offered useful services to workingmen: food, news, and a public toilet, among others. Nevertheless, liquor was neither an omnipresent nor a dominant part of working-class life. In 1889 the U.S. Bureau of Labor conducted a survey of expenditures among more than sixteen hundred families whose heads worked in the cotton, woolen, or glass industries in ten northeastern states. Among Irish-headed families, slightly more than two-fifths reported expenditures on alcoholic beverages during the previous year; among families headed by native-born persons, slightly less than one-third spent any money on liquor. Two years later a similar survey reported expenditures for liquor among 57 percent of over twelve hundred working-class families. The amounts spent averaged a little over 3 percent of annual income. The heaviest drinkers were the glass blowers, who worked in intense heat, and who spent 6.4 percent of their income on liquor.[13]

Individual workingmen's ability to control their drinking was aided by the continuing tradition of working-class self-reform. Both William H. Sylvis, head of the National Labor Union, and Terence V. Powderly, Grand Master Workman of the Knights of Labor, urged the merits of temperance upon their followers. The Knights classed saloon keepers with bankers and lawyers as social parasites and banned all three groups from their order. The first convention of the National Colored Labor Union, meeting in 1869, attacked excessive drinking along with economic exploitation as burdens of the working class. Many local leaders of the Knights and of such craft unions as the Amalgamated Association of Iron and Steel Workers and the railway brotherhoods took a similar stand. (The members of the brotherhoods, cognizant that drinking imperiled not only trains, cargoes, and passengers but also their own safety, regularly expelled members for drunkenness.) For these men, temperance promoted the self-respect and self-discipline necessary to build a workers' community and a movement to resist the depredations of capital. As a railway brakeman put it, "as soon as a man has spent all his money for drink he becomes a slave to the corporation."[14] Although working-class temperance advocates sometimes supported prohibition as well as suasionist measures, they generally distanced themselves from middle-class reformers who saw workers only through paternalistic spectacles. The expenditure statistics suggest that a substantial number of workers listened to their message. The saloon perhaps helped to assuage the effects of capitalist industrialization, but in doing so it presented a hindrance to those who wished to change the conditions that drove men to the saloon.[15]

The sturdy vine of working-class self-reform put forth several fresh blossoms in the 1870s, the most vivid of which were the "reform club" crusades led by former drinkers Francis Murphy and Henry A. Reynolds. Like the Washingtonians, the reform clubs flowered in the depths of an economic depression, appealed especially to drinkers through the use of experience speeches, and sought to create local societies through which drinkers were to maintain their own sobriety by aiding other drinkers to keep theirs. Both new groups used bits of ribbon worn on the coat as identifying badges; Murphy's followers adopted a blue ribbon, while Reynolds founded Red Ribbon reform clubs. Unlike the Washingtonians, both Murphy and Reynolds considered religious renewal an important part of self-reform. The two men differed, however, in their attitudes toward legal coercion: The middle-class Reynolds advocated prohibition as an adjunct to self-reform, while Murphy, who came from a working-class background, rejected legal means. Although neither the Blue Ribbon nor the Red Ribbon clubs appealed solely to working-class drinkers, they, along with one other national association, became the principal organized manifestations of the temperance ideal among the mass of workers during the late nineteenth century. The other was the Catholic Total Abstinence Union, a federation of local societies usually affiliated with a parish church, which held its organizing convention in 1872. Like Murphy, the Catholic temperance societies employed moral suasion almost exclusively.[16]

Drinking behavior of both working-class and middle-class men was affected by larger economic and social changes, but in different ways. The increased pace and complexity of economic life created pressure for temperance, but workers' experience of these changes in a setting over which they had little control drove many of them to seek opportunities for relaxation and self-expression in the saloon. Although the most rapidly growing middle-class group was salaried employees, a majority of middle-class men were self-employed during this era. Accelerating pace and complexity in economic life created for them a generalized insecurity that was experienced personally; the pressure they felt was relieved mainly through creation of an intense family life. Middle-class men formed no such primary male group as those that flourished in the working-class saloon and the upper-class club. Middle-class men could better afford to drink than their working-class counterparts, but their drinking took place either during the course of business activity or alone at home. Such drinking, stripped of its primarily sociable meaning, came to be viewed as an emblem of self-restraint, while middle-class men interpreted the drinking-cum-fellowship among classes above and below as an expression of indiscipline. Such perceptions implied that any temperance appeal directed to middle class men must focus on drink's social rather than personal costs and put forward manipulative rather than redemptive strategies.[17]

Wartime Doldrums and Postwar Revival

As the Civil War began, temperance leaders found evidence for both optimism and gloom. On one hand, the antebellum campaigns had produced considerable support for the temperance ideal; on the other, their constituency was fragmented and much of it was disillusioned by the apparent failure of the Maine Law. The war years were a passive interlude for temperance reform that on first glance seem to have represented a continuation of the string of setbacks that marked the last years of the 1850s.

Nevertheless, several developments of significance to the future of the reform took place during the war. Probably the least momentous and most ironic was the coming of some variety of prohibitory legislation to southern states where only recently the Maine Law had been resisted as a Yankee innovation in the use of confiscatory power. State laws in Virginia, Mississippi, and North and South Carolina prohibited the distilling of scarce grain into spirits. By early 1864 the Confederate government was forced to order blockade runners to stop using precious cargo space for liquor to meet the demand thus created. Even at the antebellum height of temperance power, reformers never dared to demand such use of federal authority. In a final twist, the Confederacy established government distilleries in four states to produce alcohol for medical purposes and military rations. In a fifth state, Mississippi, the state government took similar action. Never again were southern antitemperance advocates able to rely upon limited-government arguments in their opposition to legal coercion. Indeed, the later willingness of southern counties and one state, South Carolina, to pioneer in establishing public liquor stores—the "dispensary" system—may have derived from lessons learned through these wartime expedients.[18]

Although they gave loyal support to their respective governments, temperance reformers regarded the military experience itself as a setback for their cause. The Union government restored the army's liquor ration in 1862, thereby reversing a significant victory of the first temperance movement, and the Confederacy also considered liquor a necessary part of army supplies. Temperance spokesmen claimed ever after that the liquor ration introduced the taste of alcohol to young men who

otherwise would have been unsullied, but, given the widespread availability of alcoholic drink in civilian society, this claim was exaggerated, a
means of blaming the troubles of a becalmed reform upon someone else.

During these dark years for temperance organization, medical initiatives flourished that were eventually to change the ways in which many
Americans thought about alcohol's effects. Temperance folk, as we have
seen, moved toward a disease concept of chronic drunkenness when they
accepted the notion that some drinkers lost control of their drinking. By
the 1870s at least, leading temperance activists came to believe that
heredity caused some drinkers to drink to excess. They refused, however, to draw the conclusion that such drinkers were not responsible for
their actions. Other temperance spokesmen saw intemperance simply as
an entrenched habit having no physiological basis. Many physicians supported the temperance cause, but they apparently did so while perceiving
chronic drunkenness as an essentially voluntary disorder. In the 1850s
some physicians, led by Dr. Joseph E. Turner, sought to institutionalize
Benjamin Rush's view of habitual drunkenness as a disease through the
founding of asylums specifically for the medical treatment of inebriety.
Specifically, he and his followers argued for state-chartered and state-
funded asylums and for legislation allowing involuntary confinement. In
Turner's view inebriety was a physical affliction that resulted from the
effect of a poison, alcohol, on a constitutionally (hereditarily) weakened
system. Abstinence was the preferred cure, and confinement was necessary to ensure abstinence.

The efforts of Turner and his colleagues bore fruit in several ways.
First came the founding of special institutions for the treatment of inebriety; the earliest state institution was the New York State Inebriate
Asylum in Binghamton (1864), whose superintendent Turner became. By
1902 more than one hundred institutions for the treatment of inebriates
were in operation, although only three were state institutions. Second,
asylum superintendents and associated physicians in 1870 founded a
professional association, the American Association for the Cure of Inebriates, which soon spawned a scholarly journal, the *Quarterly Journal
of Inebriety* (1876–1914). Finally, various states in the late nineteenth and
early twentieth centuries enacted laws permitting confinement of chronic
drunkards and habitual users of other drugs. The success of inebriety
professionals in curing chronic inebriates is unknown, although the diminished claim implicit in the renaming of their organization as the Association for the Study of Inebriety is suggestive. They probably were
successful in popularizing the disease concept, at least among the phy-

sicians and academics who formed the principal audience for their views. In this respect their efforts converged with those of other temperance reformers, with whom the inebriety professionals generally sympathized.[19]

Temperance organizations left behind their wartime doldrums soon after the war ended and, although short-lived, the revival in temperance fortunes produced lasting effects. The revival manifested itself primarily through the fraternal orders, with the Good Templars achieving greater success in attracting new members than the Sons of Temperance. By 1868 the Sons nearly doubled their 1865 enrollment, while the IOGT in the same period multiplied its membership from just over 60,000 to more than 367,000. Part of the Templars' gains came through reorganizing the South, whose members had been patriotically disfellowshipped during the war, and from organizing new western states, but fresh members flocked to the order in the older northeastern states as well. Encouraged by the revival, some temperance activists took fateful steps toward formation of an institutional innovation in temperance reform, a political party dedicated to prohibition. Their efforts came to fruition in Chicago in September 1869 with the founding of the Prohibition party.[20]

This dramatic new departure probably was motivated by a reading of the early history of the Republican party as much as by an evaluation of its current state. Temperance reformers had occasionally considered proposals to found a prohibition party previously, but the vision of a separate party was never before backed by the actual experience of a party devoted to a "moral issue" gaining control of the national government. Now that the Republican party had shown the way some temperance reformers were anxious to try their hands at rallying the "moral forces" of the nation behind a new standard.

In support of this goal they deployed the rhetoric of abolitionism. The major parties' preoccupation with Reconstruction issues made them in effect opponents of prohibition, Prohibitionists claimed; therefore voters who continued to give those parties their support could not be considered true temperance men. Unfortunately for party Prohibitionists, such arguments failed to carry much weight when the political world was not polarized over the temperance issue as the politics of the 1850s were polarized over the slavery issue. Prohibitionists persevered through a series of crushing defeats in the 1870s until Reconstruction began to lose force as an organizing issue in national politics; in the 1880s, as we shall see, they were finally to find an opportunity to rewrite the national political agenda.

In the first years after its founding the effect of the Prohibition party on existing temperance organizations was depressive. Major-party loyalists among the Templars and Sons left their societies rather than support Prohibition party work, and women, whose political participation was circumscribed by disfranchisement, abandoned the Templars in even greater numbers than men. Although the Sons after 1866 invited women to become full members of their order, few responded.[21]

Women Arise

For women concerned about the negative effects of drinking, the end of the temperance orders' brief revival represented only one aspect of an increasingly threatening situation. Per capita consumption was rising from its trough in the 1850s, and despite the emerging shift to beer, distilled spirits still contributed four-fifths of absolute alcohol consumed, a fact with ominous implications for the incidence of both acute and chronic alcoholic damage. As measured by the number of retail liquor sellers relative to population, availability of alcoholic beverages reached its highest level in at least a decade.

Women confronted the results of these societal trends firsthand when they ventured onto the streets of their communities; complaints of verbal and physical harassment by drunken men arose from women in both small towns and large cities. Drunken violence invaded churches—Methodist services in Washington Court House were rudely interrupted by missiles hurled through the church windows by a drunken rowdy—and homes—newspapers regularly reported attacks on women at home by husbands and, occasionally, by strangers; one Crusade, in Westboro, Ohio, was directly provoked by an intoxicated man's assault upon a sick woman at home in her bed. An affidavit in a Washington Court House damage suit against a saloon keeper in 1872 summarized the basic facts of many domestic conflicts. According to the plaintiff, her husband "beat, struck and kicked the plaintiff, and drove her from her . . . house, and caused her to be exposed to the cold during a large portion of the night whereby she was made sick, and, otherwise injured said plaintiff, and the said [husband] by reason of said drunkenness failed to furnish the said plaintiff the necessary food and clothing."[22] Divorce from drunkard husbands was technically available to women in some states, but lack of resources to launch suits and, more generally, to support themselves and their children if given custody discouraged women from resorting to the law.[23]

The workings of the law dismayed and frustrated women in other ways, too. Laws that promised to restrain the liquor trade often failed to do so for lack of enforcement. Ohio, for example, had prohibited the sale of distilled liquor by the drink since 1854, but on the eve of the Crusade all but 2 percent of the state's retail liquor dealers paid a higher federal tax rate that entitled them to sell distilled spirits as well as beer. New Hampshire and Michigan were legally under statewide prohibition in 1873, but the ratio of liquor dealers to population equaled the national average in the former and far exceeded it in the latter. Legislators unwilling to expose their political flanks by supporting enforcement of restrictive liquor legislation tried to create a safety valve for women's frustration by enactment of civil-damage laws. If the experience of Fayette County, Ohio, women was typical, however, that safety valve was almost completely plugged by the courts. In their operation, therefore, civil-damage laws achieved an effect precisely opposite to that intended: they heightened women's awareness of themselves as a group threatened by male drinking but without providing an adequate remedy. The situation was particularly acute in Ohio, where passage of a strict civil-damage law in 1870 was followed by a sharp drop in local prosecutions for violating the state's liquor laws; officials in charge of enforcement seem to have decided to leave women and liquor dealers to fight out their differences in the civil courts. Meanwhile, the Prohibition party attempted to lead the temperance forces on a new crusade to remake the law, promising that this time, with the help of women (the party advocated women's suffrage, too), government would finally remove the dangers created for women by male drinking and the activities of the liquor trade. Considering the party's poor showing thus far, not to mention the recent record of men in government, women in most states had reason to be skeptical.[24]

From such soil sprang the grass-roots action by women that unfolded across the Midwest and Northeast in the winter of 1873–74. Dio Lewis's lectures in four towns provided the initial catalyst, but the Crusade quickly spread beyond the sphere of Lewis's influence, adopted a view of women and drinkers different from his, and sometimes employed tactics that he declared anathema. For Lewis, women's benevolent nature justified their participation in reform. He regarded drinkers and sellers as morally responsible agents, whose actions justified neither protection nor punishment by the state, and he therefore remained an outspoken advocate of moral suasion long after most other temperance activists became prohibitionists.

In contrast, the Crusaders regarded women primarily as victims of male drinking, which in turn was fatally encouraged by the liquor trade. Women's welfare and sometimes their survival were endangered by men's drinking, which threatened mothers, wives, sisters, and daughters with shame, loss of financial support, and physical injury. In community after community Crusaders described women as "the greatest sufferers" from male intemperance. As victims left helpless by lawmakers and other officials, women possessed the basic right to take action to defend themselves. They exercised that right, however, according to the "law of love," which directed them to make a "tender, respectful, and earnest appeal to the moral nature of those whom they address[ed]." Crusaders therefore approached liquor dealers with hymns, prayers, and requests to desist from their ruinous business. They also circulated total-abstinence pledges among the citizenry at large, an action which suggests that they viewed drinkers and would-be drinkers as having some control over their propensity to drink. But the focus of their action remained the retail liquor trade, a decision that implied a view of the drinker too as victim. This view of drinkers as victims of uncontrollable temptation justified the Crusade's primarily coercive approach to them, namely cutting off their sources of supply. The approach to liquor dealers was usually more evenly balanced between suasion and coercion: "Tender, respectful, and earnest appeals" were the Crusaders' principal tool, but when employed by eighty women (the average number of marching Crusaders) bringing all their moral force to bear upon a lone saloon keeper—often before a crowd of onlookers—such appeals contained an undeniably coercive element. In about 10 percent of Crusades women took part in election or referendum campaigns, but the most common attitude of Crusaders toward the use of law was cautious. Coercion without the use of law or physical force and suasion through the massed moral influence of women gave the Crusade a unique place in the history of temperance reform.

In each town where it appeared, the Crusade had a chance of success only if it could rally support from both women and men for its objective and tactics. Most women were told from childhood that their proper role was passivity and their rightful setting the home. If women feared to act unconventionally, public ridicule heaped upon the Crusaders by newspaper and magazine editors, as well as verbal abuse, harassment, and occasional violent attacks committed by men individually and in mobs reinforced their fears. Where women won the "inner battle" with their fears they usually did so through exposure to a woman who had already taken part in the Crusade. Like the Washingtonians, the Crusade spread through personal contact and experience speeches.

Various male ideologues, including spokesmen for the German-American community, tried to rally men against the Crusade by arguing that the marching women represented an attack upon male privilege and power. The potential of such an appeal was demonstrated when some evangelical ministers who professed to be fast friends of temperance publicly deplored women's autonomous activity in its behalf. Defenders of the liquor industry pictured the Crusade as a subversion of property rights and free enterprise. German-American spokesmen added the charge that the Crusade sought a revival of Know-Nothingism. In all the criticism of the Crusade, however, none could be found to gainsay either the virtue of temperance as an ideal or women's claim to be the chief sufferers from male intemperance. This focus on the Crusaders' means rather than their goal or rationale no doubt robbed objections of some force. Crusaders capitalized on this weakness by reemphasizing their basic premises. They also subdued their critique of male sins and omissions while appealing to others as members of a community whose common welfare required sacrifice of certain individual rights.[25]

The Crusade's appeal worked better than anyone at the time expected. In all the Crusade appeared in at least 911 communities spread across thirty-one states and the District of Columbia. It enlisted the support of more than 56,000 women, and the actual number may have been closer to 150,000. Abolition societies during the 1830s drew support from thousands of women and temperance societies then and since attracted even more, but not for the sort of direct-action tactics that marked the Crusade. Moral reformers sometimes mounted direct-action campaigns against brothel clients in the 1830s, and temperance women in the 1850s violently attacked saloons, but these actions found no mass support among women. Indeed, not since the pre-Revolutionary period had so many Americans of either sex adopted such militant tactics in civil conflict. Testifying to its source in shared grievances, this remarkable uprising spread without planning or central control and with virtually no coordination of its numerous local forces.[26]

The Crusade varied in its impact. In some parts of the country women never heard about the new mode of action or they received such sketchy information about it they were unable to launch a local counterpart; in other areas, such as some western states and territories, women were so vastly outnumbered by men or so scattered that concerted action was impossible or futile. Southern women generally did not face as drastic a situation as their northern sisters since the number of retail liquor dealers relative to population was lower in their defeated and impoverished region; they were also handicapped by a lack of information since newspaper circulation was far lower than in the North. The status of liquor law enforcement affected women's readiness to march. Ohio, where enforcement languished and liquor dealers proliferated in the years before the Crusade, was the scene of more than a third of the Crusades with a membership of three-fifths of the Crusaders. Massachusetts officials, in contrast, had vigorously enforced their state's restrictive legislation, causing a decline in the number of dealers; despite a higher ratio of liquor sellers to population at this time, the Bay State witnessed far fewer Crusades than Ohio. After Ohio the next leading Crusade states were Indiana, Illinois, Michigan, and New York. Within Ohio, counties containing more liquor dealers generally experienced more Crusades. Within counties small towns became the focal points for the marching women largely because the county's liquor trade clustered there. While most large cities experienced Crusades, they were generally weaker than in small towns because of the spatial segmentation and cultural diversity of city life. Social structure, culture, and politics influenced both the impact of drinking and the spread of the Crusade, but in the last analysis the Crusade's timing and distribution demonstrate that its root lay in the threats male drinking posed to women. Like the first two mass temperance uprisings—those of the American Temperance Society and the Washingtonians—the Women's Crusade arose as a direct response to drinking.[27]

The Crusade attained its extraordinary size by bringing into the temperance reform thousands of new recruits. Present and former members of the Good Templars provided a core of experienced workers, but the upsurge in drinking, the proliferation of dealers, and the apparent success of the Crusade's new method convinced thousands of women having no experience in the reform to organize or join a local Crusade band. The new recruits probably were temperate or abstinent in their personal habits, but previously they saw no need for activism or perceived no hope for women in male-dominated and increasingly politicized temperance organizations. A married woman in her thirties or forties living at home with her husband and children, the typical Crusader depended, as Bethiah Ogle did, upon the integrity of the family. In the small-town context her husband was likely to be a member of the local elite in terms of wealth, but she found that her social position offered little safeguard against the effects of drink. (Moderate wealth did, however, support a domestic servant who could watch the children while Mother marched.) Nor did association with an evangelical congregation bring much more than sympathy and mutual support after drink's damage was done. A long-time member of her community, the Crusader needed to believe that she could walk its streets unmolested, that her sons' worldly prospects would not evaporate in an alcoholic fog, and that her daughters would marry men who cared for them more than for the bottle. Such a background and such concerns produced recruits who brought to the cause courage, fortitude, and commitment in abundance, but the scope of their commitment was in many cases limited to their own community. The task of creating an ongoing movement from the Crusade was formidable.[28]

Few male temperance leaders made a serious attempt to understand why the Crusaders chose to proceed as they did. Temperance men were unable to fit the marching women into conventional images of female passivity, and in addition, most believed strongly that moral suasion was an obsolete mode of action since only prohibition was capable of putting an end to drinking in an increasingly diverse society. Social diversification was matched by growing social interdependence, which implied that local victories, even numerous ones, were insufficient: left alive anywhere, the liquor traffic would eventually creep back everywhere. This cosmopolitan perspective helps explain why the national Prohibition party was created after only a few brief, scattered, and unsuccessful experiments with partisanship at the state level. Cosmopolitan perspective and prohibitionism together created a barrier of condescension between male temperance regulars and the Crusaders. From their side of the barrier Crusaders perceived prohibitionist calls for enlistment in a political campaign as an invitation to join the exercise in futility they had observed men pursuing for a generation. The task of organizing the new recruits therefore fell to women.[29]

Women Organize

The women who stepped into the organizational vacuum generally shared the national perspective of male temperance leaders. Some of them in fact were contemplating formation of a national women's temperance organization even before the Crusade began. Such an organization was envisioned as undertaking benevolent and educational temperance work more consistent with the conventional image of womanhood than the marches and saloon prayer meetings of the Crusaders. From this perspective, national organization of women was necessary not primarily to end women's victimization by the work of the liquor traffic but rather to rectify women's failure to discourage drinking among those whom they were capable of influencing. Seizing the opportunity provided by the Crusade, several cosmopolitan, experienced temperance women called for a national convention to meet in Cleveland in November 1874. The Cleveland convention founded an organization that both institutionalized and domesticated the Crusade.[30]

The history of the WCTU during its first quarter-century may be divided into two phases: the years before Frances Willard's election as president in 1879 and the Willard era that followed. During the first phase the organization remained small in numbers and timid in approach, deviating from a benevolent and educational strategy only to endorse prohibition, and turning aside from a narrow pursuit of "gospel temperance" only grudgingly and under pressure from Willard and her followers. Most former Crusaders did not join the new organization, and those who did were women whose concerns extended beyond their communities or who lived in places where the Crusade had failed to reduce the number of liquor dealers. In Illinois Willard demonstrated that large numbers of women could be organized through a campaign for the "Home Protection" ballot—women's suffrage on issues involving regulation or prohibition of the liquor traffic—but the national leadership of the WCTU refused to follow her example. They failed to realize that, with the decline in drinking and the reduction in the number of liquor dealers brought about by the Crusade and the economic depression, temperance was no longer as pressing an issue for many women as it had been in the early years of the 1870s. The plateau in per capita consumption and the consolidation of the retail liquor trade, both of which were to continue through the 1880s and 1890s, meant that temperance organizations had to become more flexible and creative in order to survive. Willard met that challenge brilliantly and in the process she and her colleagues transformed the WCTU into a new kind of temperance organization.

Frances Willard came to temperance reform at the age of thirty-five from an apparently conventional midwestern rural background. After a short schoolteaching career and two years' travel in Europe she was chosen as the first president of Northwestern Ladies' College, and then became dean of women at Northwestern University when the college merged with the university in 1873. She resigned this position after a battle with the university president in the spring of 1874. Willard became corresponding secretary of the national WCTU at the Cleveland convention in November, but for the next few years temperance competed with public lecturing, evangelism, and even newspaper editing for her attention. Beginning in 1877 she clashed publicly with WCTU president Annie

Benjamin Rush.
*Courtesy of the Historical Collections
of the Library, College of Physicians
of Philadelphia*

Edward Delavan.
*Courtesy of the New York Historical
Society, New York City*

Neal Dow

Crusaders besieging a saloon.
Courtesy of the Ohio Historical Society/Westerville Public Library

Frances Willard

Wayne Wheeler

Ernest Cherrington.
Courtesy of the Ohio Historical Society/Westerville Public Library

The Anti-Saloon League National Convention, 1921.
Courtesy of the American Council on Alcohol Problems, Inc., Papers,
Michigan Historical Collections, Bentley Historical Library, University of Michigan

Bill Wilson

E. M. Jellinek

Marty Mann.
Reproduced with permission of the
National Council on Alcoholism Inc.

Wittenmyer over the organization's narrow focus on temperance. Two years later, Willard defeated Wittenmyer for the presidency and turned her formidable abilities solely to the temperance cause. She now redefined temperance advocacy to include far more than it ever encompassed before.[31]

Serious challenges faced not only temperance reformers in the late nineteenth century but also other middle-class persons who perceived that national unity, so dearly won in the Civil War, was splitting along new fault lines. Chronic conflict between capitalists and workers—which became acute in 1877, 1886, 1892, and 1894—was the most obvious and persistent sign of stress. The human costs of economic change, which became most apparent during the depressions of 1873–79 and 1893–97, grated upon middle-class sensibilities and raised disturbing questions about the meaning of "progress." The opulent display of great wealth produced the same effect, and the blatant contrast thus presented between wealth and poverty fed middle-class fears for social order. Some reformers, such as the prominent minister Henry Ward Beecher, reacted to labor-capital conflict by calling for Gatling guns to shoot down striking workers; other reformers tried to formulate a more positive response. Women of the WCTU, led by Frances Willard, stood foremost among the latter.[32]

In their organization's early years, WCTU women regarded temperance activity among the working classes from some distance, as the appeal of their own organization seems to have been primarily to members of the middle class, and whatever cross-class contact took place in the course of WCTU activity occurred in a paternalistic (or maternalistic) context. No studies of local membership exist, but examinations of leader's backgrounds reveal husbands with middle-class occupations and wives having considerable formal education. Those WCTU leaders who worked outside the home usually did so as lecturers, authors, editors, teachers, professors, or professional temperance workers. Leaders were native-born and likely to belong to an evangelical Protestant church. When they came to the WCTU, middle-class women probably had had little direct exposure to the conditions of working-class life or culture. But as they cast about for instruments with which to reknit the unraveling fabric of their society that situation changed.[33]

The women at first approached the working class with manipulative intent. One of the earliest activities undertaken was visits to jails, launched to bring benevolence and to extract conversion to religion and abstinence. An easy trade: flowers and hot meals for bodies and souls.

Then the visitors began to notice who ran the jails and who was incarcerated therein. Soon political action followed, as the visitors began petitioning for the hiring of police matrons to oversee women prisoners, demanding reformatories for rehabilitation, constructing women's halfway houses, and seeking appointment of women to state boards of charities and corrections. In 1886 Frances Willard stated that the principal question for the working class was not "how to get higher wages" but rather "how to turn present wages to better account." Three years later, Willard gave new life to an old but distinctly minor theme in temperance debate when she told the WCTU national convention that intemperance was a product of harsh working conditions. During the 1880s the WCTU created special departments for work with miners and timber workers, intending thereby to organize voting support for prohibitory legislation. Probably few votes for prohibition materialized as a result, but the views of the women who saw the actual conditions of workers certainly changed, as delegates to the WCTU national convention soon discovered. The superintendent of the department for work among miners, Minnie English, lectured her colleagues on the need for mine safety laws and increased wages. "Better that rich corporations should lose heavily on their present contracts," she announced, "than that the lives of men, women, and little children, who at best have a pitifully meager living, should go out in hunger and want." Both mining companies and consumers must make sacrifices, she concluded, in order to bring justice to the mine worker.[34]

Broadening of middle-class perspectives was evident in other areas of WCTU activity as well. The WCTU became the first temperance organization to proselytize among children, but its initiatives were at first designed only to secure eventual recruits for the temperance army. Then the needs of children forced themselves upon WCTU workers, and agitation began for establishment and state funding of day-care centers and industrial schools. Juvenile work became even more political in widespread petition and lobbying campaigns for "scientific temperance instruction," which demanded state laws requiring curriculum reform, use of WCTU-approved textbooks on physiology and hygiene, and teacher training in these subjects; by 1901 such campaigns were successful in every state. A department for peace and international arbitration, begun in 1887, opposed military training in schools; it enlisted WCTU workers in twenty-four states by 1895. After mobilizing to rescue and convert prostitutes WCTU women discovered what seemed to be a structural condition underlying seduction: laws made the age of consent ten years in twenty states, and seven years in one state. Massive petition and lobbying campaigns for "social purity" secured laws in twenty states raising legal consent to sixteen years, and by 1894 only four states held the age at ten. The WCTU workers only gradually overcame their skepticism about the ballot for women, as Willard and others won them over first to the home-protection cause and then to full suffrage. By the 1890s the WCTU took part regularly in statewide suffrage campaigns. Inspired by reading Edward Bellamy's popular utopian novel, *Looking Backward* (1888), Frances Willard tried to turn her colleagues in a socialist direction. In 1889 she told delegates to the national convention that "the land and all resources of the earth [must] be held and controlled in some way by the community as a whole"; in 1893 she returned to the same theme when she declared that "in every Christian there is a socialist; and in every socialist a Christian."[35]

If Willard's calls for socialism evoked a sympathetic response from her listeners, they did so because in the WCTU, as Ian Tyrrell points out, "woman's consciousness was harnessed to a hierarchical, evangelical impulse that valued service and self-sacrifice over the achievement of individual aspirations."[36] WCTU thinking was shaped by the positive aspect for women of the doctrine of separate spheres: the belief that women's nature was inherently finer, more sensitive to moral and ethical concerns than that of men. This allowed WCTU members to see women as a group uniquely fitted to lead society toward a better day, and acceptance of community and cooperation as "natural" values for women may have made them receptive to larger schemes for cooperation. Furthermore, since the Crusade at least, temperance women had been accustomed to claiming priority for community welfare over individual property rights.

While the WCTU never adopted a socialist program, WCTU women remained far more interested in improving the condition of the working class than were suffragists at the time. WCTU initiatives also represented a greater challenge to patriarchal authority than most American socialists were prepared to countenance. In addition, the WCTU was more zealous to advance both the rights of women and working-class concerns than were most male temperance reformers. The WCTU drew from others, but the result resembled none.[37]

While granting the WCTU's contributions to the cause of women's rights, some historians have nevertheless argued that its commitment stopped short of a full challenge to patriarchy. Specifically, they claim, the WCTU accepted the continued existence of a family structure— the patriarchal nuclear family—that oppressed women. The WCTU did support the family as an ideal, but the ideal it envisioned was quite different from the reality its members saw about them. Through their advocacy of social purity, voluntary motherhood, and "a white life for two," WCTU members sought to change the sexual balance of power within the family by holding men to a standard of behavior appropriate to women's needs and desires. Since American society at the time offered women few avenues to a satisfying life outside the family, their campaign to improve women's position within the family represented a direct response to the interests of the vast majority of women. But that was not all. The WCTU recognized that domesticity was not the only road taken by women, and sought as well reforms aimed at changing the world beyond the family to meet women's needs. WCTU women advocated dress reform to liberate women from the cumbersome, restrictive, and unhealthy attire prescribed by contemporary fashion. In addition, they made the Prohibition party the first national political party to advocate equal pay for equal work. If women were to remain within the family, they argued, women's needs must be the basic criterion by which the family's most important decisions were made. And if women worked outside the home, they must be accepted as equals there as well.[38]

This view of the WCTU ideology, like any other based upon the organization's national program, must be informed by recognition of the WCTU's size and diversity. The WCTU was a large organization by 1890—it claimed nearly 150,000 members—and its growth was accomplished by deliberate encouragement of a wider diversity in program than in the backgrounds of its membership. Such diversity produced both strengths and weaknesses.

In its first years the WCTU's leaders envisioned a closely coordinated, centrally controlled organization, but Willard and other suffragists successfully fought for toleration of local initiative in order to mount home-protection campaigns in the states while such activities were officially discountenanced at the national level. When Willard came to power the WCTU adopted her "Do Everything" policy, an official stance that encouraged a proliferation of activities and a broadening of vision. Departments were created to pursue various interests, groups, and causes; thirty-nine departments existed at the national level by 1896, twenty-five of which had little obvious connection with temperance. No member, however, was required to undertake any particular activity endorsed at a higher level. While delegates to national conventions debated the social policy, economic basis, moral condition, and political direction of the Republic, local WCTU workers may have been engaged in nothing more revolutionary than circulating temperance pledges and constructing floral arrangements for the local jail. Tireless and indomitable organizing campaigns during the 1880s by Willard and other organizers spread the organization into the South and West. Numbers and geographical representativeness increased—by 1890 more than half the counties in the United States contained WCTU organizations—but Willard downplayed suffrage and antiprostitution commitments in order to bring southern women into the organization alongside radical westerners. For the two decades of Willard's ascendancy, the Do Everything policy provided a successful solution to the temperance reform's perennial problem of fragmentation as well as a cement for rapid construction of the largest American women's organization before the twentieth century. During the years of Willard's leadership the WCTU was central to women's reform not because it encouraged links with other organizations but because it subsumed a multitude of reform activities within itself.[39]

By encouraging diversity, Willard, of course, risked generating tension and conflict within the organization. To a considerable extent local freedom served as a safety valve, but on some issues the tension became too great. The suffrage fight was bitter, but the suffragists' victory at the 1881 national convention provoked few defections, perhaps because opposition was primarily tactical; in addition, suffrage was an issue to be dealt with by the states, and state WCTUs could still refuse to mount their own campaigns. Having won the suffrage fight, Willard then began to push the WCTU toward endorsement of the Prohibition party, which she hoped to make into the chief political vehicle for temperance and other reforms. Willard secured WCTU endorsement of the Prohibition party in 1884 after strenuous efforts to demonstrate that neither of the old parties was prepared to make any concessions to the prohibition cause. The conflict over endorsement at the 1889 convention produced a walkout led by J. Ellen Foster of Iowa and the subsequent founding of the Non-Partisan WCTU (NPWCTU). Foster took with her about two hundred of the more than seven thousand local unions, scattered across eleven states. Founding of the NPWCTU represented an embarrassment, not a disaster, for its parent organization, but those who walked out with Foster may have been only the last of a number of women repelled by the protracted controversy.[40]

Party Politics

Despite such defections the WCTU doubled its membership during the 1880s, and the Prohibition party vote climbed rapidly from 10,000 for its presidential candidate, Neal Dow, in 1880 to 150,000 four years later.

For most of its long history the Prohibition party has been essentially a set of leaders without followers, voices in the political wilderness, but in the 1880s a different destiny appeared to be in store for the party. During the previous decade many Republican prohibitionists who had lived through the Maine Law battles may have been willing to grant the party's argument that prohibition must be enforced by a party elected for that purpose, but they could not wrench free of the Republican party and its short but glorious tradition of action on "moral" issues.

By the early 1880s, however, the Republican party's antislavery birthright was sold for the mess of pottage known as the Compromise of 1877, which peacefully inaugurated a Republican president at the cost of abandoning the freedmen to the mercies of their former masters. Moreover, the party's boasted devotion to "moral" issues was increasingly overshadowed by the tarnished but rising star of the reputed corruptionist James G. Blaine. When Blaine won the Republican presidential nomination in 1884 the trickle of Republican voters draining into the Prohibition party became a rushing stream. Blaine was not the party Prohibitionists' only benefactor, as a series of actions by Republican state officials in the decade before the 1884 election convinced Republican voters in various key states that the party of Lincoln could not be trusted on the liquor issue. Republican complicity in repealing Pennsylvania's local option law in 1875, for example, more than doubled the Prohibition party vote to an off-year total that was only marginally exceeded in the presidential election nine years later. The Prohibition party's surge continued after Blaine's defeat, as its total vote rose to 294,000 in the state and congressional elections of 1886. The party appeared well placed to become the Republican party's successor as the national party of reform if not at the seat of power.[41]

This briefly emergent party has been described as an avatar of political moralism and antipartyism, but such a reading mistakes a tool for a basic trait. Antiparty rhetoric served a crucial purpose for third-party politicians, whose chances for success depended in the first instance upon the willingness of major-party voters to acknowledge that their parties no longer deserved confidence. Although some prohibitionists saw prohibition primarily as a means of rescuing individual drinkers, this view was not shared by other leading spokesmen for prohibition. Party Prohibitionists in particular aimed at neither the salvation of drunkards nor the moral regeneration of society, although they hoped that these would follow in prohibition's train. Instead, they perceived the liquor traffic as the source of numerous specific social evils including crime, disease, poverty, and political corruption. Their materialistic arguments ignored the scriptural basis for social action asserted by the churches and thereby assisted the secularization process to which their predecessors in the temperance reform had similarly contributed. When clergymen refused to move as fast or as far on the issue of liquor control as prohibitionists wanted, prohibitionists (like most other political combatants in the late nineteenth century) were unsparing in their denunciations of their opponents' hypocrisy and immorality; by the early 1890s such attacks thoroughly alienated most leaders of the evangelical churches.

The nature of the prohibitionist appeal should be kept in mind when evaluating the view of some historians that conflict over the prohibition issue in this era represented a species of religious conflict pitting aggressive pietists against defensive liturgicals. The prohibitionist appeal did not depend upon allegiance to a particular set of ethnic or religious values, but instead spoke directly to the material interests of every citizen, citing the direct and indirect costs of intemperance to society because of drink's responsibility for crime, poverty, and disease. Such arguments were designed for an increasingly diverse and interdependent society in which appeals based upon pietist values—or those of any other subgroup—were incapable of finding a hearing among enough citizens to support successful political action.[42]

For party Prohibitionists political success entailed winning the power to govern. National party platforms in the 1880s took positions on many issues besides prohibition and women's suffrage. Such breadth was intended to demonstrate the party's ability to govern, not merely to enact and enforce a single reform. Each plank was carefully evaluated for its possible effects in repelling as well as attracting support. For party Prohibitionists the suffrage demand became a barometer for their current resolution of the conflicts between political principles and constituencies: a weak suffrage plank indicated frenzied courting of white southern prohibitionists; a strong suffrage plank signaled rejection of white southerners in favor of reformist northern voters. Despite party Prohibitionists' condemnation of the Republican party, until the late 1880s the Republicans represented their model of a successful reform party and the Republican conquest of power their ideal.[43]

The Prohibition party was capable of drawing support from a strategic constituency. Both its leaders and most of its voting strength came from the Northeast, the most urban and industrial region, which contained nearly half of the nation's population and even more of its wealth. Since the South and West were bastions of the Democrats and Republicans, respectively, the Prohibitionist heartland was also the nation's political cockpit. In New York State the Prohibition party drew disproportionately from the rural areas and small towns upstate, but in Massachusetts the party attracted a strong urban vote. Its leadership was overwhelmingly urban in origin and place of residence. While the national leadership was thoroughly middle-class, the party ran working-class candidates in various regions. Leaders were predominantly native-born and evangelical in background; Prohibition votes generally came from similar areas, although Scandinavian evangelicals added a significant component of immigrant support. The Republican party involuntarily furnished most of the Prohibition national leadership; most Prohibition voters were probably former Republicans too.[44]

Republican party leaders in the 1880s took great interest in the size and contours of the Prohibition vote, but to them probably the most important fact about the third party was that it did not capture all or even most of the prohibitionist vote. If it had, Republican leaders could have devoted themselves single-mindedly to pursuing antiprohibitionist voters, but the persistent attachment of large numbers of prohibitionists to the party of Lincoln made them a force to be reckoned with so long as the Prohibition party continued to present an alternative. Antiprohibitionists, in the form of nonevangelical immigrants and their increasingly numerous male offspring of voting age, were unfortunately growing in numbers faster than those groups who were likely to support prohibition, and so the Republican party faced a hard choice between its present prohibitionist supporters and tomorrow's majority. Republicans tried to cover all bases by focusing on the tariff issue while stealing the prohibitionist argument from time to time, but every such larcenous act risked turning their constituency into the hands of the party Prohibitionists.[45]

Into this situation stepped the women of the WCTU with a new weapon for the prohibition cause: constitutional prohibition in the states adopted by statewide referendum. Kansas pioneered the new method with a victory for a prohibition constitutional amendment in 1880, and nineteen more statewide referenda were held in seventeen states and territories during the following decade. The principal force behind the launching of these campaigns was the desire of major-party politicians, most of them Republicans, to find a means of blunting prohibitionist demands for a party commitment to the cause, demands backed implicitly or explicitly by the threat of shifting to the Prohibition party. The main instrument by which this desire materialized was J. Ellen Foster, then superintendent of legislation for the national WCTU, leader of the pro-

Republican forces in the WCTU, and director of the successful Iowa referendum campaign in 1882, the second held. Foster wrote the WCTU's campaign manual for constitutional referenda and relentlessly prodded state WCTUs to begin petition drives for a referendum in their state. In many states the WCTU took the initiative, and even where it did not, WCTU members often provided a significant proportion of campaign workers. The proximate stimulus for the campaigns was the rise in Prohibition party fortunes at both the state and national levels. Iowa provides a good example of the pattern at the state level. There, a sharp jump in the Prohibition party vote in 1877 deprived the Republicans of a majority for the first time since the 1850s, and the next Republican state convention declared for submission of a prohibitory constitutional amendment. The Prohibition vote thereupon dropped by two-thirds. Sixteen of the twenty referenda took place after the Prohibition party's national breakthrough in 1884.[46]

The South also witnessed considerable temperance activity during the last two decades of the nineteenth century, although only Texas, Tennessee, and West Virginia held statewide referenda (in all of which prohibition lost). Virginia, Georgia, and Mississippi enacted local-option laws in the 1880s; in Virginia the threat of Prohibition party organization helped the process along. Of the three states, prohibitionists in Mississippi made the best use of local option, drying up four-fifths of the state's counties by the late 1890s. Prohibition parties appeared in Alabama and North Carolina during the early 1880s. Athens, Georgia, in 1891 established the first municipal monopoly over liquor sales in the United States, and its example was followed by other Georgia counties and by the state of South Carolina. Despite giving constitutional prohibition only 45 percent of a statewide vote in 1887, Tennessee came close to achieving prohibition in a different way through the operation of its Four Mile Law, first enacted in 1877 and later strengthened, which prohibited the retail sale of liquor within four miles of a school, except within incorporated towns. Through use of this law Tennesseeans brought much of the rural area of the state and many small towns under local prohibition.[47]

This revival of southern temperance forces is instructive for several reasons. It did not derive from hostility between abstemious native-born citizens and drinking immigrants, since the South received little immigration. Nor did an evangelical-nonevangelical or pietist-liturgical split fuel the southern prohibition conflict, since most church members were evangelicals or pietists and they could be found on both sides of the issue. Southern temperance is often described as primarily an attempt by whites to control blacks. Blacks do seem to have voted heavily against state or local prohibition in Tennessee and Virginia, but blacks gave substantial help in voting Atlanta, Georgia, dry under local option, and in Mississippi twenty counties with black majorities split evenly for and against local prohibition in the first round of local-option elections in 1886. In Virginia, the eastern counties with large black populations generally voted wet or not at all under the local-option law, even when blacks were in the minority. In short, racial conflict does not seem to provide an adequate explanation for alignments on the liquor issue. Nor was the conflict between urban and rural populations: Atlanta, one of the New South's most dynamic cities, voted for local prohibition in 1885, and in Virginia Norfolk, Charlottesville, Harrisonburg, and Roanoke all went dry.

Instead, temperance seems to have struck a responsive chord in those parts of the South where the gospel of the New South was preached most fervently, and where economic growth was most rapid. Cities such as Atlanta and Norfolk, of course, were entrepôts of the New South, but predominantly rural areas such as southwestern Virginia, which was growing rapidly in population and property values because of mining and railroad development, also demonstrated a link between market expansion and temperance support. In effect, the economic changes that transformed much of the North before the Civil War and that helped galvanize the temperance cause then were now beginning to produce the same results in the South. As their northern counterparts had before them, the increasing numbers of southern entrepreneurs and workers discovered that traditional drinking patterns made a poor fit with the exigencies of life under the new regime. After the turn of the century, continuing integration of the South into the national economy was to make the region much more prominent on the temperance stage.[48]

In the North the prohibition issue aligned those who embraced the new industrial morality against those who clung to traditional ways and existing interests. Among the most fervent apologists for the social order of industrial capitalism stood the party Prohibitionists, since they worked harder than any others to put the blame for society's ills upon the saloon alone. For prohibitionists the greed and corruption they found intertwined with the liquor traffic was a plant that grew only among one species of businessmen, the "criminal capitalists" of liquor. After the bloody battles between miners and mine owners' private armies at Coeur d'Alene, Idaho, in 1892 a Prohibition party organizer declared that prohibition would have prevented it all. Such an analysis also found favor with the 1.6 million voters who cast ballots for prohibitory constitutional amendments during the 1880s, as they differed from party Prohibitionists only in their attachment to a major party. Most prohibitionist voters did not live in the areas most threatened by the work of the liquor traffic; in direct contrast to the Women's Crusades, the prohibition vote increased from county to county as the number of liquor dealers declined. If they were urban residents, they had no basis for fears of growing drunken disorder, since residential segregation proceeded apace in these years while drunk-and-disorderly arrest rates declined in the nation's largest cities. Although the bulk of the prohibition vote probably came from the middle class, some working-class spokesmen endorsed prohibition too. Most members of a working class that was heavily foreign-born and strongly attached to its male club in the saloon or its political machine centered in the saloon voted against prohibition, thereby helping to ensure its defeat in twelve of the twenty referenda.

Protestant pietism lent strength to the prohibition upsurge, although church members' minority status in the population probably prevented their weight from being decisive. Like others, pietists welcomed an argument which insisted that the responsibility for society's flaws lay elsewhere. Poverty and class conflict had to be acknowledged, but devout supporters of the new industrial order wanted to believe that the roots of these ills were nourished only by liquor. In voting for prohibition, men expressed their unease over existing conditions, their hopes for change, and their desire that reform be accomplished without disturbing the basic economic or political institutions of their society.[49]

After a decade of work covering much of the nation, those most responsible for the referenda claimed few victories. Of the two legally dry states at the end of the 1870s, Maine reaffirmed its commitment to prohibition and New Hampshire voted to reject constitutional prohibition and thereby retained a statutory facade for unenforced prohibition. Four western states (Kansas, Iowa, North Dakota, and South Dakota) were added to the prohibition ranks. In the shadow of the prohibition referenda, campaigns for high-license and control of dealer numbers went forward. High-license, at first rejected by the liquor industry, took on new luster as prohibition loomed in the offing and was embraced by the industry in an attempt to appease some prohibitionists. It did have the effect of reducing the number of licensed dealers; a similar result was achieved by Massachusetts legislation in 1888 limiting licenses to one per five hundred population, which cut the number of licenses in Boston by two-thirds. [50]

The Republican party generally fared no better than the prohibitionists. A Republican legislative caucus's vote for submission of a prohibition amendment to popular vote seldom removed the pressure for party commitment, and where the party declared its support for prohibitory law it usually drove out more voters than it attracted. Such secessions from Republican ranks played a large part in ending the stalemate between the major parties that had endured for a decade and a half by tipping the electoral balance in the Democrats' favor. As the Republicans in the early 1890s scrambled to regain lost voters, their party's temperance commitment became one of the first casualties. The Prohibition party, however, was in no condition to benefit from Republican backsliding because the referendum campaigns trapped the party in a cruel dilemma. If party Prohibitionists held aloof from such campaigns, they became vulnerable to charges that they put party above principle, the precise charge they themselves levied against the Republicans. Participation in referendum campaigns, however, undercut their essential claim that prohibition could succeed only when enforced by a party elected for that purpose. Party Prohibitionists generally did work for prohibition in the referenda, and such work had the additional effect of absorbing time and money that otherwise would have been devoted to party organization. When combined with the effects of the high-license campaigns in drawing off potential support and the alienation of Prohibitionist voters caused by the party's platform oscillations, the referenda put a stop to party growth, which peaked in 1886. The new weapon had backfired in the party's face. [51]

As the Republican and Prohibition parties withered, a new reform party appeared on the horizon. The drift of the Southern Farmers' Alliance toward political action brought a serious challenge to the major parties when the Alliance attempted to reorganize the national political agenda around the economic demands of southern and western farmers. In 1890 the Alliance's success within the Democratic party in the South and as a separate People's party in Kansas left politicians of all existing parties groping for their bearings. Detecting prohibitionist sympathies among the insurgent farmers, a few male leaders of the Prohibition party broached the subject of coalition, but Frances Willard was the leader who took decisive action. In January 1892 she attracted Populist and Prohibitionist leaders to a conference at the Sherman House in Chicago and hammered out a platform that most of them could accept. Unfortunately for Willard, the Sherman House platform entailed too much compromise of prohibition for the Prohibition party leadership as a whole and too little compromise of prohibition for the Populists, who did not wish to see their own developing coalition disintegrate under the cross-pressure of the prohibition issue. Willard's push for coalition came to an end a month later in St. Louis, where a national Populist conference refused to accept a prohibition plank despite Willard's heroic efforts on its behalf. Although Willard was to live for another five years, this incident virtually brought to an end the American political career of the most visible woman in late-nineteenth-century politics. [52]

The failure of coalition in 1892 put a seal to party Prohibitionists' hopes for power and provides an end point to the third cycle of temperance reform, as the future of the cause lay with the Anti-Saloon League, a quite different kind of organization from the Prohibition party or the WCTU. Temperance reform had emerged from the disappointments of the Civil War years with the revival of the fraternal orders and the great uprising of the Crusaders and then in the 1880s once again became a political force through the WCTU, the Prohibition party, and the constitutional referendum campaigns. The gulf during these years between men's drinking and women's abstemiousness, together with women's economic dependence upon men, impelled women to take the lead in temperance reform. Women's leadership in turn kept temperance reform vibrant during a period of relatively low per capita consumption.

The increased scale and diversity of American society now made creation of a dry America through moral suasion inconceivable for most temperance reformers. Their hopes for the future, fears for social order, and unease about the direction in which their society seemed to be moving flowed into campaigns to make, amend, or enforce law. While temperance reformers shifted once again from less coercive to more coercive means, this cycle began in the Crusade with a more coercive brand of moral suasion than was employed in the 1820s and again in the early 1840s. Francis Murphy's and Henry Reynolds's reform clubs, which used a purer form of moral suasion than the Crusade, rallied the temperance forces and brought new supporters to the cause, but Murphy did not attempt to recommit the temperance movement as a whole to suasion. The cycle continued when the Prohibition party emerged as a political force during the 1880s promising a stronger form of coercion than the Maine Laws represented. As a national party the Prohibition party if elected would presumably squeeze the liquor traffic even out of states whose citizens wished to keep it. Bethiah Ogle and her fellow Crusaders demonstrated the force that could be mustered through voluntarism, informal networks, and localism, but by the end of another generation men and women like Frances Willard, a professional reformer with a cosmopolitan perspective, organizational skills, and a coercive agenda, controlled the temperance movement. During their reform's next cycle most temperance reformers were to follow the Anti-Saloon League even farther into the land of coercion.

Chapter Four

The Anti-Saloon League
Era (1892–1933)

To youth, more than to age, the pressure group presents both a challenge and an opportunity. To dare enlist with groups of forward-looking people, to become identified with a cause that has not yet become popular, to stand for right and progress and growth is the historic position of youth. The group with which you ally yourself may number no more adherents than the original nationalists in the Thirteen Colonies, the first anti-slavery advocates, the early champions of women's suffrage or national prohibition. If your cause is right, your loyalty genuine, your methods legitimate, you will move your nation both onward and upward. It may be safer to follow in the old ruts, but it still is "man's perdition to be safe when for the truth he ought to die." The days of martyrdom have passed but the day of opportunity for heroic service in a noble cause is with us now as never before in history.[1]

These words, delivered to a class in practical politics at Columbia University in the fall of 1923, were spoken by a slight, balding, middle-aged man wearing pince-nez spectacles above a close-trimmed graying mustache. He could easily have been taken for an academic, but the speaker was in fact one of the most powerful politicians—and arguably the most powerful nonelected politician—in America at that time: Wayne B. Wheeler, general counsel and legislative superintendent of the Anti-Saloon League of America. His power and his prominence as a leading spokesman for the Anti-Saloon League brought the invitation to speak at Columbia, since the League was viewed as the organization chiefly responsible for adoption of a national prohibition amendment to the Constitution (the Eighteenth Amendment) and as the principal force pushing for compliance with the Volstead Act, the amendment's enforcement legislation. Wheeler himself played a large part in drafting both the amendment and the Volstead Act, in securing their enactment and ratification, and in defending them in the courts. Political victory brought social change: as Wheeler spoke before the Columbia students, drinking in America stood at its lowest level ever. After a century of effort temperance reform had reached a pinnacle of triumph. Wheeler's words on that autumn day evoked the idealism that kept their vision alive for the generations of temperance folk who labored before him. The fact that the inspiring words were spoken by a salaried professional politician who spent his entire public career within a political temperance organization indicated at the same time that new elements had been added to the persistent idealism of reformers.

Nonpartisan political temperance organizations were formed at various times and places—for example, by Neal Dow in campaigning for his Maine Law in the 1840s—but the first such organization to last was the Anti-Saloon League of Ohio, which was created in 1893 by a Congregational minister and temperance activist named Howard Hyde Russell. In contrast to the Prohibition party, the League was to be staffed by paid workers. One of Russell's first recruits was young Wayne Wheeler, who was just completing his studies at Oberlin College. Wheeler's later observations to the Columbia students were drawn from personal experience, as the early workers for the Anti-Saloon League were few in number, their salaries meager, their work unrecognized or denounced by other reformers, and their efforts unrewarded by success. Beginning his work as a speaker and local organizer for the League, Wheeler by 1903 had become the superintendent, or chief executive officer, of the Ohio League, and two years later he led a successful campaign to unseat the Republican governor, Myron Herrick, who opposed a local-option law advocated by the League. Herrick's defeat—while the rest of the Republican state ticket swept to victory—established the League's leadership within the temperance movement by demonstrating the potency of its single-issue focus, balance-of-power tactics, and nonpartisan method.

In beating Herrick, Wheeler and the League also defeated Herrick's patron, Republican party boss George Cox of Cincinnati. This triumph brought to Wayne Wheeler's office in Columbus journalist Lincoln Steffens, a muckraking writer crusading against political machines and bosses. Steffens came to learn how this quintessentially Progressive battle was won. "I do it the way the bosses do it," Wheeler confided, "with minorities." "There are some anti-saloon voters in every community. I and other speakers increase the number and the passion of them. I list and bind them to vote as I bid. I say, 'We'll all vote against the men in office who won't support our bills. We'll vote for candidates who will promise to. They'll break their promise. Sure. Next time we'll break them.' And we can. We did."

"You'll sacrifice everything else?" Steffens inquired.

"Yes," Wheeler replied. "One thing at a time."

But, Steffens rejoined, the prohibitionists were interfering with the Progressive battle against big business. "We have no quarrel with business," said Wheeler. "The employers of labor are with us."

"So you are with them," shot back Steffens.

"One fight at a time," repeated Wheeler.[2]

In 1920 Wheeler, a Republican, became the Anti-Saloon League's chief spokesman to the incoming Republican administration under President Warren G. Harding, another Ohioan. (As the League's man in Washington he succeeded James Cannon, Jr., a bishop in the Methodist Episcopal Church, South, who wielded much influence during the administration of Woodrow Wilson.) In drafting the Volstead Act Wheeler had already seen to it that employees of the federal enforcement bureau were political appointees rather than civil service workers so that the League would be able to involve itself in the recruitment of prohibition agents. He also took part in convincing President Harding to appoint as federal commissioner of prohibition an undistinguished Ohio politician whom Wheeler felt would be responsive to Anti-Saloon League direction. Neither initiative turned out well, as the federal prohibition agency quickly became a synonym for scandal and corruption. Nevertheless, Wheeler invoked League unity—the organization's unofficial slogan was "It is better to be united in a bad fight than divided in a good one"—to prevent criticism of his decisions.

Within a few months after his address to the Columbia students Wheeler was turning the balance-of-power tactic to his own purposes within the League. Early in 1924 the final illness of long-time national superintendent Purley A. Baker made evident that a successor had to be chosen for the Anti-Saloon League's top office. The leading candidate was Ernest H. Cherrington, the League's chief financial officer, head of its extensive publishing operation, and founder of the World League Against Alcoholism. By virtue of his advocacy of an educational strategy, Cherrington became the principal rival to Wheeler, who stood for a focus on law enforcement. Wheeler did not aspire to the national superintendency himself, but he hoped to keep it in the hands of a leader who would not restrict his power. At a crucial meeting of the League Board of Trustees a member of Wheeler's faction falsely announced Baker's imminent recovery, and the board reelected the dying man. During the remaining two months before Baker died, Wheeler organized support for himself and undermined Cherrington's candidacy. When the election was held Wheeler received enough votes to deny Cherrington election on the first ballot, and he then delivered sufficient votes to ensure the election of Cherrington's opponent, a man with no experience in national affairs. Wheeler thus kept a free hand in Washington as the nation's self-styled "dry boss" until his death three years later.[3]

Although Wayne Wheeler no doubt overstated his own importance, he and other leaders of the Anti-Saloon League certainly wielded more power in national affairs than any temperance leaders before them. Similarly, his Anti-Saloon League dominated the temperance reform during its fourth cycle. Wheeler's jump from the Oberlin campus into the rough-and-tumble of prohibition politics is representative of the careers of his colleagues in the League's national leadership, although he entered the service of the League at a younger age than most. Leaders of the League generally were not members of temperance organizations before their commitment to the League or had been involved only in short-lived local organizations. Few belonged to the Prohibition party. Similarly, most of the League's followers were not party Prohibitionists, a fact evident in the League's ability to mobilize far more votes to swing as a balance of power than the party ever attracted. Most of its adherents did not become committed to the ideal of temperance or the cause of prohibition through the Anti-Saloon League, as the League devoted little energy to proselytizing for new converts. As historian Robert Bader says, "The league's genius came, not in . . . exhortation, but in focusing in an intense, laserlike beam the influence of those who had already been converted."[4]

The Anti-Saloon League represented a new solution to temperance reform's perennial problem of a fragmented constituency. Whereas the Woman's Christian Temperance Union and the Prohibition party sought to unite temperance supporters behind a multifaceted program of reform, the Anti-Saloon League advocated concentration on the lowest common denominator upon which temperance folk could agree. This approach brought the League the greatest political triumphs in the history of temperance reform and contributed as well to the reform's most resounding political defeat. Despite its eventual downfall, the Anti-Saloon League became the prototype of the political pressure group, a species that has flourished in the soil of American politics since the early twentieth century. The League's organization and strategy were not, however, simply seeded and cultivated according to instructions drawn from a textbook in political science. They sprang instead from a particular garden, the prohibition politics of the 1880s and 1890s, which was dominated by other shrubs to whose shadow the League adapted itself.

Origins of a New Approach

The principal influence upon the appearance and early growth of the Anti-Saloon League was the Prohibition party. As an organization the Prohibition party looked very much like the major parties of the nineteenth century: voluntaristic, decentralized, and relatively open and democratic in its decision-making procedures. Fund-raising was sporadic, operating primarily during presidential election campaigns, and was devoted mostly to sending out mass mailings of the party newspapers. Between campaigns the party's papers formed the principal nexus connecting party members to the leadership. Through their letters columns party members debated policy, and every four years they elected delegates to a national convention that decided the party's strategic course. The national chairman, state chairmen, and national and state committee members were all elected directly or indirectly by party members. Among its officials only the national chairman might be paid by the party. Most lecturers touring on behalf of the party lived by the contributions they received from their audiences.[5]

Rising vote totals in 1884 and 1886 had encouraged the party faithful; the results in 1888, however, gave pause even to the most optimistic. Despite an extremely close presidential contest and an increase in the party's vote, neither the Prohibition party nor its principal issue played a determining role in the outcome, as it had done four years earlier. Intraparty debate intensified as Prohibitionists sought an answer, until in 1896 the debate ended by rupturing the party. Before that happened, Prohibitionists undertook new initiatives that were to prove critical in shaping the political direction of their Anti-Saloon League successors.

One new initiative threatened to sunder existing ties between Prohibitionists and their churches. On the surface such a conflict appears surprising, since most evangelical Protestant churches were staunchly prohibitionist, and gatherings of the Prohibition party could easily be mistaken for revivals. The trouble was that evangelical clergymen and laymen, while prohibitionist in principle, were not prepared to abandon their major party (usually the Republican party) in favor of the Prohibition party despite the Democrats' consistent, and the Republicans' inconsistent, refusals to endorse prohibition. Like their predecessors in temperance reform, party Prohibitionists pushed along the secularization process by employing arguments emphasizing drink's social rather than spiritual damage and by putting forward a secular means of reform, the Prohibition party. These aspects of the party appear to have bothered church voters much less, however, than the radicalism they perceived in the party's advocacy of women's suffrage. Since the major parties provided—in the referenda of the 1880s—a means for voters to express themselves on prohibition without voting Prohibitionist, most prohibitionists were content to retain their old-party loyalties.

The spectacle of millions of church members piously praying for prohibition, adopting resolutions for prohibition in denominational assemblies, voting for prohibition in referenda, and then refusing to vote for the Prohibition party drove party members to distraction. By the mid-1890s their dissatisfaction with the churches was vigorously expressed through editorials and letters in the party press and took concrete form in a series of annual conferences and in several new "prohibition churches" scattered across the country from New York to California. For many party men and women the evangelical Protestant churches no longer served the cause of reform and therefore they no longer represented fit institutional expressions of religion either.

At the same time as they severed ties with existing churches party Prohibitionists worked to create links with the farmer's insurgency rising in the South and West. Frances Willard's efforts in Chicago and St. Louis in 1892 represented the closest Prohibitionists came to forming such a coalition, but her failure did not put an end to their attempts to do so. The Prohibition party in 1892 received its largest presidential vote ever, but its vote was still only slightly higher than its 1888 harvest, and represented only 2.25 percent of the total cast; the Populists, with 8 percent, did much better in their first presidential contest. This outcome converted some of Willard's former opponents into dedicated advocates of coalition, and fusion with the Populists became a major theme of intra-party debate for the next three years. By 1895 a majority of the national committee favored taking steps toward coalition with both the Populist and the Socialist Labor parties. The coalitionists failed, however, to muster their full strength at a key meeting of the national committee in December 1895, and a vote taken at that meeting stopped further attempts at creation of a grand union of reformers and radicals.

In the process of pursuing the Populists, Prohibitionists changed their own party's ideological stance both by formulating new demands on issues other than prohibition and by questioning their party's commitment to prohibition itself. After their rebuff by the Populists at St. Louis, Prohibitionists gathered in Cincinnati where, in their 1892 national convention, they adopted a platform that shifted their party toward the radical end of the 1890s political spectrum. The platform demanded government control of railroad, telegraph, and "other public corporations"; a government-issued currency (a controversial demand in the late nineteenth century since private banks issued much of the nation's currency); a progressive tax on wealth; limitation of individual and corporate ownership of land (a plank more radical than the Populists'); an end to lynching; unqualified women's suffrage; and equal pay for equal work by men and women. The last three planks bespoke an end to Prohibitionists' courtship of conservative southerners, and the last two (at least) were equally offensive to many churchmen in the North. Prohibition was identified as the "dominant issue" in the platform, but after the election a debate erupted within the party over proposals for "nationalization of liquor," a state-monopoly system of liquor distribution that promised to change the existing liquor business by eliminating both the saloon and private profit.

These intertwined issues—the value of the churches, coalition with other reformers and radicals, economic and social policy, prohibition versus nationalization—aroused vigorous debate within the party during the mid-1890s and eventually tore it apart in 1896. At the national convention in that year, the supporters of coalition and radicalism, the advocates of nationalization, and the antiecclesiastical Prohibitionists clashed with a "narrow-gauge" faction that arose in response to their initiatives and urged instead a renewed appeal to middle-class Protestant voters on a platform limited to prohibition alone. The party split, and neither of its fragments attracted many votes in that polarized and hard-fought campaign. For our purposes, however, the split is less important than the intraparty debate that preceded it, because that debate formed the matrix that shaped the Anti-Saloon League. It was a debate over the fundamental issues of the identity, purpose, and constituency of temperance reform, and such a discussion of basic issues never took place again.

The fundamental problem that caused the debate was the same fragmentation of their constituency that had plagued temperance activists for half a century. The problem took concrete form in a phenomenon revealed by the constitutional prohibitory referenda of the 1880s, namely the existence of a substantial body of voters who were sympathetic to prohibition but not to the Prohibition party. They numbered at least a million and a half men, were probably middle class, and were likely to be affiliated with one of the evangelical churches. Most important, they seemed frightened of any political or social change except prohibition. They clung tightly to the major parties, and they demanded that their parties refuse to entertain any policy that seemed likely to threaten their own position or power despite the nation's evident need to reconcile its divided classes, races, regions, and sexes. In contrast to the spirit of exemplary sacrifice that prevailed among early temperance reformers, prohibitionists came increasingly to see their reform as a means of self-protection from the higher taxes needed to support jails, asylums, and poorhouses, and from political machines organized around the saloons. By focusing on liquor as the primary source of social ills, prohibitionists also blinded themselves to other possible causes for poverty, corporate power, and industrial conflict.

During the 1880s the Prohibition party tried to accommodate this fearful conservatism by weakening its women's suffrage plank and proclaiming that, despite its advocacy of other reforms, prohibition was its "dominant issue." Neither worked, and so many Prohibitionists, forced by the polarizing effects of the farmers' revolt to choose sides, chose to move to the left; by doing so they turned away from those whom they previously considered their special constituency. But the conflict that tortured and eventually sundered the Prohibition party was witnessed by other eyes, those of the men who were to create the Anti-Saloon League, and they drew from it the same conclusions that impelled the narrow-gauge Prohibitionists. Indeed, the founders of the Anti-Saloon League shared with the narrow-gaugers of the Prohibition party the same fears of radicalism and class warfare that motivated the prohibition constituency. They therefore set out to design and build an organization capable of attacking the liquor traffic without disturbing any other institution in American society.[6]

Strategy and Structure

The first institution to which Anti-Saloon League men turned was the churches. Where Prohibition party editorialists had vilified the evangelical churches, the Anti-Saloon League announced that it was "the Church in Action Against the Saloon." The League was organized at the grass roots by contacts with local pastors, who were encouraged to enroll their congregations as League affiliates. Lists of church members willing to vote for politicians sympathetic to League measures were drawn up from these contacts. Each cooperating local church set aside one Sunday each year for an "Anti-Saloon League Field Day" on which a League representative spoke from the pulpit outlining the League's progress and prospects and soliciting pledges of financial support. Representatives of supportive denominations were placed on the governing boards of state leagues and the national League; after 1903 they were given procedural control over the affairs of the state and national organizations. (Day-to-day operational control remained in the hands of the paid staff.) In its own leadership the League did appear to be "the Church in Action Against the Saloon": whereas businessmen, lawyers, and clergymen each contributed about one-fifth of Prohibition party leaders, clergymen alone made up three-fifths of Anti-Saloon League leaders, and among the paid officials of the League the proportion of clergymen was even higher.[7]

If they were to secure cooperation from church members, League activists recognized that their organization must remain a single-issue pressure group. Therefore, the Anti-Saloon League normally focused on prohibition alone. Typically a state League drafted a liquor-control bill during each legislative session and directed all its efforts toward securing the bill's passage. In the following election the League worked to reelect its legislative supporters and defeat its opponents. Then in the next session the legislature found itself confronted with another demand by the Anti-Saloon League——for the same bill if the League had been unable to win its enactment previously or for a more advanced piece of legislation if the League had won its law. The League was prepared to accept allies wherever they could be found. In California and Colorado, for example, the League worked with Progressives while in Virginia it cooperated with a distinctly un-Progressive political machine. But the League always put its own issue first.[8]

In its attitude toward the major parties the Anti-Saloon League was unequivocal. "The League does not seek the disintegration of any political party," proclaimed an official statement. "It avoids all efforts that would tend to destroy party integrity or effect the overthrow of any political organization." League officials targeted individual candidates, questioning them concerning their attitudes toward League measures, publicizing their responses, and endorsing them or not depending on their position relative to those of their opponents. The League pursued this program in both party primaries and general elections. Although most leaders of the League were Republicans and therefore regarded Republican officials as more sympathetic to their cause, they were capable of acting in a genuinely nonpartisan manner.

By wooing the churches, keeping to its single issue, and reassuring the major parties of its peaceful intentions, the League demonstrated its willingness to accept American society as it was except for the existence of the liquor business. After the party split in 1896 the Prohibition party followed a parallel course under the leadership of its narrow-gauge wing, making renewed appeals to church voters and returning in its platforms toward the political center. But the League still distinguished itself from the party not only by its rejection of third-party action but also by its gradualism, its opportunism, and its use of balance-of-power tactics.[9]

In each state the immediate League goal was determined by the existing situation. "Do not strive after the impossible," the Ohio headquarters instructed local agencies. "Study local conditions and reach after the attainable."[10] Where the sale of liquor was licensed the League sought to elect local officials committed to no-license and demanded local option in the largest jurisdiction it deemed politically acceptable. If ward or precinct local option prevailed, the League sought to dry up localities and pressed state legislators for a county local-option law. In states allowing county option the League sought to make as many counties as possible dry before proceeding to a campaign for statewide prohibition. National prohibition, their ultimate goal, waited upon the spread of dry territory through local option and statewide prohibition.

When choosing candidates to endorse, League officials balanced two principal factors: the candidates' willingness to vote as the League wished and their chances to win. Prohibition party candidates were recommended by the League only when both major-party nominees were totally unacceptable. As this practice suggests, the personal habits and values of candidates were considered to be less relevant than their legislative behavior; the League endorsed numerous officials who lived wet because they voted dry. In fact, the League did not require a total-abstinence pledge from its own members.

The League won the confidence of prohibition voters not by occupying more advanced ground than the Prohibition party—indeed, the League usually advocated less restrictive measures than did the party—but rather by picturing itself as successful in obtaining the measures it advocated. Therefore its credibility in the eyes of its constituents, hence its power, depended upon maintaining an image of success. When various states adopted the initiative and referendum allowing voters to propose or enact legislation, the WCTU or party Prohibitionists often pushed for immediate statewide prohibition campaigns, whereas the Anti-Saloon League was usually found dragging its heels in order to avoid needless losses. Advocates of such campaigns saw them as educational tools even if their measure lost; League officials simply regarded lost campaigns as advertisements of prohibitionist weakness.

According to the League, prohibitionists should play only melodies of success, and this it proceeded to do in a symphony of propaganda that poured forth from its printing plant at League headquarters in Westerville, Ohio. Perhaps the most famous means of self-advertisement was the maps of each state contained in the League's annual *Yearbook,* with dry areas in white and wet counties colored in black. Such maps, together with accompanying tables of statistics and reports of dry progress, gave an impression of careful attention to detail, but in fact they were sometimes grossly inaccurate and exaggerated League achievements.[11]

In its advocacy of national prohibition the Prohibition party represented a highly coercive mode of temperance reform. Nevertheless, the party required assent to its program by a majority of voters if it were to implement prohibition. Although the opportunism of the Anti-Saloon League was intended to maximize support for League measures, the same opportunism as expressed in the use of balance-of-power tactics showed that League officials were willing to accept any forward movement that could be attained, with majority support if possible, but without it if necessary. Balance-of-power tactics simply meant swinging the prohibitionist vote between candidates in closely contested races according to their sympathy for League measures. "'Balance of power' may not represent a majority sentiment," wrote one League spokesman, "but it *controls* it."[12] The League's willingness to accept national prohibition imposed by a minority made its brand of temperance reform the most coercive Americans had yet seen.[13]

The structure of the Anti-Saloon League distinguished it from the Prohibition party in yet other ways. The party's reliance on occasional donations from party members was replaced by the systematic solicitation and collection of funds from supporters, principally those within the evangelical churches; by 1919 the state and national leagues together were collecting about $2.5 million annually from about 300,000 regular donors. The League had received large donations since its early days from John D. Rockefeller, and it later organized a committee, headed by dime-store magnate S. S. Kresge, to secure donations from other businessmen. About 14,000 businessmen responded to Kresge's call. Proceeds from these fund-raising measures were used to pay the staff members who performed the day-to-day work of building and running the organization.

During the League's first decade low pay and meager results produced a higher rate of turnover among its state superintendents than among Prohibition party state chairmen, and few but clergymen could be persuaded to work for the League. After 1904, however, staff members stayed with the organization longer, and the League found that it could now attract more men from careers other than the ministry, although clergymen remained by far the largest single group among the League's leadership.[14]

In relying upon a professional leadership acting in specialized bureaucratic roles the League marched in step with the emerging business corporation. So, too, in its operations did the League depart from the Prohibition party model in favor of a mode of decision making more centralized and less democratic, in short, more businesslike. League boards of trustees were selected not by local members of the organization but by denominational governing bodies. Trustees then appointed the state superintendent as well as district superintendents. Decisions about League policy were made at the top with minimal participation by the membership. Annual conventions were held, but, as historian Austin Kerr points out, "like the stockholders' meetings of the typical modern corporation, they were carefully staged events for exhortation and education, not for involving large numbers of people in reaching decisions vital to the organization."[15]

Prohibition Victories and Social Change

The Anti-Saloon League of America was born in 1895 when Howard Russell's Ohio reformers joined a similar group in the District of Columbia to create a national organization. The League's history from its founding to the coming of national Prohibition in 1920 can be divided into two phases demarcated by its decision in 1913 to mount a campaign for a prohibitory constitutional amendment. During the first phase the Anti-Saloon League consolidated the temperance forces under its leadership and drove the liquor business from territory where the strength of prohibitionist battalions was greatest; the second phase was the League's triumphant crusade for national prohibition. Although both the Prohibition party and the WCTU retained distinct organizational identities, many party members as individuals and the WCTU as an organization cooperated with the League in most states and in most of its endeavors. In addition, the League mobilized support from prohibitionist voters outside the party and the WCTU. In winning its victories the Anti-Saloon League was aided by larger changes in American society, which sometimes produced effects sufficiently powerful to spread prohibition even without the aid of the League.[16]

During the years 1907–09 six southern states—Oklahoma, Tennessee, Georgia, Alabama, North Carolina, and Mississippi—adopted statewide prohibition, but in the last four of these the Anti-Saloon League played little or no part in the victorious campaigns. Even before the beginning of the new prohibition wave much of the South was legally dried up through local option; by one estimate, 825 of the 994 counties in the states of the Old Confederacy were dry by 1907.[17]

In these southern campaigns prohibitionists employed racist arguments, such as the claim that liquor must be proscribed because its use inflamed black men and provoked assaults upon white women. But racist arguments were also used against prohibition, as in accusations that a federal prohibition amendment would lead to further interventions in the area of personal morality and behavior, including federal challenges to antimiscegenation statutes. Whites who lived in areas having the largest black populations, who should have been most interested in controlling blacks' behavior, generally provided the strongest resistance to prohibition.[18]

Prohibition attracted strong support from the southern middle class in both rural and urban areas, probably for the same reasons that persuaded northern farmers and businessmen during the nineteenth century. To emergent manufacturers confronting workers who brought traditional attitudes toward work to their new jobs in the mills, prohibition seemed to offer a means of inculcating the discipline of machine production. If resistance to the new order continued, drink furnished a useful explanation. To those who preached the virtues of "rational" farming practices and to those who listened to them, agricultural reform and drink reform went hand in hand, as both promised success in meeting the shifting imperatives of the market. Southerners who wanted to cleanse their cities, purify politics, and promote public health turned to prohibition. After disenfranchisement of most blacks and many poor whites, the white native-born middle class made up a disproportionately large segment of the southern electorate, and in bringing prohibition to the region they imposed their new values upon their fellow citizens.[19]

The prohibition cause also benefited from social changes affecting various western states during this period. During the late nineteenth century the mining frontier contained populations consisting largely of young men engaged in intermittent labor under the direction of others; there were many saloons and much drinking. By the 1890s, however, Colorado and Idaho began to attract farmers and their families as new techniques of irrigation and dry-land farming brought a fresh wave of people emigrating from older midwestern states. Mining counties, which once held most of the population and dominated state politics, stagnated while commercial agriculture underwrote prosperity and population growth in new farming areas. Many immigrants came from states such as Kansas and Iowa that had adopted prohibition, but more important were the conditions the immigrants found in their new homes. Raising potatoes or sugar beets for the market required careful planning and disciplined labor, neither of which was compatible with traditional drinking practices. European immigrants, who made up a substantial component of the mine workers, retained such practices, and when bloody conflicts between workers and bosses erupted, prohibitionists rallied support for their cause by blaming the emergence of class hostility upon the saloon. To safeguard their families and to enforce "modern" values, farmers and their wives voted rural areas dry under local option. Then they joined with native-born allies in the urban middle class to restore order by voting their states dry.[20]

The impetus for the third wave of prohibition victories, which began in 1907 and crested a decade later, came from states in the South and West. In political matters, however, the nation's center of gravity lay in the Northeast because of that region's wealth, population, and control over national media of communications. Prohibitionists in the South and West were sometimes able to construct a voting coalition embracing commercial farmers and the urban middle class; where the urban working class consisted largely of native-born workers, prohibition sometimes succeeded in cities before it prevailed statewide, thereby blunting the edge of urban-rural conflict. In the Northeast, in contrast, the prohibition issue normally mobilized the countryside against the city.

Prohibitionists everywhere sounded appeals that they hoped would prove resonant in an atmosphere of Progressive reform, striking chords of belief in moral law, commitment to material progress, faith in science, opposition to the corrupting influence of plutocracy, humanitarianism, and uplift of the lower classes. Such appeals often succeeded in wooing members of the urban middle class, especially when the saloon rather than drinking was to be proscribed. The content and constituency of Progressivism shifted from state to state, however, and in northeastern states where Progressives found support among the urban working class the prohibitionist appeal to urban voters generally fell on deaf ears. Organized workers whose unions had long advocated temperance resented paternalistic rhetoric that portrayed workers as helpless objects of middle-class concern or as suitable targets of employers' campaigns for increased efficiency. Prohibition laws forbidding retail sale—workers' source of supply—while allowing personal importation and consumption of liquor clearly favored wealthy drinkers. Finally, workers rightly suspected prohibition campaigns under the Anti-Saloon League of diverting attention from pressing issues of wealth and power.[21]

Rural-urban conflict in the Northeast over prohibition drew sustenance from other sources as well. Most northeastern farmers were taught market discipline by the spread of commercial agriculture before 1900; one lesson they learned was a hostile attitude toward drinking. Small towns formed the cockpits of struggles over liquor because they concentrated the social effects of drinking within a small space and exposed more of their populations to those effects than did cities. Support for prohibition by groups living outside the large cities therefore represented a direct response to drinking and its attendant damage, adaptation to modern work patterns, or both together.

The groups holding the most traditional attitudes toward drinking were the recent immigrants from southern and eastern Europe, who clustered in the cities. These groups brought with them drinking customs similar to those that most native-born rural dwellers had renounced long before, and such customs were reinforced by the work experience in America. Once again, populations composed predominantly of young men who held insecure jobs requiring hard but intermittent labor performed in extreme heat or cold, and who lived in transient communities containing more men than women, formed the core of both the drinking population and the resistance to prohibition. Traditional attitudes were hardened by lack of opportunity for social mobility: calls for sober self-improvement tended to be lost on Slavic steelworkers in factories where only Yankees became foremen. The saloon provided a principal avenue of mobility for some new immigrant groups, as it had for the Germans and Irish before them, and thereby reinforced those groups' hostility to prohibition.

This being said, however, important qualifications must be made. Budget studies of working-class families revealed that families of European origin spent less for liquor than similar families in Europe. Budget-study findings also suggested that the cultural difference between native and immigrant families in their perceptions of liquor merely resided in the more common tendency of poor immigrants to regard it as a necessity. Confirming this view, among all working-class families alcohol expenditures rose and converged as family income increased. The massive immigration of the early twentieth century furnished both new drinkers and new antiprohibitionist voters, most of whom resided in large cities. But the American environment appears to have modified immigrant drinking patterns in the direction of temperance, and cultural differences operated within a framework of conditions affecting both native and immigrant workers.[22]

Although new immigrants provided the bulk of voting power behind urban antiprohibitionism, they were not the only groups to be found in the cities. Middle-class prohibitionists and working-class temperance men and women lived there, too, but also important was an emerging cultural orientation that appeared among middle-class and, especially, upper-class urbanites. This was a set of attitudes that historians call "cultural modernism"—actually only the most recent in a series of "modernisms"—which appeared in direct opposition to the Victorian culture from which temperance reform drew nourishment. Where Victorianism preached thrift, industry, and sobriety, cultural modernism exalted consumption and display, identified self-expression as the key to the good life, and sought fulfillment in leisure. This orientation was consistent with the changing needs of an industrial economy that produced more goods than it could sell, an economy that relied increasingly on advertising to foster new needs and thereby to create fresh markets for its surplus. "Men must enjoy," a leading economist proclaimed. "The new morality does not consist in saving but in expanding consumption."[23] Reinforced by a declining workweek, a new openness to pleasure manifested itself in growing audiences for public amusements. Perhaps the clearest expression of the new style could be found in the cabaret life of New York City, which burst forth in the 1890s and became more lavish, participatory, and public after the turn of the century. Yet in other cities as well rural observers found "a bunch of day-sleeping, night chasing gilded cockerels and hens of the café crowd."[24]

Hedonistic attitudes were anathema to prohibitionists because they undercut both specific injunctions against drinking and the general spirit of sacrifice for the common good that prohibitionists invoked as rationale and justification. Prohibitionists' ability to present a positive alternative was weakened, however, by another change in attitudes that also bolstered the growing emphasis upon leisure: the degradation of work. This change, too, can be traced to industrialization, which during the late nineteenth century gradually destroyed each of the major justifications for work. In an economy of abundance, scarcity no longer called men and women forth in the service of production, and work could no longer be linked easily or automatically with social utility. Nor did work as creativity make sense in a world of factories and increasingly bureaucratic offices. Finally, the correlation between work and upward mobility became more uncertain as the ranks of the self-employed dwindled. Ironically, the process of industrialization, which temperance reformers historically embraced, became a corrosive agent undermining the ideal of sober workmanship that occupied such a prominent place in the temperance utopia. Gradually the degradation of work and the emergence of cultural modernism were to turn the Anti-Saloon League, its allies, and its supporters into yesterday's modernists.[25]

The Drive for National Prohibition

Cultural changes took decades to unfold, and meanwhile the prohibition forces won most of the political battles. By the beginning of 1912 the Anti-Saloon League had claimed considerable success for its cause. Through the operation of statewide prohibition laws much of the South had been rendered legally dry. Local option produced the same result throughout wide areas in the South and elsewhere. Despite the corrosive effects of cultural modernism, drinking as a cultural ideal claimed few friends in strategic places. Almost one quarter of daily newspapers refused liquor advertising, as did most of the popular family magazines. Although the nineteenth-century flood of temperance plays and novels ebbed after 1900, temperance values and beliefs permeated the novels, plays, and films of the time, which presented to their mass audiences few positive portraits of drinkers amidst an ocean of negative images.[26]

Much that we know about the liquor situation around 1912 suggests an equilibrium. Prohibitionists had successfully driven the liquor business from the areas where it was least welcome, but without imposing excessive burdens on minorities of drinkers within such areas. In Missouri before national Prohibition, for example, 97 of the state's 115 counties voted dry under local-option legislation. The dry areas held slightly less than half of the state's population, and access to wet cities did not present a formidable difficulty for most residents of dry counties, nor did the law forbid bringing liquor back with them. In 1917, Missourians decisively rejected statewide prohibition in a popular referendum. Nevertheless, in the same year three-quarters of the state's congressmen voted to submit a constitutional amendment for national prohibition to state legislatures for ratification. Fourteen months after the referendum, and without any intervening elections, the Missouri General Assembly ratified the Eighteenth Amendment.[27]

The high-water mark of prohibitionist success came at different times in different states, but the basic pattern was the same everywhere. The number of counties voting dry under local option increased up to a certain point and then stabilized, as the majority of dry and wet counties retained their status while a few counties changed their stance each way, some dry-to-wet and some wet-to-dry, during each round of elections. A similar situation appeared on the state level.[28]

This slowing of progress confronted Anti-Saloon League leaders with a dilemma, which became acute as the result of a victory in Congress. After a short campaign the League in 1913 convinced Congress to adopt the Webb-Kenyon Act, which prohibited interstate shipment of liquor into a state contrary to the laws of that state. Webb-Kenyon extended an 1890 prohibition against shipment into a prohibition state for sale to ban interstate shipment for personal consumption when the state law was "bone-dry," that is, when it forbade possession or consumption of liquor. Passage of the act represented a significant achievement for prohibitionists, and in addition it demonstrated the League's ability to influence Congress, an ability that seemed particularly impressive in view of the law's enactment over a veto by President Taft.

The League's easy conquest of Congress tempted its leaders to launch a campaign for submission of a national prohibition amendment. Such a campaign was particularly suited to the League's balance-of-power tactics, which were more effective in swaying individual legislators than in influencing political parties or winning popular referenda. Furthermore, the potency of the balance-of-power tactic itself would be enhanced by several facts. Because of lagging reapportionment in the House and constitutional design in the Senate, rural residents were overrepresented in both Houses. In the state legislatures rural areas were also typically overrepresented. State and federal legislatures, where submission and ratification of an amendment would be decided, therefore seemed to be likely targets for a single-issue pressure group whose mass constituency largely resided in rural areas and states.[29]

If national prohibition were enacted through skillful manipulation of a minority, however, the Anti-Saloon League risked outrunning its popular support and thereby endangering effective enforcement. To leaders who typically followed an incremental approach the dangers of premature action were clear. Three considerations seem to have swayed them to launch the crusade for a national prohibition amendment in 1913. In the first place, simply to stand still and hope to protect territory currently dry was dangerous. Stung by prohibition victories, the liquor business had started a counteroffensive, which began to roll back prohibitionist gains. The spirits trade in 1908 formed a new organization for self-regulation and political action, the National Model License League, which advocated licensing as a regulatory measure, and claimed successes in several states within three years of its founding. Brewers, many of whom previously eschewed political action in the belief that the self-evident virtues of beer would protect them from prohibitionist assaults, began to realize their mistake and to contribute heavily to fund parallel efforts toward saloon reform and political mobilization in Texas and Ohio. Headed by Percy Andreae, an officer in a Cincinnati brewery, the brewers' vigilance bureau in Ohio hired detectives to report saloons' violations of restrictive laws. In addition, Andreae organized voters in a Personal Liberty League, which attempted to operate as a single-issue lobby like the Anti-Saloon League. Andreae's efforts contributed to the rolling back of prohibitionist gains in Ohio's second round of county-option elections held in 1911, to the state's repeal of its 1851 no-license constitutional clause in a referendum in 1912, and to the repeal of county option itself after another referendum in 1914.[30]

Losses in these and other referendum campaigns exposed the League's basic weakness in failing to attract majority support for its cause. The League had also not obliterated its rival for leadership of the dry forces, the Prohibition party, and as prohibitionist momentum slowed that failure began to loom large in the eyes of League leaders. In 1907 party Prohibitionists struck at a vulnerable point in the League's armor by organizing denominational temperance forces under a new flag, the Inter-Church Temperance Federation; four years later the Federation evolved into an even larger organization, the National Church Temperance Council. This action cast doubt on the League's claim to be "the Church in Action Against the Saloon." After 1909 many leaders of the party who previously cooperated with the Anti-Saloon League rejected the League and turned to an effort to rejuvenate their party.[31]

Finally, most national leaders of the Anti-Saloon League believed that the campaign for national prohibition would be a protracted one. Howard Russell and Purley Baker thought it might require two decades. A long campaign would enable the League to educate public sentiment as it worked for national prohibition and so to avoid the second horn of its dilemma. To reverse its recent defeats, to maintain its leadership of the temperance forces, and to achieve a long-cherished goal the Anti-Saloon League in 1913 launched the campaign for national prohibition.

During the next seven years the Anti-Saloon League won the greatest political victories in the history of the temperance reform, victories that came so quickly they surprised even those most responsible for winning them. The means by which these triumphs were achieved contributed to their eventual reversal, but in the rush of momentous events few paused to consider such a possibility. The key to the success or failure of national prohibition was popular support, and in the heady days after 1913 many signs indicated that the prohibition cause was winning the battle for public opinion. Numerous states held referenda on statewide prohibition, and in most prohibition prevailed. During 1914 Arizona, Colorado, Oregon, Virginia, and Washington State all voted dry, while only California and Ohio voters rejected prohibition. In 1915 South Carolina joined the dry ranks; Ohio voters again voted wet. Nine states returned majorities for state prohibition in 1916; only three voted against. Four referenda in 1917 were split evenly between wets and drys, but in 1918 prohibition's progress resumed, with seven state referenda approving prohibition, while in only two was it rejected. Meanwhile, four states in 1915, three in 1917, and another in 1918 adopted statewide prohibition by legislative action without a referendum.[32]

Even while campaigns in the states went forward, the Anti-Saloon League turned its attention more and more toward Congress. In 1914 the dry forces won a majority vote in the House of Representatives for submission of a prohibition constitutional amendment (the resolution failed because the majority fell short of the constitutionally required two-thirds). The League then focused its energies on the 1916 elections, and its efforts were rewarded with the return of sufficient dry congressmen to provide the necessary two-thirds majority for submission.

From the opening of the new Congress the prohibition issue became entangled with the United States' involvement in the European war and the political issues arising therefrom. First, the League lobbied success-fully for an amendment to a food-conservation bill that banned the use of grain in distilling, a move that effectively shut down the distilling industry for the duration of the war. Then in December 1917 Congress voted to submit the proposed constitutional amendment for national prohibition to the states. Finally, League lobbying brought about enactment in 1918 of a wartime prohibition law, to remain in effect during the war and subse-quent demobilization, which went into force on 30 June 1919. Early in 1917 Congress also approved an amendment proposed by a wet senator to embarrass the League, which League representatives accepted reluc-tantly (because of a perceived lack of public support); this was the Reed-Randall Bone-Dry Amendment forbidding transportation of liquor into any state under statewide prohibition, whether state law forbade it or not. The League's work in 1916 for a dry Congress paid off bountifully.[33]

When James Cannon and his Anti-Saloon League colleagues brought their demands to Congress, they found little effective opposition from the liquor business. Although prohibitionists typically pictured the liquor trade as an aggressive and monolithic force, in reality the liquor forces were usually defensive and divided. After the coming of the federal income tax in 1913 they failed to recognize the full effect of this new source of revenue in lessening federal dependence upon their industry. The most debilitating fissure separated the two largest and wealthiest groups, the brewers and the distillers. The distillers first sensed the potential of the Anti-Saloon League, but they were rarely able to convince the brewers of the need for united action. To the brewers beer was a true temperance drink, and only fanatics classed it with whiskey. Therefore, their instinctive reaction to prohibitionist pressure was to distance themselves from the distillers. Furthermore, brewers' love affair with their beverage led them to deny their own responsibility for the conduct of the saloons, most of which they owned.

Brewers were also divided among themselves. The large breweries in Milwaukee and St. Louis that shipped beer across the country found little incentive to fight state prohibition statutes that allowed personal consumption while shutting down breweries serving local markets. A similar conflict of interest undermined brewers' willingness to cooperate within states in fighting the spread of dry territory under local option. In Michigan, brewers in safely wet Detroit gained an increased market share as county after county went dry, closing local breweries while leaving county borders open for shipments of bottled Detroit brew. After the promising beginning of the liquor industry's counteroffensive in Texas and Ohio, an influential group within the United States Brewers' Association (USBA) stopped the association's antiprohibition campaign, replacing it with a strategy that accepted prohibition while seeking exemptions for beer and wine. The federal government's action against the distilling industry in 1917, which left brewing and winemaking untouched, only strengthened the position of this group and made the prospect of united industry action even more remote than before.[34]

While thousands of Americans were voting at the ballot boxes against the liquor business, saloonkeepers, brewers, and distillers were hearing another kind of vote being registered in their tills and balance sheets. After its long plateau in the late nineteenth century per capita consumption began to rise. As during the years since 1850, the increase in beer consumption was most dramatic, rising from 16 gallons per capita in 1900 to more than 21 gallons by 1913. Unlike previous periods of growth in beer consumption, however, this one did not represent substitution of beer for spirits; per capita consumption of distilled liquors also rose, by about one-fifth between 1900 and 1913. As a result, per capita consumption of absolute alcohol rose to 1.7 gallons by 1906, the highest level since the 1840s, and remained there for the next decade. To some extent the rise resulted from the addition to the drinking population of a prime drinking group, young males, through the massive immigration of the early twentieth century. But the rise in consumption proportionately outstripped the growth of the adult male population and must be explained in other ways as well. Increasing prosperity provides a large part of the answer, as national income rose even faster than expenditures on alcoholic beverages during this period. This prosperity, of course, furnished the basis for shifts in popular values toward attitudes friendly to consumption. In the short run, however, the increase in drinking lulled some brewers and distillers into a false sense of security and so contributed to sapping the liquor industry's determination and unity.[35]

By producing injury to health and by contributing to alcoholic violence, the increase in drinking gave a powerful stimulus to prohibition victories in the state referenda of this period. Many people came over to the temperance side in these referenda or in legislative campaigns as a direct response to the personal and social damage they saw around them. Yet the threat from drinking may have been less serious at this time than in previous periods of high consumption. Before the Civil War spirits contributed most of the alcohol consumed and by the early 1870s, despite a great increase in beer's popularity, distilled liquors still represented four-fifths of absolute alcohol consumption. By 1915, however, the positions of fermented and distilled beverages were nearly reversed, as beer provided three-fifths of all the alcohol consumed. If beer's increasing popularity implied the presence of a growing number of moderate drinkers, as some analysts believe, then the extent of drunkenness and alcoholic damage may not have been so great as in earlier periods of high per capita consumption. The death rate for cirrhosis of the liver fell after 1911, and the death rate for "alcoholism" began to drop after 1916 or 1917. The post-1900 rise in consumption nevertheless caused extensive alcoholic damage, which gave credence to prohibitionist propaganda since few if any realized that such damage was less severe than during the nineteenth century. If the rise in consumption implied a growing population of moderate drinkers, however, the meaning of this shift for the prohibition cause was ominous, since it signaled that a growing portion of the population rejected the prohibitionist vision of a dry utopia, even though they might be willing to embrace prohibition for other reasons.[36]

One reason was radicalism, which seemed to be spreading in step with liquor consumption. Radicalism and labor militance appeared on several fronts: in the strikes and "free-speech" fights led by the Industrial Workers of the World (IWW), in the rising vote totals won by the Socialist party, in violent conflicts between labor and capital, and even in the increasing numbers of workers enlisted by the unions belonging to the American Federation of Labor. Middle-class men and women may have been sympathetic to radicals' and reformers' demands for social justice, but they were repelled by the sacrifices satisfaction of such demands might entail for them.

To the middle class, prohibition offered an attractive way of understanding and responding to the radical program. The prohibitionist argument portrayed social conflict and disorder as products of personal and social vices, removable by a stiff dose of state-enforced morality. Insofar as prohibitionists focused attention on working-class drinking and blamed workers' drinking for industrial conflict, their indictment was false. The working-class tradition of temperance reform flourished in most of the craft unions and among Socialist party organizers and the IWW; agrarian radicalism and temperance advocacy often went hand in hand; and social surveys conducted at the time showed that the average share of working-class family income spent on liquor consistently fell below the national average. When middle-class voters accepted a link between working-class drinking and labor conflict, they revealed their own need to divert attention from other sources of disorder. As pressing as this need may have been at times, middle-class men and women could not deny that charges of corporate arrogance and rapacity were well founded, and prohibitionists managed to fit their panacea to this perception as well. Prohibition in fact constituted a minimal agreement with the radical program. This agreement was embodied in willingness to dispossess the capitalists of the liquor industry, a form of destruction of private property that became tolerable to middle-class voters only when more extreme proposals appeared on the political agenda. To take that step was to demonstrate middle-class concern for the welfare—and the good order—of the working class, but without embracing a program for fundamental change.[37]

The United States' entry into World War I in April 1917 furnished another reason for some to support prohibition. Calls for sacrifice gained resonance as young men were called to risk their lives in battle. Specific wartime needs, such as those for food and fuel conservation and for preservation of military discipline and sobriety, led to the suspension of distilling, reduction in the alcohol content of beer, restriction of saloons' opening hours, and prohibition of liquor selling near military bases and to servicemen in uniform. In addition, wartime hatred of things German destroyed the German-American Alliance, one of the few large popular organizations opposing prohibition, and the Anti-Saloon League seized every opportunity to associate beer with the enemy. For the prohibition crusade, however, American involvement in the war came too late and ended too soon to be of great assistance. By April 1917 most of the states that were to vote themselves dry had already done so, and the Anti-Saloon League had elected its compliant congressmen in the previous fall elections. The ratification process may have been hastened by the wartime atmosphere, but the process was completed suddenly by the actions of twenty-one state legislatures during the month of January 1919, more than six weeks after the war's end. The Eighteenth Amendment came into effect one year later.[38]

The rapid ratification of the Eighteenth Amendment demonstrated once again the ability of the Anti-Saloon League to influence the actions of legislators. In mobilizing public opinion behind national Prohibition, however, the League was not so successful. Most of the states holding prohibition referenda and voting dry were among the less-populated states of the South and West. Of the ten largest states, five never held a referendum on state or national prohibition, and two others voted wet in their last referendum held before national Prohibition went into effect. Michigan voters in 1916 approved a constitutional amendment bringing prohibition to the state while allowing personal importation and consumption. Texas voted dry in 1919. After defeating state prohibition in 1912, 1914, 1915, and 1917, Ohio voters approved it in a light vote in 1918; in 1919 they returned both pro- and antiprohibition majorities in four referenda.[39]

The coming of national Prohibition was not the result of long-term trends in American society nor of long-standing conflicts, although both of these set the stage. Expansion of the market economy made temperance a widely accepted ideal, but public respect for temperance did not necessarily imply prohibition. Conflicts between labor and capital and among ethnic groups could have been addressed in other terms than those supplied by prohibitionists. In the coming of national Prohibition, the key actors were a specific organization and a short-term development. The development was the upsurge in drinking in the early twentieth century, and the organization was, of course, the Anti-Saloon League, which capitalized on antiliquor sentiment arising in response to the upsurge.

In Congress and the state legislatures skillful use of prohibitionist minorities created legislative majorities, and in both electoral and lobbying campaigns the Anti-Saloon League outmaneuvered its poorly organized, divided, and dispirited opposition. To enforce and maintain the law required both continued influence over legislatures and a considerable degree of popular support. Prohibition probably did not command majority assent as the time of ratification of the Eighteenth Amendment, but the amendment's placement of its reform in the Constitution gave the cause much prestige and power, which were reflected in some favorable referendum results during the first years after national Prohibition went into effect. Once prohibition was implanted in the Constitution nearly everyone thought it would stay there. After nearly a century's effort temperance reformers had finally achieved major goals: the dismantling of the liquor business and enlistment of the state on behalf of their cause. No one foresaw what changes these achievements were to bring for temperance reform and for the nation.[40]

National Prohibition

In its effects, national Prohibition did not entirely prohibit, but it did reduce drinking considerably. The Eighteenth Amendment banned the manufacture, sale, transportation, importation, and exportation of intoxicating liquors, and the Volstead Act defined "intoxicating" in most cases as one-half of one percent alcohol by volume. Most alcohol production was thereby rendered illegal, and for the period of national Prohibition estimates of consumption, which are usually derived primarily from production figures, are therefore highly provisional. The best estimates place consumption of absolute alcohol per capita in 1921–22 at about three-quarters of a gallon, the lowest level in American history. Consumption rose thereafter as bootleggers and rumrunners became better organized, and by 1927–30 per capita consumption of absolute alcohol stood at about 1.1 gallons, which was slightly below the average level of the late nineteenth century and well below the immediate pre-Prohibition peak of 1.7 gallons reached in most of the years between 1906 and 1917. Decline in alcohol consumption accelerated the widening use of nonalcoholic beverages including milk, coffee, carbonated drinks, and fresh fruit juices.[41]

The impact of Prohibition fell unequally upon the different alcoholic beverages. Beer suffered most because its bulk in relation to alcoholic content made its manufacture, transportation, and sale least profitable and easiest to detect. Its massive decline reversed fifty years of growth in consumption. Grape growers were surprised and delighted to find that concentrate could be legally produced and sold to an enlarged market of home wine makers; per capita consumption of wine nearly doubled between 1911–14 and 1927–30, reaching an unprecedented level, although wine still furnished a smaller proportion of total absolute alcohol consumption than beer. After a drop in the early years of Prohibition, spirits recovered by the latter years of the 1920s to a point slightly below the pre-Prohibition peak of 1917. The decline of beer left distilled liquors contributing a much larger proportion of absolute alcohol consumed than during the decade before Prohibition, about two-thirds of the total.[42]

Beer's decline meant that Prohibition's impact on drinking fell heaviest upon the working class, which contained most of the nation's beer drinkers. Per capita consumption among the working class dropped considerably because the principal substitute, distilled spirits, became too expensive for most workers to afford on a regular basis. The money thus saved was either spent on other consumer goods or swallowed up in an inflationary surge that accompanied the drive for national Prohibition. By the late 1920s per capita consumption among the middle class seems to have regained its pre-Prohibition level; the higher cost of Prohibition liquor drew from middle-class pockets about a billion dollars more each year than was spent on its better-quality predecessor. The upper class too continued to drink at its pre-Prohibition rate, but Prohibition placed upon the wealthy a double burden. In addition to paying more for illicit liquor, the rich paid higher income taxes and suffered lower dividends because of increased corporate taxation levied to make up for lost federal revenues from the liquor business.[43]

A desire to shift the financial burden imposed by Prohibition back onto the rest of society therefore provided part of the motivation that impelled members of the upper class to take the lead in the campaign to repeal the Eighteenth Amendment. The repeal campaign was led by the Association Against the Prohibition Amendment (AAPA), founded in 1918 by a businessman, lawyer, and former naval officer, William H. Stayton. Although prosperous, Stayton was not himself among the most wealthy, and his reasons for opposing Prohibition were primarily ideological. Stayton's ideology anticipated the conservatism that was to become a powerful political force in the late twentieth century, as he was repelled by any increase in the power of the federal government except that which was necessary to augment the size and strength of the armed forces or to suppress radicalism. "This prohibition business," Stayton proclaimed, "is only a symptom of a disease, the desire of fanatics to meddle in the other man's affairs and to regulate the details of your lives and mine."[44] Although this anticentralization argument remained basic to its criticism of Prohibition, the AAPA seized upon other issues including the cost of enforcement, increasing criminal activity, corruption in government, and an alleged spread of disrespect for law as a result of extensive violation of the Volstead Act. After failing to attract wide support, the AAPA made itself into an elite lobby and propaganda machine that could bring to bear upon policymakers and the public the influence and resources of the wealthy. By the late 1920s the AAPA had attracted such men as the three du Pont brothers, Pierre, Irénée, and Lammot, who controlled the vast Du Pont industrial empire (which included the General Motors Corporation), and John J. Raskob, a top executive first at the Du Pont Company and then at General Motors.[45]

These men and others of similar wealth and connections opposed national Prohibition both because it represented a significant increase in federal power and because that power was not being exercised as they wished. Some had previously supported the Anti-Saloon League, and all believed that temperance was good for workers, even to the point of enforcing it in their plants. Like Stayton they seem to have believed that some purposes justified augmentation of federal power, and none of them are known to have protested government excesses in suppressing radicalism during World War I or the postwar Red Scare. With the radical threat removed, however, the specter of a federal government strong enough to wipe out an entire industry at a single stroke—while increasing the tax burden of the rich—became too frightening to tolerate any longer. Furthermore, although AAPA members' interests and activities extended across the nation—indeed, across the world—and their outlook was cosmopolitan, their power and prestige were greatest in localities or states and they could not reliably depend upon control of the federal government. They needed the federal government, however, to protect their far-flung interests. When its authority was eroded by widespread violation of its laws, the federal government's ability to foster their aims diminished. John Raskob warned, "If the Prohibition Amendment and laws at present on our books (remember I say 'if') are resulting in a lack of respect for law in our institutions, it is but a short step to such a lack of respect for property rights as to result in bolshevism."[46] Despite its denunciation of the Volstead Act, the AAPA consistently refused to endorse attempts to flout the law. Probably because of their source in upper-class interests, the arguments of the AAPA received little popular support during most of the organization's history.[47]

Although its prestige and power were far greater than those of the AAPA, organizationally the Anti-Saloon League was not flourishing either. League adherents soon after ratification of the Eighteenth Amendment stopped giving their time and their money to the cause, although they continued to vote as the League instructed. Even some national leaders of the League, such as the aging Purley Baker, relaxed their efforts in the belief that victory at last was theirs.[48]

The WCTU's interest in other issues than Prohibition and women's suffrage allowed it to retain support better than the Anti-Saloon League after its leading causes were embodied in the Constitution. Increasingly as the twenties wore on, however, the WCTU was crippled by societal controversy over Prohibition and beset as well by a handicap that was not shared with the Anti-Saloon League. Along with many other suffragists the women of the WCTU assumed that because of their gender women experienced common conditions and shared common interests and perceptions. The WCTU arguments for the vote therefore usually consisted of variations on the theme that enfranchised women would benefit public life by bringing to it their unique moral insight. Women's entry into the political world of the 1920s, with its male-defined issues and male-designed institutions, provided little evidence, however, of women's power for change. Large numbers of women stayed at home on election day, as did large numbers of men. The women who voted divided their support among the existing parties, none of which advocated significant change in women's condition. These developments seriously undermined the assumption of women's unity of purpose.[49]

In addition to assuming unity of purpose among women, the WCTU claimed to articulate that purpose, and in the absence of credible competing claims its assertion generally passed unquestioned. Late in the twenties, however, an organization arose that brought into question the WCTU's right to speak for women on the issue of liquor control. This was the Women's Organization for National Prohibition Reform (WONPR), a creation of the same class that produced the AAPA. The husbands of some WONPR leaders held leadership positions in the AAPA, but the women acted independently in founding and running their new organization. Nevertheless, the Women's Organization for National Prohibition Reform for the most part simply repeated arguments for repeal long made familiar by the AAPA. The fact that anti-Prohibitionist arguments were voiced by women, however, dissipated much of the credibility that WCTU support brought to the defense of prohibition. Leaders of the WONPR realized this and consequently devoted much effort to increasing their membership rolls and publicizing the results. The Prohibition cause suffered accordingly when, in December 1931, the WONPR announced that its total membership now exceeded that claimed by the WCTU.[50]

If the WCTU's constituency was thus divided, the WCTU itself seems to have been united during the political battles of the twenties. The same cannot be said of the Anti-Saloon League, which in addition to declining support was troubled by a debilitating internal struggle between factions headed by Wayne Wheeler and Ernest Cherrington. At issue was the relative priority to be given to enforcement and education. Both men realized that Prohibition did not enjoy unanimous assent, that many were likely to violate the law in order to continue drinking, and that the Anti-Saloon League, whatever its triumphs in winning the Eighteenth Amendment and the Volstead Act, did not win the power to rule. Wheeler believed, however, that the League could continue to wield its balance of power so as to compel elected officials to enforce the law so rigorously that drinking would become too costly to be continued.

The Eighteenth Amendment called for "concurrent" enforcement by the federal government and the states, and in Wheeler's view this meant that federal officials were only to bolster the primary enforcement thrust that was to be made in the states. Wheeler also felt that demanding substantial enforcement budgets along with creation of a large new bureaucracy would confess the strength of popular opposition to Prohibition. As Wheeler assessed the situation, the principal advantages held by the Anti-Saloon League were the amendment with its enforcing legislation and the League's political balance of power. Wheeler granted a need for educational activity by the League, but he perceived such activity as consisting mainly of calls to obey the law. The weakness in Wheeler's strategy was, of course, the very real possibility that the minimal enforcement effort he was willing to demand would be insufficient to compel acquiescence. Especially was this outcome likely in the cities, which represented the real testing ground for national Prohibition, since most rural areas had long since voted themselves dry under local option or state prohibition.[51]

Cherrington agreed with Wheeler that symbolic victory was not enough, but he disagreed on the means to be used to achieve Prohibition in substance as well as in law. In Cherrington's view, recalcitrant drinkers should be offered not the iron fist of the law but rather the blandishments of dry propaganda, which would point out the personal and social benefits to be derived from abstinence. The Eighteenth Amendment and the Volstead Act represented educational forces, teaching social norms that would be underpinned by temperance pedagogy. As such they were to be maintained and enforced, but by governments rather than by temperance reformers acting through political lobbies. The Anti-Saloon League should be transformed into an agency of moral suasion.[52]

Cherrington's vision led to consensus rather than conflict, but the pursuit of consensus would cost the Anti-Saloon League something. Perhaps most distasteful to the other major leaders of the League was the prospect of basic change in the nature of their organization and the possibility that even a fundamental transformation might still eventuate in the loss of what they had gained. To advocate personal abstinence was to question the values and personal behavior of some League supporters as well as many of its opponents and to bring into question as well the League's basic assumption that the liquor trade, not the individual drinker, was at the root of the liquor problem. Most leaders of the League no doubt preferred to pursue both educational and coercive strategies, but the reduced resources of their organization foreclosed this possibility and forced a choice. The likely costs for an uncertain gain entailed by Cherrington's proposals convinced the leadership of the League to reject them until Wheeler's strategy proved its bankruptcy.

Imprisonment within a rigid and coercive strategy produced rhetorical excess, inability to compromise, detachment from reality, and a callous disregard of individual rights and democratic principles. Modification of the Volstead Act to allow manufacture and sale of light wines and beer, a proposal that gained widespread support and no doubt would have satisfied many of Prohibition's opponents, was considered by the League to be unacceptable. In the face of widespread and increasing violation of the law, and with federal courts flooded by Prohibition cases, the Anti-Saloon League in California typically "maintained . . . a dogged insistence that the letter of the law be observed; and until the very end it continued to meet the repeated breakdown of enforcement machinery with bright predictions of future improvement."[53] In Michigan, the superintendent of the Anti-Saloon League, R. N. Holsaple, throughout the twenties opposed reapportionment of the state legislature, which would have increased representation for wet Detroit. When wets proposed a referendum on Prohibition, Holsaple responded that America was not a democracy: "As long as we have representative government," he announced, "it is the duty of the legislator who is dry to oppose a referendum."[54] Proposed legislation to prevent police entry into private homes without search warrants was perceived by League spokesmen solely as a threat to Prohibition enforcement. Federal law required that industrial alcohol, whose diversion provided a bountiful source of illicit liquor, be poisoned, and the Anti-Saloon League opposed efforts to change the law: "Not only did the League consider the law essential to its cause, but it viewed a run of poisonings as a healthy sign."[55]

Repeal

The Anti-Saloon League's organizational enfeeblement and strategic rigidity combined with other developments to turn Prohibition's political triumphs to dust. Ironically, one of those developments was the reduction in drinking and consequently in alcoholic damage brought about by Prohibition itself. The incidence of alcoholic psychoses and alcohol-related diseases such as cirrhosis of the liver dropped as first state and then national Prohibition took effect, although psychosis rates later rose to about their pre-1910 level. Most of the large hospitals for treatment of inebriates closed or were turned to other uses. With these changes the personal and social costs of drinking became less widely apparent, and dry warnings lost the resonance they held for many people during the early twentieth century.[56]

Like other reformers, prohibitionists taught governmental responsibility for curing social problems, and with the coming of the Great Depression in 1929 their teachings turned on them with ironic force, as did their previous attempts to claim credit for prosperity. While unemployment spread and bread lines lengthened, Anti-Saloon League insistence that Prohibition remained the most pressing issue made its cause ridiculous. Other developments produced reinforcing effects. The League reached its peak of national power in the presidential election of 1928, when it mustered all its resources to elect the dry Republican Herbert Hoover over the wet Democrat Al Smith. One significant ingredient in Hoover's victory was the anti-Smith campaign led in the South by Bishop James Cannon. The League's successful effort to save Prohibition in 1928, however, tied the Prohibition cause more closely than ever before to the fortunes of the Republican party. Meanwhile John Raskob, named by Smith to the Democratic national chairmanship, quietly consolidated that party's attachment to the cause of repeal. Immediately upon taking office Hoover appointed former attorney general George Wickersham to head a presidential commission to investigate the administration of criminal justice. The commission's report, delivered in 1931, accepted AAPA arguments that drinking had increased since 1920, that bootlegging and official corruption were widespread, that the judicial and penal systems were overburdened by prosecutions under the Volstead Act and state enforcement statutes, that states were slackening their efforts at enforcement, and that respect for law was eroded by Prohibition. Nevertheless, the commissioners' conclusion, upon which Hoover focused as he endorsed their report, opposed repeal. This performance inspired composition of the following widely quoted verse:

> Prohibition is an awful flop.
>   We like it.
> It can't stop what it's meant to stop.
>   We like it.
> It's left a trail of graft and slime
> It don't prohibit worth a dime
> It's filled our land with vice and crime,
>   Nevertheless, we're for it.[57]

Unfair as it was, the indictment stuck.[58]

In 1929 for the first time scandal attached itself to a national leader of the Anti-Saloon League. Following Wheeler's death and Cannon's partly successful campaign to split the solid South from its Democratic party allegiance, the Southern Methodist bishop became the most visible symbol of the Anti-Saloon League. The League and the Prohibition cause therefore suffered when in the summer of 1929 political enemies of the bishop brought charges against him ranging from flour hoarding during World War I, through patronage of a fraudulent dealer in stocks, to misuse of campaign funds and adultery. Cannon eventually vindicated himself, but not until after several years of hearings and trials preoccupied an able leader, shattered his political influence, and tarnished the dry leadership's reputation for probity.[59]

In Cannon's downfall the Anti-Saloon League paid dearly for its victory over Al Smith in 1928, and the next presidential election cost it even more as a result of its abandonment of nonpartisanship. Neither major party's platform in 1932 was friendly to Prohibition, but the Republican party's position left room for continued federal action on liquor control, while the Democrats declared outright for repeal. The Republicans nominated the dry Hoover. Franklin Roosevelt, the Democratic nominee, finally ended years of straddling the Prohibition issue when the 1932 national convention pulled him onto the wet side of the fence by adopting a repeal plank by a convincing majority. The election was to determine the fate of national Prohibition and, since the Republicans were saddled with political responsibility for the worst depression in the nation's history, its outcome was hardly in doubt.

Nevertheless, the election results suggest that Prohibition dragged down the Republican party as much as the unpopularity of Herbert Hoover doomed Prohibition. Aided by a long-delayed reapportionment that finally began to reflect urban predominance, the Democrats gained numerous seats in Congress, but the congressional balance shifted from dry to wet even more dramatically than from Republican to Democratic. Furthermore, voters in nine states repealed their state prohibition statutes in referenda held at the same time as the presidential poll. Since its founding in 1918 the AAPA sought in vain for an audience; now in the space of a few years and with no change in repeal arguments, sentiment for repeal burst forth so rapidly and apparently spontaneously that even the repeal organizations failed to appreciate its growing strength.[60]

Politicians saw the election as a mandate. During the interval between election and inauguration the lame-duck Congress, which had earlier proven unsympathetic to repeal, voted to submit a repeal amendment to the states. Nevertheless, Congress lagged behind some states, where legislatures were already preparing—for the first time since adoption of the Constitution—for ratification by conventions rather than by legislatures. Ratification by convention was the method desired by leaders of the repeal campaign because they realized that the developing drive for repeal could be frustrated by the legislatures of only thirteen states, and rural overrepresentation remained a fact of life in many state legislatures. To ensure the maximum advantage for their cause members of a repeal organization called the Voluntary Committee of Lawyers circulated a model bill authorizing a ratification convention, which included a key proviso for election of convention delegates at large rather than by districts. Such a procedure gave greatest possible weight to the votes of city residents, who were usually wet, as against those of their fellow citizens living in rural areas. Twenty states adopted the model bill with no more than minor changes, and many others borrowed its ideas.[61]

In most states delegates were elected as slates pledged for or against repeal, so the convention elections represented a referendum on Prohibition. The Anti-Saloon League was so short of resources that it could not mount a credible defensive campaign, and for the most part dry counterattacks were limited to ineffectual court challenges. A tidal wave of enthusiasm for repeal swept away the drys. Within a short time after congressional submission of the amendment, forty states made provisions for holding repeal elections. Thirty-seven states conducted state-wide votes on repeal between April and November 1933, and voters in thirty-five of those endorsed repeal. Overall nearly 21 million voters turned out for the repeal elections, and nearly three-quarters of them voted for repeal. Only in North and South Carolina was the repeal drive turned away. Fears among the AAPA of the rural dry vote turned out to be largely unfounded; although urban areas provided the largest majorities for repeal, most rural areas also voted wet.

The repeal elections represented a sweeping and decisive rejection of Prohibition, and by the autumn of 1933 what was thought only a short time before to be impossible became a certainty. Since they were elected to vote for repeal, the delegates usually went about their work with a minimum of debate; in New Hampshire's convention they required only seventeen minutes. On 5 December 1933 Utah became the thirty-sixth state to ratify the new Twenty-first Amendment, and the Prohibition amendment became the first to be repealed. Meanwhile in April 1933 a special session of Congress passed a bill changing the Volstead Act's standard of "intoxicating" to 3.2 percent alcohol, and weak beer once again became legal. For most people, the return of beer marked the end of Prohibition.[62]

National Prohibition's departure, like its arrival, was caused more by short-term forces than by long-term changes. Repeal therefore did not imply rejection of temperance as an ideal or put an end to temperance reform, although reform during the next cycle was to appear in quite a different guise than during the Anti-Saloon League era. Hedonistic attitudes and their expression in mass consumption spread during the expansionary twenties, but they played a minor part in the repeal of Prohibition, which took place in the radically dissimilar atmosphere of depression. Furthermore, cultural modernism seems to have had greater impact upon intellectual and social elites than upon public opinion at large. The large minority of voters who embraced Prohibition at the end of the First World War was augmented during national Prohibition's first years by other citizens who accepted the reform as the law of the land. When federal and state agents found they had to kill some people, imprison many others and prosecute thousands more in order to enforce the law, and when drinking continued while prosecutions increased instead of diminishing, Prohibition alienated some among both its old and its new supporters. Nevertheless, until the coming of the depression in 1929, Prohibition continued to enjoy much popular support, as the election results in 1928 indicated.[63]

The depression caused massive slippage in that support, but not because voters agreed with the AAPA and the WONPR that the federal government had accumulated too much power. Instead, in a world of disappearing jobs and impotent governments, resurrection of the liquor business offered one concrete way to put some people back to work and to provide one source of government revenues badly needed to care for the needs of others. The consequences in alcoholic damage were forgotten in the exigencies of the moment or were never learned by a generation that came to maturity during an era of diminished consumption. Through the repeal organizations a wealthy elite played a key—and ironic—role by manipulating the political process so as to allow a newly emergent anti-Prohibition majority to express its wishes quickly and decisively. By its decision to launch a campaign for national Prohibition the Anti-Saloon League gambled, won a great victory, and then suffered an even greater defeat. In national Prohibition temperance reformers discovered a way to reduce drinking on a large scale, but they were unable to avoid pitfalls inherent in pursuing a political solution to a social problem. Both their success and their failure cast long shadows over the next cycle of reform.

Chapter Five

Governments, Alcoholics, and Academics (1933–80)

Bill Wilson wanted a drink. As he paced the lobby of his hotel in Akron, Ohio, the erstwhile Wall Street manipulator heard from a nearby lounge the familiar sounds of alcoholic conviviality. Wilson knew, however, that for him to walk into the lounge and order a drink would be disastrous. To put the matter mildly, Bill Wilson had a drinking problem. His drinking had wasted business opportunities, brought him to jail, and confronted him with the specters of approaching insanity and death. Although he recognized the inevitable consequences of his virtually constant drunkenness, Wilson could not stop. Six months before, in November 1934, he had been visited by an old drinking companion whom he regarded as a hopeless drunkard; Wilson was amazed not only to find his friend sober but also to learn that his sobriety resulted from religious commitment. Their conversations revealed to Wilson that a "drunk," as he called himself, could talk openly and honestly with another drunk about their mutual affliction. But Wilson, a self-proclaimed rationalist, could not at first accept the existence of a power greater than the human mind. Finally, after falling into deep despair Wilson underwent a spiritual experience that gave him the strength to stop drinking. Reformed, he immediately tried to reform others by telling them how he had done it. In five months many listened, but none stopped drinking. Recently Wilson had returned to Wall Street, a scene of former triumphs, and his attempt to rebuild his business career brought him to Akron. Now he was alone in a strange city, and tempted. Just one drink! Mustering all his resolve, Wilson turned instead to a telephone booth, picked the name of a minister from the directory, and asked to be put in touch with another drunk.

Wilson found Dr. Robert Smith, an Akron surgeon who was in the process of destroying his medical practice through chronic drunkenness. Indeed, when Wilson's contact called, Smith was lying at home in a drunken stupor. Waking the next day with a hangover, Smith agreed to meet the stranger from New York, but on the way he told his wife they would stay only fifteen minutes. Smith expected preaching and was surprised to find that Wilson wanted to talk to him for Wilson's own sake, not his. They talked for six hours. Smith later described the meeting:

[Bill] was a man who experienced many years of frightful drinking, who had had most all the drunkard's experience known to man. . . . *He was the first living human with whom I had ever talked, who knew what he was talking about in regard to alcoholism from actual experience. In other words, he talked my language.*[1]

Aside from one binge several weeks later Smith never took another drink; Wilson also remained abstinent for the rest of his life. Bill Wilson's action in reaching out to another drunkard in order to preserve his own sobriety became the central dynamic behind the spread of a most unusual organization, Alcoholics Anonymous, founded by "Bill W." and "Dr. Bob." Wilson's recognition that he suffered from an affliction that was incurable without the aid of a higher power provided the rationale for AA's distinctive approach to drunkards. And the bond established by the two men that day became the model for the ties that by the 1980s were to bind into small, tightly-knit groups hundreds of thousands of people who call themselves "alcoholics" in the United States and in diverse societies across the world. Alcoholics Anonymous dates its founding from the moment when Dr. Robert Smith took his last drink, on 10 June 1935.[2]

The alcoholic afflictions of William Wilson and Robert Smith did not begin with the repeal of Prohibition. Their drinking, as well as that of other heavy drinkers, had flourished during the twenties, as Prohibition had not cut off the flow of liquor to those who wanted to drink most desperately. Instead, Prohibition had worked, especially in its early years, to discourage drinking among those who had been social or moderate drinkers and to make access to alcohol difficult for those who were coming of age to drink. This was, of course, exactly what the Anti-Saloon

League was trying to do. Although the League received no credit for it, per capita consumption remained at a level below that of the immediate pre-Prohibition period for a quarter of a century after Repeal. But if Prohibition ignored the needs of habitual drunkards, American liquor-control policy after Repeal did no better. Poor people who became intoxicated in public were often arrested and jailed, or perhaps committed to an asylum. Well-to-do drinkers whose drinking disrupted careers or families were placed in one of the remaining institutions for the care of inebriates; Bill Wilson's spiritual experience occurred while he was hospitalized in one of these. Neither the founding of Alcoholics Anonymous nor its early growth can be traced to larger changes in drinking behavior or in social policy toward drinking.

Although the number of habitual drunkards in American society may have varied over time, drunkards' need for help was persistent; that need had been met in various ways and to varying degrees by the American Temperance Society, the Washingtonians, the fraternal orders, the reform clubs, and the inebriety asylums. The shutting down of most of the inebriety asylums and hospitals with the coming of national Prohibition created a vacuum that was filled by the emergence of Alcoholics Anonymous. When AA took on the job of reforming drunkards, it adopted some of the tools—such as experience speeches, secrecy, and mutual support networks—used by those who had previously sought the same goal. In one crucial respect, however, the founders of AA gave a new twist to an old idea. Although they agreed with earlier temperance reformers that alcohol was addictive, they insisted that alcohol produced unique effects among one group of drinkers whom they labeled "alcoholics." This effect was a loss of control over drinking, an irresistible craving that drove the alcoholic toward destruction. Acceptance of this idea was crucial to their strategy for recovery: unless the alcoholic conceded his or her powerlessness over alcohol, Wilson and Smith believed, he or she had no hope for recovery. This view of alcohol's effect drove a wedge between "normal" drinking (that which was controlled) and pathological drinking, and therefore between social drinkers and alcoholics. By defining only the drinking of alcoholics as problematic, the new view undercut strategies for prevention of drinking problems.

This new view of drinking and addiction is usually referred to as the "disease concept of alcoholism," although its originality lies not in the claim that chronic drunkenness is a disease but rather in the distinction it makes between drinkers who are and are not susceptible to the affliction. Attachment of the "disease" label to habitual drunkenness in the minds of the public at large is the unique achievement of the latest cycle of temperance reform, an achievement that was made possible by emphasizing the distinction between "normal" drinkers and "alcoholics." Other developments, such as the emergence of a drinkers' movement for self-reform and the growth of state intervention, resemble phenomena that appeared in other cycles. The disease concept gained currency because of its employment by Alcoholics Anonymous and also because of its advocacy by a crucial handful of academic experts. The principal means by which the new view was propagated was the National Council on Alcoholism, whose work was fostered both by the academic alcoholism experts and by leading members of Alcoholics Anonymous. These new temperance reformers—in Alcoholics Anonymous, in the National Council on Alcoholism, and in a cloistered corner of the academic world—presented themselves as citizens who sought to control drinking without bringing on the excesses of past reform. Indeed, they rejected the label of "temperance reformers" and sought to distinguish themselves from all those who had previously tried to control drinking. The story of the new reformers' emergence and their uneasy triumph is the story of the fifth cycle of temperance reform.

Liquor Policy, Drinking, and the Old Reformers

Repeal of national Prohibition returned liquor control to the states; the federal government reserved the shared power to tax and retained by virtue of the Twenty-first Amendment an obligation to prevent shipment of liquor into states whose laws prohibited its possession or consumption. While the states were formulating new systems of control over the liquor industry, however, the federal government sponsored a unique attempt at central direction of the industry. This occurred with the formulation during 1933 of a "code of fair competition" as directed for all industries by the National Industrial Recovery Act. Drafting of such codes was supervised by the National Recovery Administration (NRA), but businessmen themselves were given responsibility for the actual writing. The brewing industry code revealed the brewers' understanding of why they were put out of business thirteen years earlier, how they planned to avoid the same fate in the future, and what shape they wished to see their industry assume.

The central feature of the NRA code for the brewing industry, as in more than four hundred other NRA industry codes, was a requirement for price posting, after which the price could not be changed for ten days. Code authorities created by the brewers were empowered to invalidate any price they considered to represent "destructive price-cutting or dumping." Such price-fixing was sanctioned for the brewing industry, as for other industries, in order to reduce competition and to raise prices to a level that would provide a satisfactory return to producers. Limitation of competition seemed especially necessary to the brewing industry, which had already been entered by about five hundred firms during the short period since brewing had become legal again.

Brewer spokesmen justified price-fixing, however, not only in the terms used by spokesmen for other industries but also as a measure to prevent the return of the saloon. For the brewers price-fixing meant a first step toward eliminating financial ties between producer and retailer, which they described as a principal source of evil in the days before national Prohibition. Control by a brewer over a saloon keeper supposedly produced relentless pressure to sell unlimited amounts of the brewer's product, which in turn spawned practices such as treating, sales to minors and habitual drunkards, and prostitution. Public posting of prices was intended to prevent discounted sales to preferred outlets. The NRA code also included bans on other practices that tended to make the retailer dependent in any way upon the producer of his or her product. Federal sponsorship of the brewing industry's code in effect endorsed the view that the tied saloon rather than drinking was the source of alcohol problems.

Stigmatizing the tied saloon obviously served the interests of the liquor industry as a whole, but it also suited the needs of the largest brewers, those who shipped beer across the nation as well as serving their own cities. Although companies such as Pabst, Schlitz, and Anheuser-Busch owned large numbers of saloons themselves in the days before national Prohibition, they regarded the tied saloon as particularly suited to attempts by small local brewers to protect their own markets against the shipping brewers' campaigns to create brand loyalty through large-scale advertising. For the shipping brewers price maintenance and elimination of the tied saloon were part of an effort to restrict competition through political tools where economic means had failed. Although the code died with the NRA in 1935, the brewers remained committed to the model embodied therein, and its basic elements reappeared in the new liquor-control systems constructed by the states.[3]

Other forces were at work on the states as they cast about for a foundation on which to build a new system. In January 1933 John D. Rockefeller, Jr., announced his sponsorship for a study of the liquor problem that was to provide the necessary guiding principles. Rockefeller's main concern was the disrespect for law that he believed to have been engendered by national Prohibition; six months before, this concern led him to part company with the Anti-Saloon League, to which he and his father had been major contributors, and to advocate repeal of the Eighteenth Amendment.

The resulting study, published in October 1933 under the title *Toward Liquor Control,* was less a product of scientific research than a discussion of means to achieve renewed obedience to law where drinking was concerned. Rockefeller outlined this purpose in his introduction: "Rightly, the first objective is the abolition of lawlessness. Any program offered in lieu of the Eighteen Amendment must make that its chief aim, even if— and I weigh carefully what I say—the immediate result is temporarily away from temperance."[4] *Toward Liquor Control* recommended a state monopoly over retail sale for off-premises consumption of distilled spirits, fortified wine, and beer with more than 3.2 percent alcohol. An alternative system was recommended for states unwilling to create a state liquor monopoly. They were advised to establish a state licensing board to replace the local authorities that issued liquor licenses before Prohibition. Under both systems state authorities were to exert power over a wide range of matters including prices, advertising, design of outlets, time of sales, and the number and location of outlets. Tied saloons were prohibited. The Rockefeller program sought to bring under state control an industry—the liquor industry—and a type of mass behavior—drinking—that flourished totally uncontrolled during the period of national Prohibition. To accomplish this end it called for an exertion of state power exceeded only by national Prohibition itself.[5]

Nothing in the Rockefeller program ran counter to the interests of the producers of alcohol. On the contrary, the control systems proposed in *Toward Liquor Control* promised a stable legal framework for the sale of their product, and prohibition of the tied saloon echoed a part of the brewers' own strategy. Consequently producers offered no opposition as the states proceeded to construct alcohol-control systems along the lines laid down by Rockefeller and his associates. By 1936 fifteen states had created state monopolies for sale of heavier alcoholic beverages and issued licenses through a state agency for outlets selling lighter liquors. Except for a handful of states that retained state prohibition, the remainder of the states adopted license systems, all of which centralized control at the state level, although some allowed local option on the questions of whether and what type of licenses should be issued. The new state agencies possessed wide powers over the conditions of sale and consumption, and in exercising these powers they generally favored off-premises consumption and discouraged the sale of liquor by the drink. By 1940 every state but one had passed legislation prohibiting tied outlets.

The alcohol-control system created during the 1930s was later modified, but its main features remained the same. The number of prohibition states steadily dwindled, with Kansas repealing its prohibitory amendment in 1948, Oklahoma in 1957, and the last, Mississippi, in 1966. Licensing authorities became less hostile to on-premises consumption. In general, the new system worked not so much to suppress drinking as to discourage public drinking and to exert behind-the-scenes control over that which persisted. Arrests for public drunkenness and disorderly conduct continued their long decline which began in the late nineteenth century. Placement of responsibility for alcohol control in a state-level bureaucratic agency effectively removed the liquor issue from the political sphere, which it had persistently troubled since the 1830s. The proportion of Gallup poll respondents favoring the return of national Prohibition dropped steadily from nearly two-fifths in the late 1930s to less than one-fifth by the early 1980s. Meanwhile federal and state governments levied special taxes on liquor, which became responsible for an increasing share of the retail price; by 1970 federal taxes accounted for more than a quarter of consumer expenditures on alcoholic beverages, compared to about one-sixth in the 1930s. Including state taxes, the total government share in 1970 came to more than one-third.[6]

Within the framework created by the states the liquor business developed in a pattern similar in most respects to that found in other businesses. Distilling quickly became dominated by four corporations, which by the end of the 1930s were producing more than three-quarters of all whiskey distilled in the United States. Concentration occurred more slowly and less completely in brewing, where the 703 firms of 1935 dropped to 45 by 1979. Nevertheless, by 1984 the six largest brewers controlled about 94 percent of the market, and the two largest brewing corporations, Anheuser-Busch and Miller, shared about 55 percent. In brewing, concentration was aided by regulations supporting price maintenance and opposing the tied saloon that were adopted by many states following the principles of the NRA code.

Another prod toward concentration was provided by the coming of the aluminum beer can in 1934, since many smaller brewers could not afford the capital outlay necessary to purchase canning equipment; furthermore, the lower costs of a distribution system based on cans compared to one using bottles (when neither is returnable) eroded the disadvantage that transportation costs always imposed on shipping brewers in relation to their local competitors. Traditionally beer was sold in kegs, and the introduction of bottled beer in the 1880s—in part as a reaction to the growth of dry territory—did not change this practice significantly. By the 1930s the spreading use of home refrigeration provided a necessary condition for emergence of a home market for packaged beer. In addition, state liquor-control authorities often encouraged proliferation of outlets for off-premises sale by setting lower license fees than for on-premises sellers and by outlawing credit advances by producers to retailers as part of the campaign to prevent the return of the tied saloon. Such regulations facilitated the entry of grocery chains into beer retailing, a move that helped make beer buying a normal part of everyday life and made drinking increasingly a private rather than a public activity. Clearly the development of the liquor business since Repeal has not been shaped by market forces alone; instead, the state has intervened continuously in order to create conditions that influence every aspect of the business from production to sale to consumption. And in the making of every part of alcohol-control policy the experience of national Prohibition had a profound impact.[7]

Because of abstinent or temperate habits learned during the period of national Prohibition, and because the Great Depression left most families little income to spend on liquor, the level of alcohol consumption per capita hardly changed with Repeal and for nearly a decade afterward. During the remainder of the thirties the principal change in drinking patterns was replacement of distilled spirits by beer, a reversal of the trend that appeared during national Prohibition. Beer's return came slowly, however, and throughout the thirties the brewing industry was plagued by overcapacity, which added a poignant note to brewers' cries for protection from excessive competition. Although beer production rose gradually during the quarter century after Repeal, by 1960 per capita consumption still fell well below pre-Prohibition levels. Wine consumption rose more rapidly, and by 1960 it stood at its highest point ever; even at that level, however, wine contributed far less to total consumption of absolute alcohol than either beer or distilled spirits. Per capita spirits consumption had dropped by 1940 to one gallon, the lowest point in American history, and rose only slightly during the following two decades. In 1960 beer contributed almost one-half the absolute alcohol consumed and spirits about two-fifths, with wine representing the remainder. Total alcohol consumption per capita itself rose after World War II to about the level of the 1890s and remained there until the 1960s.[8]

Neither the level of consumption per capita nor the changes in drinking patterns that occurred in the quarter-century after Repeal distinguished the United States from other national societies. American society after national Prohibition was remarkable, however, for its large proportion of abstainers. In 1939 the Gallup poll reported that 42 percent of respondents did not use alcoholic beverages, and by 1960 that percentage dropped only to 38 percent. The American combination of a moderate level of per capita consumption with a large proportion of abstainers meant that alcohol consumption per drinker ranked among the highest in the world. This juxtaposition of heavy drinkers and numerous abstainers provided abundant fuel for rekindling of a powerful temperance movement in the classic mode. Despite abundant smoke, no fire ever appeared, however, owing to the stifling effect caused by memories of Repeal.[9]

World War II provides an accurate gauge for the weakness of temperance forces in the aftermath of Repeal. As American participation in the conflict drew near, prohibitionists renewed the demands they made so successfully during World War I, such as insulation of servicemen from alcoholic beverages and a ban on distilling to conserve grain supplies. The liquor industry braced itself for a new prohibitionist onslaught. Both sets of antagonists were surprised when federal officials turned a deaf ear to dry advice. No new proscriptions on military drinking were enacted; instead, the federal government required brewers to set aside 15 percent of their production for military consumption and authorized deferments for brewery workers because of the essential nature of their work. Distilled spirits production was banned in 1942, but this only drove up the price of the five-year supply stored in warehouses. Meanwhile the federal government paid the distillers' full costs of conversion to manufacture of industrial alcohol, offered cost-plus, fixed-profit contracts for filling wartime orders, and included industry representatives in policymaking. In addition, the government allowed distillers three "liquor holidays" in 1944 and 1945, when they were allowed to produce beverage alcohol. Production of beer, wine, rum, and brandy went ahead during the war without government hindrance. Per capita consumption of both beer and distilled spirits increased between 1941 and 1945, and heightened wartime taxes nearly tripled federal tax revenue from alcoholic beverages during the same period. Although more than one-third of survey respondents during these years endorsed national prohibition, prohibitionists' undeniable minority position, together with the organizational debility of the Anti-Saloon League, the Prohibition party, and the WCTU, left them utterly without influence upon the politics of the nation and most states.[10]

The Rise of Alcoholics Anonymous

Because of the bitter battles waged between wets and drys during the last years of national Prohibition, public opinion after Repeal was highly polarized over the liquor issue. That a substantial body of prohibitionists remained—leaderless, bitter, and defiant—ensured that polarization was to continue. Having first banished liquor to the nether world of forbidden substances and then welcomed it back again, governments acted as if drinking problems were caused only by drinking that occurred in a certain kind of place, the saloon. For its own reasons the most powerful segment of the liquor business agreed, although, as always, liquor industry spokesmen argued as well that the drinker, not the substance, was the primary source of drinking problems. Meanwhile, the high level of per-drinker consumption ensured that liquor problems continued. Those who wanted or needed to address such problems, however, could find few rationales or methods from which to choose.

The new movement for drinkers' self-reform founded by William Wilson and Dr. Robert Smith drew its inspiration from several sources. One was the Oxford Group (later known as Moral Re-Armament), a twentieth-century nondenominational evangelical movement based on an attempt to return to the ways of primitive Christianity. The aim of the Oxford Group was not to establish a distinct theological position but rather to promulgate the means to live a Christian moral life. Local chapters in New York and Akron worked with drunkards, and both Wilson and Smith were exposed to Oxford Group teachings during the period when they achieved sobriety and founded Alcoholics Anonymous. Both were influenced by the group's principles of self-survey, confession, restitution to those harmed by one's previous actions, and giving of oneself in service to others, and they incorporated these principles into AA practice. Through and beyond these specific principles, the Oxford Group emphasized the importance of a "changed life" which was to be attained by stages. As historian Ernest Kurtz points out, the notion of a "changed life" was important to AA in providing "a way of understanding sobriety as something positive rather than the mere absence of alcohol or drunkenness."[11] Also passed from the Oxford Group to AA was the importance of surrender to a higher power as a prerequisite to changing one's life.[12]

The early AA groups—in New York, Akron, and Cleveland—at first remained part of Oxford Group chapters, but within a few years AA groups separated from their sponsors. Basic purposes differed; as Wilson later put it, "The Oxford Group wanted to save the world, and I only wanted to save the drunks."[13] In trying to save "drunks" early AA members discovered that insistence on the Oxford Group's "Four Absolutes" (absolute honesty, purity, unselfishness, and love) only turned away potential recruits, who rejected absolutes of any kind. Instead, AA assumed that complete "cure" was impossible and advised drunkards to work at being sober "one day at a time." Public identification with the Oxford Group threatened AA's ability to attract Roman Catholic members, since the Oxford Group was proscribed by the pope. Most important, AA discovered that the aggressive public evangelism practiced by the Oxford Group required sacrifice of individual anonymity. Although the rule of anonymity was not codified until the end of the 1940s, early AA members realized that anonymity was useful—if not necessary—in attracting drunkards who needed to be assured that their affliction would not become public knowledge. Alcoholics Anonymous also recognized—as did the secret fraternal orders of the nineteenth century—that anonymity protected the group from discredit in case of relapses by members.[14]

Another important source of inspiration for Wilson was Dr. William D. Silkworth, a specialist in neuropsychiatry who served as physician-in-charge of the Charles B. Towns Hospital in New York City, essentially a detoxification center for the well-to-do. Silkworth held that habitual drunkenness was a disease consisting of both a psychological craving for alcohol and a physiological condition that he described as an allergy. "The patient," Silkworth wrote, "cannot use alcohol at all for physiological reasons. He must understand and accept the situation as a law of nature operating inexorably. Once he has fully and intelligently grasped the facts of the matter he will shape his policy accordingly."[15] Silkworth was the one who informed Wilson that his condition was hopeless from a medical standpoint, and he also reassured Wilson after the latter's spiritual experience that the sensations he had felt were not produced by insanity.

Silkworth's understanding of alcoholism as allergy has never been confirmed by research. From its very first days, however, Alcoholics Anonymous found the concept of a physiological basis crucial in persuading potential recruits that they were indeed "powerless over alcohol." This recognition led in turn to AA's central theme, the message of human limitation. Acceptance of limitation made possible drunkards' search for wholeness through an agency beyond the self, which might be a concept of God or the AA group itself. Belief in a physiological reaction to alcohol in the alcoholic also necessitated total abstinence as the means of recovery. Finally, it set the alcoholic apart from the nonalcoholic majority and thereby served to justify a passive stance toward debate over alcohol policy made prudent by polarization of public opinion. [16]

The fellowship created by Wilson and Smith spread very slowly at first. Three years after Smith stopped drinking, two groups were meeting, one in New York under Wilson's leadership and a larger one in Akron inspired and led by Smith. Altogether, they numbered about threescore members. In an attempt to publicize the group and to attract financial support Wilson began to draft a manuscript that would contain a statement of principles and a demonstration of what could be accomplished if those principles were followed. After considerable discussion and revision the book was published in 1939 under the title *Alcoholics Anonymous: The Story of How More Than One Hundred Men and Women Have Recovered from Alcoholism*. Wilson's hopes for the book were not initially fulfilled; few copies were sold and few reviewers noticed it. Hopes for growth were raised again in the fall of 1939 when a series of favorable articles in a Cleveland newspaper sparked formation of nearly thirty local AA groups within a year. [17]

Beginning in 1940 the Cleveland experience was repeated on a national scale. In that year much favorable publicity followed public discovery that AA members had won to sobriety a national sports figure, Cleveland Indians catcher Rollie Hemsley, the battery-mate of star pitcher Bob Feller. An article published the next year in the *Saturday Evening Post* also brought widespread recognition, and numerous AA groups began to organize on the basis of the principles explained in *Alcoholics Anonymous* and without benefit of personal contact with an existing AA group. Much more publicity—most of it favorable—resulted from the founding in 1944 of the National Committee for Education on Alcoholism (later the National Council on Alcoholism), which devoted itself to winning public acceptance for the view of alcoholism as a disease. The efforts of the National Committee were reflected during the period of 1945–50 in a proliferation of articles in mass-circulation magazines portraying chronic drunkenness in terms of a medical model. This was the period of most rapid growth for Alcoholics Anonymous, whose estimated membership slowly rose to about 15,000 by 1945, then jumped to more than 100,000 by 1951. [18]

During the 1940s Alcoholics Anonymous gradually evolved an organizational ideology to facilitate putting into practice the therapeutic principles it defined in its first years. Anonymity was understood from the beginning as necessary both to attract new recruits and to protect the group if a member faltered. Those who attended AA meetings were therefore ritually cautioned not to reveal the identities of those they saw there. Early efforts to publicize the fellowship, however, involved breaches of anonymity, such as in Rollie Hemsley's announcement of AA's leading part in his battle with drunkenness. In the early 1940s William Wilson also undertook a national speaking tour on behalf of the group, and similar public appearances as a self-confessed "alcoholic" were made after 1944 by Marty Mann, the founder of the National Committee for Education on Alcoholism. Gradually, however, Alcoholics Anonymous came to define such public activity as a manifestation of the egocentrism that AA perceived as a basic cause of chronic drunkenness itself. When Wilson codified AA's organizational principles in 1952, therefore, he wrote that anonymity was the "spiritual foundation" of AA's traditions, "ever reminding us to place principles before personalities."[19]

Defined thus in a manner consistent with AA's central theme of human limitation, anonymity became a more fundamental and pervasive element in AA's approach than secrecy was for any of AA's predecessors in the ranks of self-help groups. The group was viewed as the essential element in reform, and principles were established to protect both the group and its members from the temptations of self-seeking. Leaders were defined as "but trusted servants; they do not govern."[20] Therefore, although AA established a headquarters in New York City, the General Service Office, and a national convention, the General Service Conference, no central body was given authority over local members or groups. Alcoholics Anonymous gave up the right to determine its membership, declaring that a desire to stop drinking—and that only—made one a member. Contacting new recruits and maintaining the sobriety of present members were defined as the sole purposes of the fellowship, and the AA name was not to be used to endorse any outside activity. Unlike all other temperance groups, AA took no public position on any issue, even on questions—such as moral suasion versus coercion—on which its own activity suggested a definite stance. After unsuccessful early attempts at attracting donations from the wealthy, AA adopted a policy of self-support and resolved to accept no outside contributions, including bequests; even member contributions were explicitly limited.[21]

Viewed in historical perspective Alcoholics Anonymous represents a flowering among middle-class and upper-class men of the self-help tradition that flourished primarily within the ranks of working-class men from the early nineteenth century to the early twentieth century. A powerful motivator of the self-help impulse among workers was the search for security in the face of periodic economic depressions and technological change; with the spread of unions in the early twentieth century and again during the thirties, many workers discovered in them new and more effective vehicles for the pursuit of security than temperance self-help societies. Surveys of drinking behavior, first conducted after World War II, found the incidence of drinking to be higher among men than among women and to be higher among the middle and upper classes than among the working class. The surveys seemed to show the opposite relationship between social class and some kinds of problems associated with drinking such as poor health, difficulties at work, conflicts with police, family, and community, and binge drinking. This apparently paradoxical finding—more drinking in the middle and upper classes and more drinking problems among the working class—is explainable by researchers' tendency to define these drinking problems in such a way as to include aspects of working-class behavior that derived from imperatives of the working-class situation rather than from the effects of alcohol consumption. Poor health, for example, is more likely among those with inadequate nutrition; difficulties at work will probably be found more commonly among those who work under close supervision; and conflicts with police are more likely among those who spend more time in public places, or whom police will arrest rather than escort home. Family or community conflict will probably more often occur among those who live in a social environment in which drinking is less tolerated (and where less drinking in fact occurs); finally, binge drinking is more common among those who live from paycheck to paycheck. While finding that these social problems were more common in the lower ranges of social class, drinking surveys showed psychological dependence upon alcohol to be more frequent in the upper ranges. Actual needs among middle-class and upper-class men that went unmet by any other institution therefore provided the soil in which the transplanted self-help tradition flourished.[22]

By the late 1970s Alcoholics Anonymous claimed a million active members worldwide, with 350,000 members in 14,000 groups in the United States and Canada. In addition to its own increase in members and local groups, AA has served as a model for those wishing to bring self-reform to bear on conditions as diverse as asthma, obesity, cancer, compulsive gambling, excessive smoking, schizophrenia, and acne. A parallel but distinct organization has been established for the families and friends of alcoholics (Al-Anon), with a youth division (Alateen). The spread of AA and its use as a model by others have been based on AA's claims for success in helping drunkards attain sobriety. Such claims are of course inherently unverifiable given the nature of the fellowship. The growth of Alcoholics Anonymous has nevertheless demonstrated what many living in the shadow of Repeal wish to forget, that drinking remains a troublesome presence in some people's lives. The publicity given to AA's claims for success in helping drunkards to attain sobriety has convinced many that chronic drunkenness can be treated. Both the reminder of drink's damage and the perceived demonstration of therapeutic accomplishment contributed in turn to public willingness during the 1960s and 1970s to accept extension of government support for the treatment of habitual drunkenness. Despite AA's growth and the publicity it received, such an introverted organization could not have carried out the propaganda work necessary to sway public opinion and to gain the attention of governments. These elements were provided by a handful of academics and other professionals working in uneasy alliance with a thinly staffed, mainly volunteer publicity agency.[23]

Popularizing the Disease Concept of Alcoholism

Professional social scientists—sociologists, economists, anthropologists, and others—appeared in American universities during the late nineteenth century and began to influence intellectual life shortly thereafter. Drinking, however, was never an important focus of their investigations. Social scientists' lack of interest in drinking as a topic of research probably resulted from agreement with the view of drinking held by temperance reformers. Social scientists saw drinking as a social problem, but one whose causes and remedy were obvious. Research into drinking was left in the hands of medical researchers, mainly those affiliated with the Association for the Study of Inebriety.

As we have seen, members of the Association for the Study of Inebriety developed a concept of habitual drunkenness as a disease. Although in their view inebriety could take several forms, one of its manifestations was as a physiological addiction. Addiction implied increased tolerance for the addictive substance as the disease advanced, so that larger and larger amounts were required to produce the same effect. Cutting off an addicted person's supply produced withdrawal symptoms that might include nervousness, acute pain, and delirium. Attempts at reducing an inebriate's consumption revealed an irresistible craving for alcohol, which was caused by bodily changes brought about as a result of long-term heavy drinking. Over a long period the disease was progressive, as minor symptoms mushroomed into major damage to the body and mind. This analysis of inebriety as a disease implied that the inebriate was not responsible for his or her condition and that medical treatment rather than punishment was the appropriate societal response. As preventive measures the leading spokesmen for inebriety professionals endorsed both temperance education and prohibition. In turn, other temperance reformers generally looked with favor upon the work of inebriety researchers. The triumph of the former, however, accompanied and perhaps caused the downfall of the latter. The organ of the association, the *Quarterly Journal of Inebriety,* ceased publication in 1914, and nearly all research into drinking lapsed during the period of national Prohibition.[24]

In the years immediately following Repeal, research into drinking and alcoholic damage fell largely into the hands of psychiatrists, who succeeded to the role of the asylum superintendents of the late nineteenth and early twentieth centuries as the principal professional specialists responsible for the care of habitual drunkards. In 1937 psychiatrists joined with a few physiologists interested in the metabolism of alcohol to found the Research Council on Problems of Alcohol. Those who established the Research Council were friendly to the disease concept of alcoholism, but their part in spreading the concept was transitory though significant. The Research Council funded a review of the scholarly literature on habitual drunkenness that brought E. M. Jellinek to a strategic position at Yale University.[25]

When he came to Yale in 1939 Elvin Morton Jellinek had already constructed a distinguished career as a biometrician (applying statistical methods to biology). Born in New York City in 1890, Jellinek studied at the Universities of Berlin, Grenoble, and Leipzig, from the last of which he received an honorary doctorate of science. During the twenties he was employed in plant research in Central America, and during the thirties he pursued physiological research at a hospital in Worcester, Massachusetts. Jellinek apparently showed little if any interest in alcohol research before 1939, and his reasons for accepting this short-term position are unknown. Soon, however, he became the nation's leading expert on drinking and alcoholic damage and the principal academic proponent of the concept of alcoholism as a disease.[26]

The basis for Jellinek's new expertise was his review of published research on drinking and drunkenness, which included the work of those affiliated with the Association for the Study of Inebriety. The ideas with which he emerged differed in no important respect from theirs. The term "inebriety" was replaced by "alcoholism," a disease which appeared in several forms, only some of which were addictive. The addictive forms of alcoholism were characterized by bodily changes that increased tolerance to alcohol and produced withdrawal symptoms when alcohol was withheld. The disease of alcoholism was progressive from psychological to physiological dependence, but treatable.[27]

Despite its lack of originality Jellinek's formulation of the disease concept of alcoholism "framed most aspects of the modern debate over the nature of alcoholism and its treatment."[28] That it did so is due less to the force of the formulation itself than to Jellinek's work as publicist, which in turn seems to have profited enormously from the connection of Jellinek and his closest associates with Yale University. After completing his literature review Jellinek was hired by Howard Haggard, director of the Laboratory of Applied Physiology at Yale, to work in the laboratory's Section on Alcohol Studies. Haggard believed that the best way to prevent intemperate drinking was to encourage habits of moderate drinking. In Haggard's eyes Jellinek's formulations served this purpose, and so he encouraged expansion of the Section on Alcohol Studies and its eventual transformation into a new institution, the Yale Center for Studies of Alcohol (later the Yale Center of Alcohol Studies).[29]

As Haggard and Jellinek saw it, the mission of the Yale Center of Alcohol Studies was to promulgate a "scientific" view of drinking and drunkenness in contrast to the "moralistic" view whose prevalence they attributed to the success of the temperance crusade. What was scientific about the disease concept of alcoholism besides its articulation by scientists is, however, not apparent. Neither of its key terms—*alcoholism* and *disease*—was clearly or consistently defined. Jellinek once wrote that "a disease is what the medical profession recognizes as such."[30] Nor were any of its key propositions supported by controlled empirical research. One of Jellinek's most influential statements on alcoholism, for example, was based on his analysis of ninety-eight responses to a set of about sixteen hundred questionnaires designed and circulated by Alcoholics Anonymous. Nevertheless Haggard and Jellinek were adamant in rejecting competing theories, such as those using psychoanalytic concepts, which they regarded as deficient in empirical support. The real problem with psychoanalytically based theories from the perspective of the Yale Center was that they portrayed chronic drunkenness not as a disease itself but rather as a manifestation of an underlying psychological disorder. Haggard and Jellinek associated their view with the humanitarian goals of obtaining treatment rather than punishment for the habitual drunkard and encouraging drunkards to seek treatment. Their rejection of competing—and equally well founded—theories that could have served the same purposes just as well suggests the utility of the disease concept for Haggard's desire to encourage moderate drinking in the population at large by establishing a rigid distinction between controlled and pathological uses of alcohol.[31]

Mainly on Jellinek's initiative the Yale Center donned the trappings of scientific endeavor. Building on the literature survey that originally drew Jellinek into alcohol research, the Yale Center created a fully abstracted and indexed archive of scholarly literature on alcohol, drinking, and drunkenness. In 1940 the center began to publish the first scholarly journal covering alcohol studies since the demise of the *Quarterly Journal of Inebriety* in 1914; the new periodical was called the *Quarterly Journal of Studies on Alcohol* (later the *Journal of Studies on Alcohol*). Three years later Jellinek organized the first of an annual series of summer sessions to teach the importance of a "scientific" approach to alcoholism. Designed as a lecture series for educated citizens interested in the latest research on drinking and drunkenness, the Yale Summer School of Alcohol Studies issued a certificate bearing the Yale seal to the various temperance workers, teachers, ministers, social workers, and others whom it attracted. Finally, Jellinek proposed and the center established outpatient clinics, the first of which were opened in 1944 in New Haven and Hartford, Connecticut. The clinics used group therapy and individual counseling to treat drunkards and engaged in research as well. They were known as Yale Plan Clinics.[32]

For all its efforts in disseminating the disease concept of alcoholism, the Yale Center was primarily a research institution and therefore was limited in its ability to reach the general public. Although the leaders of Alcoholics Anonymous were also interested in gaining public acceptance of the disease concept in order to reduce the stigma attached to chronic drunkenness, AA's focus on treatment and its tradition of anonymity precluded its use for propaganda purposes. The result was creation of a new publicity organization whose specific initiative came from an individual, Marty Mann, but which received crucial support from both AA and the Yale Center. The daughter of wealthy parents, Mann found her early life as a socialite brought to an end by her father's bankruptcy in the late 1920s. She supported herself as a writer and businesswoman until her career was wrecked by her chronic drunkenness. Psychiatric counseling proved unable to help her, but she discovered the AA doctrine through reading *Alcoholics Anonymous* shortly after its publication. She met Bill

Wilson, regained sobriety, and became one of the first women to join Alcoholics Anonymous. In 1944, while preparing a radio script on the life of Dorothea Dix, the nineteenth-century campaigner for better treatment of the mentally ill, Mann conceived an ambition to become the "Dorothea Dix" of the habitual drunkard. She was put in touch with E. M. Jellinek, who enthusiastically supported her plans to publicize the AA view of drunkenness, and Jellinek persuaded Howard Haggard to provide sponsorship by the Yale Center of Alcohol Studies. Mann then attended the 1944 session of the Yale Summer School. In October 1944 was born the National Committee for Education on Alcoholism (NCEA), for which Marty Mann became executive director. Its advisory board was recruited from among supporters of Alcoholics Anonymous and included both of AA's cofounders, although their connection with AA was not made explicit.

The NCEA quickly embarked on a campaign to inform Americans of "two momentous discoveries about alcoholism: FIRST that alcoholism is a *sickness,* not a moral delinquency. SECOND that when this is properly recognized *the hitherto hopeless alcoholic can be completely rehabilitated.*"[33] An effective speaker and fluent writer, Marty Mann undertook an arduous schedule of speaking engagements across the country, and the NCEA also published literature presenting its point of view. Local affiliates of the committee were established to disseminate its literature and to provide speakers. Mann used her extensive circle of contacts among the New York journalistic community to good advantage; articles on NCEA consistently presented the statement "alcoholism is a disease" as a scientifically established fact and mentioned NCEA's Yale sponsorship. News reports also noted acceptance of the disease concept by Mamie White Colvin, president of the WCTU, whom Mann met at the 1944 Yale Summer School. In addition to announcing that alcoholism was a treatable disease, NCEA attempted to establish the seriousness of alcoholism as a major public health problem and to destroy the stereotype of the alcoholic as a homeless derelict, arguing instead that drinking problems appeared in every social class.[34]

Together Alcoholics Anonymous, the Yale Center of Alcohol Studies, and NCEA formed a potent force for change. Alcoholics Anonymous provided a growing constituency, a nucleus of activists at the local level, and a demonstration of the treatability of drunkenness. From the Yale Center the disease concept received a scientific aura and NCEA gained crucial funding. The committee became the mouthpiece of the alcoholism coalition, taking on under Marty Mann's indefatigable leadership the task of disseminating a medical model for understanding chronic drunkenness.

The campaign of the alcoholism advocates was also fortunate in meeting with no organized opposition. On one side, the prohibitionist leadership had no difficulty in accepting the idea of addiction, since that idea had been a part of their reform for more than a century. Therefore prohibitionist leaders initially welcomed the academic attention bestowed upon alcohol studies, and many attended the Yale Summer School in its early years. By the late 1940s, however, their sympathy turned to opposition when they realized that the alcoholism coalition viewed alcoholism as a disease to which only some people were susceptible. But even then prohibitionists regarded the claim that alcoholism was a treatable disease not as wrong but rather as narrow and incomplete. On the other side, the liquor industry welcomed the new approach enthusiastically since it promised to provide academic benediction for its long-standing view that the source of alcohol problems lay elsewhere than in the bottle. The industry objected only to use of the term *alcoholism* because of its implication that alcohol itself held some responsibility for the damage sustained by drinkers.[35]

In changing the official positions of institutions and in shifting public opinion the alcoholism coalition was largely, though not completely, successful. One of its more complete victories was won over the press. During the period 1900–19 treatments of drunkenness in the periodical press typically attributed problem drinking to liquor industry temptations. By the 1960s, in contrast, most magazine articles dealing with chronic drunkenness discussed it using a medical model. In addition to changes in the periodical press, standard reference works such as dictionaries and encyclopedias shifted their definitions or portrayals of habitual drunkenness to conform to the disease model.[36]

The rise of the alcoholism coalition offered churches a way to manifest their traditional concern with drinking as an individual and social problem without becoming embroiled once again in political conflict. In 1946 the General Assembly of the northern Presbyterian church became the first church body to pass a resolution describing alcoholism as a disease and calling for "treatment, not punishment; understanding, not condemnation."[37] The Federal Council of Churches (1947), the National Council of Churches of Christ (1958), the General Assembly of the Protestant Episcopal Church (1958), and the General Board of the National Council of Churches (1958) adopted similar positions. Literature published by some churches presented the same view. The activists whose efforts lay behind such resolutions typically attended the Yale Summer School and received backing from the Yale Center or were associated with Alcoholics Anonymous, or both. One example was the Reverend David Works, an

Episcopal minister who organized a series of annual national conferences on religion and alcoholism in his New Hampshire parish. Works experienced drinking problems in his youth, gained sobriety through Alcoholics Anonymous, and attended the Yale Summer School of Alcohol Studies. Through church endorsements of its leading idea the alcoholism coalition gained powerful allies.[38]

Although many physicians during the nineteenth and early twentieth centuries were influenced by temperance ideology, and the American Medical Association (AMA) in 1917 officially opposed both beverage and therapeutic uses of alcohol, temperance supporters were never able to forge a consensus within the medical profession. During national Prohibition some doctors were alienated by federal attempts to restrict their discretion in prescribing alcohol. General hospitals normally refused to admit habitual drunkards for treatment because hospital authorities considered them to be excessively active, uncooperative, and unwilling to pay their bills.[39]

During the 1950s a campaign supported by E. M. Jellinek resulted in adoption by the AMA House of Delegates of a resolution (1956) urging general hospitals to admit cooperative and willing drunkards. Eleven years later the AMA Clinical Session resolved that alcoholism was a disease. The American Hospital Association in 1944 and again in 1957 urged upon its members a tolerant approach toward alcoholics. Nevertheless, a survey of fifty-two hundred hospitals in 1964 found that three-fifths still refused to accept patients for whom alcoholism was the primary diagnosis. For chronic drunkards who managed to obtain entrance to hospitals, sixty-four of the seventy-nine Blue Cross insurance corporations provided hospitalization benefits as of 1969, as did most other insurance companies under group—though usually not individual—contracts.[40]

Incomplete victory also best describes the alcoholism coalition's efforts at public education. On its face, the change in public attitudes toward chronic drunkenness seems quite dramatic. Public opinion surveys during the late 1940s typically found only about one-fifth of respondents willing to agree with a depiction of the alcoholic as sick and of alcoholism as an illness. By the early 1960s nearly two-thirds of survey respondents accepted these propositions. Many of those who agreed with statements of the disease concept of alcoholism, however, continued to view drunkenness as a moral weakness over which the drunkard exercised some degree of control; the notion of "voluntary slaves" expressed by temperance reformers a century before clearly had not died.[41]

In the years after Repeal the principal objective of governments in dealing with the liquor issue was to remove it from the public arena, and the alcohol control systems they created moved toward that goal by exerting often subtle controls over the point of sale. Viewing habitual drunkenness as a medical problem promised to aid depoliticization, and so governments typically welcomed the coming of the disease concept. Agencies were created that would uphold a medical model, although funds to make good on promises of treatment for problem drinkers often were not so readily forthcoming.

The alcoholism coalition was active on the government front, too. Scholars from the Yale Center wrote Connecticut's law establishing a state alcoholism program, one of the first enacted; the statute provided for a state-supported educational effort on the causes and treatment of alcoholism and gave state sponsorship and funding to the Yale Plan Clinics. Selden Bacon, the Yale Center sociologist who wrote the Connecticut law, became the first board chairman of the Connecticut Commission on Alcoholism. Yale Center scholars and graduates of the Yale Summer School were also instrumental in designing New Hampshire's state program shortly after Connecticut acted. By mid-1949 twelve states, the District of Columbia, and the Canadian province of Ontario had established alcoholism programs or agencies, and the directors of all of these were graduates of the Yale Summer School. By 1973 every one of the fifty states had instituted some sort of state alcoholism program, although the agencies thus created varied in their degree of autonomy and in the mixture of educational and treatment functions they performed.[42]

The first federal legislative recognition of the disease concept came in a 1947 law providing for establishment of alcoholism treatment clinics in the District of Columbia. This law was modeled after the legislation setting up alcoholism programs in Connecticut and New Hampshire; it explicitly stated that "alcoholism is a disease" and that "an alcoholic should receive appropriate medical, psychiatric, and other scientific treatment rather than criminal punishment."[43] No funding was provided to set up such clinics, however, until 1966.[44]

This long-delayed provision of funding for clinics in the District of Columbia was actually one of the least important of a series of federal actions during the 1960s concerning drinking. As a part of the general expansion of federal social programs, vastly increased appropriations were provided for alcoholism treatment facilities conducted under the guidance of state alcoholism agencies. After 1970 these funds were channeled through the National Institute of Alcohol Abuse and Alcoholism (NIAAA), created in that year within the Department of Health,

Education, and Welfare (later the Department of Health and Human Services). The NIAAA was also charged with responsibility for funding and coordinating research on alcoholism. Its first year's appropriation of $13 million grew to $175 million by 1979. Finally, through federal court decisions in several cases during the mid-sixties and through legislation enacted in the early 1970s, the federal government encouraged the removal of public drunkenness from state criminal codes.[45]

These new and significant federal initiatives resulted from the convergence of several forces. Of greatest long-term importance was the work of the alcoholism coalition in advocating a disease concept of alcoholism that set the chronic drunkard radically apart from the social drinker; acceptance of this view made research into the physiological basis of alcoholism and treatment of alcoholics more appropriate responses to problem drinking than prevention policies. Funding of research and treatment also demonstrated government concern without offending any powerful constituency, such as the liquor industry or the majority of voters who drank. Decriminalization of public drunkenness was initiated by civil liberties forces headed by the American Civil Liberties Union. It also suited the purposes of the alcoholism coalition by giving public recognition to the disease concept and by providing funding for expanded treatment facilities, while responding to the desires of police and judges to unburden themselves of the estimated one-third of all arrests caused by the criminal status of public drunkenness.[46]

The National Committee for Education on Alcoholism, as part of its campaign for recognition of alcoholism as a disease, sought to convince businessmen to establish within their firms programs to identify workers with drinking problems. Instead of being dismissed such workers were to be referred to appropriate agencies for treatment. Advocates and founders of such programs claimed that the decision to accept or reject treatment lay with the worker, but—with disciplinary action including firing as an alternative—a strong element of coercion was clearly present. After spreading slowly during the 1940s and 1950s, occupational alcoholism programs sprang up rapidly during the 1960s, and by 1971 between 250 and 300 seem to have been in operation. Expansion was fueled by a broadening of programs' scope to include other possible sources of poor work performance such as family or financial troubles and physical or mental problems. With this broadening, new rubrics ("troubled employee" or "employee assistance") were adopted in an attempt to avoid the stigma alcoholism attached to both worker and company.[47]

The founding of NIAAA in 1970 set off an explosion of occupational alcoholism programs, as the new federal agency began to promote the idea aggressively. After 1972 the type of program NIAAA recommended was the "broad-brush" variety that dealt with drinking along with other problems inhibiting satisfactory work performance. By mid-1977 nearly two thousand programs were operating in private firms as well as about four hundred in the public sector. The list of participants included half of the five hundred largest firms as ranked by *Fortune* magazine.[48]

Occupational alcoholism programs meshed neatly with policies for control of workers that were developed in the late twentieth century by leading corporations. Increasingly corporate officials sought measures that would regulate the pace of work while dividing workers from each other and binding them to the organization. Bureaucratic systems that promised upward mobility within the firm as reward for faithful execution of carefully specified tasks seemed to be a favored solution in the largest and most innovative corporations. Highly organized and interdependent systems, however, were vulnerable to disruption by a few incapacitated or intractable workers. In addition, longtime employees represented a considerable investment in training, and maintaining workers' loyalty to the organization required at least some show of concern for those whose incapacity could be seen as caused by illness. Occupational alcoholism programs promised recovery of organizations' "human resources," with the iron fist of discipline concealed in the velvet glove of therapy. Such programs also reinforced arguments by corporate spokespersons that actions that might otherwise be construed as resistance to alienating work were simply the product of personal "problems." Intrusions into workers' personal lives incidental to the successful operation of occupational alcoholism programs-especially those of the broad-brush type— were likely to increase after program evaluators announced that cost-effectiveness would be enhanced by early identification of problems.[49]

In occupational alcoholism programs coercion was used to bring workers to accept treatment. The same pattern appeared in the decriminalization of public drunkenness when police were given power to take chronic public inebriates into "protective custody" while conveying them to a treatment facility. Whether such use of the powers of the employer and the state represented a more coercive approach than the firing and jailing that preceded the new initiatives is a moot point. Whether or not the result was greater coercion, the coupling of coercion and treatment in initiatives supported by the alcoholism coalition helps clarify its place in the history of temperance reform. In rejecting prohibition as a means of controlling drinking—a step that was accomplished by drawing a line between alcoholics and other drinkers—the alcoholism advocates did not reject coercion; they disclaimed only modes of coercion that associated them with the temperance movements of the past. This helps explain why proposals for more coercive measures came to be entertained even among some elements of the alcoholism coalition itself.

Toward Coercion

Strains were present in the alcoholism coalition from the beginning. By 1949 Howard Haggard and Selden Bacon (who became director of the Yale Center in that year) were becoming increasingly sensitive to a conflict between the imperatives of research and the needs of propagating the new ideas which that research supposedly supported. Specifically, they became uneasy that Marty Mann and her National Committee for Education on Alcoholism were announcing that alcoholism was a disease when research findings were still not forthcoming to support that claim. Consequently the Yale Center terminated its sponsorship of NCEA at the end of 1949. During the 1950s Selden Bacon also began to criticize the methods of Alcoholics Anonymous, whose belief that "only an alcoholic can help another alcoholic" presented an obstacle to his attempt to win endorsement for the disease concept from the medical profession as well as to his efforts to promote professional treatment in institutions such as the Yale Plan Clinics. For Marty Mann the founding of clinics was useful primarily to buttress the disease concept, since her hopes for treatment lay with AA. The Yale Center scholars remained committed to the disease concept, but they found that placing sole emphasis on alcoholism and alcoholics also prevented them from pursuing the interest in promoting moderate drinking that made Howard Haggard receptive to the disease concept in the first place.[50]

In their attempts to redirect discussion of alcohol use toward the question of moderate drinking, the Yale Center scholars were joined—for different reasons—by a new group, the administrators of the state alcoholism programs. In 1949 these administrators formed a professional association, which became the North American Association of Alcoholism Programs (NAAAP; later the Alcohol and Drug Problems Association of North America). Probably because of the broad mandate given such programs in their enabling legislation, program directors became interested in dealing with drinking problems other than those manifested by the small population of habitual drunkards. This interest was echoed by clergymen such as David Works, who found a focus on alcoholism too restrictive in dealing with the manifold problems among their congregations that seemed to be related to drinking. For researchers, administrators, and clergymen, broadening the scope of discussion from alcoholism to "drinking problems" seemed necessary. The instrument for their purpose was to be a new research organization that was to conduct a comprehensive survey of issues related to alcohol and set a fresh direction for alcoholism programs. In 1960 NAAAP applied for and received from the National Institute of Mental Health a five-year grant to create such a research organization; thus was founded the Cooperative Commission on the Study of Alcoholism. The commission's report, issued in 1967, failed to achieve the hoped-for impact on liquor policy, but it furnishes a useful point of entry into an evolving debate.

True to its origins, the Cooperative Commission recommended broadening the scope of discussion over alcohol to include other "problems" besides alcoholism, a shift reflected in the report's title, *Alcohol Problems*. Instead of "alcoholics" and "alcoholism" the Cooperative Commission spoke of "problem drinkers" and "drinking problems." In developing its view of drinking problems and their causes the Cooperative Commission relied on research by Selden Bacon and other social scientists on cultural differences in rates of alcoholism and other behaviors associated with drinking. A principal conclusion drawn from this research was that drinking problems were caused by societal ambivalence about drinking. Ambivalence in American society was believed to stem from the success of temperance reformers in stigmatizing drinking, thereby confusing Americans about whether or not social use of alcohol was legitimate. The Cooperative Commission therefore recommended formation of a national consensus to encourage "responsible drinking." To this end the commission's most widely reported conclusions recommended an educational campaign that—among other aims—was to teach young people to drink in a temperate manner.

In several ways the report of the Cooperative Commission departed from the beliefs of the alcoholism coalition. Broadening the population believed to be subject to drinking problems beyond chronic drunkards revived the perception of the problem held by reformers during previous cycles of temperance reform. Both the scientific validity and the practical utility of viewing alcoholism as a disease were explicitly questioned. In other ways, however, the commission simply extended the line of thought already underway within the alcoholism coalition. The report advocated greater involvement by various types of health-care professionals in treatment of drinking problems and denigrated what it regarded as the narrow approach espoused by Alcoholics Anonymous. The commission also recommended formation of a federal agency concerned with alcoholism within the National Institute of Mental Health; this was the only one of its recommendations to have any direct institutional effect, as the agency thus created became the forerunner of NIAAA.[51]

The report of the Cooperative Commission helped stimulate renewed debate over alcohol policy that both built upon and rejected its major conclusions; that debate continued through the seventies and into the eighties. The drinking behavior of the large majority of the population who were not habitual drunkards became the focus of debate for the first time since Repeal; academics and bureaucrats now discussed how the majority's drinking was to be regulated so as to reduce both personal and social costs. The Cooperative Commission intended its educational campaign to result in individuals developing the ability to control their own drinking, and this approach was adopted for a time by NIAAA during the tenure of its first director, psychiatrist Morris Chafetz, a leading advocate of "responsible drinking." Chafetz's views essentially repeated early temperance reformers' advocacy of moderate drinking.

In opposition appeared a set of arguments dressed in modern social-scientific garb but which echoed arguments first made in the 1830s. These proposals aimed at increasing the number of total abstainers and reducing overall consumption by invoking social controls. Such arguments were presented under various labels—"public health," "alcohol problems," and "problem-drinking" approaches—but all joined in the Cooperative Commission's attempt to dismantle the conceptual wall the alcoholism coalition had built between the habitual drunkard and other drinkers; at the same time they rejected promotion of "responsible drinking" in favor of more coercive preventive measures. These included reducing the accessibility of alcoholic beverages through price increases brought about by taxation, controlling the number and location of retail outlets, reducing opportunities for on-premises consumption, restricting liquor advertising, and raising the legal drinking age. Chastened by the political failure of national Prohibition, however, these new advocates of coercion accepted the essential durability of drinking habits, and some joined to their endorsement of coercion calls for other measures to "make the world safe for drunks" through the improvement of general public safety.[52]

Increasing rejection of the disease concept of alcoholism by academics and other professionals, deepening divisions within the alcoholism coalition, and growing openness toward broad social controls stemmed from several causes. The disease concept contained conceptual weaknesses and lacked empirical support, but these qualities had never before in its long history hindered its acceptance; the concept always functioned as it had since Repeal, as a call for compassion toward rather than condemnation of habitual drunkards. The claim for a scientific basis, however, made the disease concept vulnerable when professionals began to enter alcohol studies in large numbers, as they did after federal funding began to flow during the late 1960s. In particular, the rigid distinction erected between habitual drunkards and other drinkers by the concept's most recent partisans limited the scope of efforts by social workers, psychologists, rehabilitation counselors, clergymen, and psychiatrists, as well as spokespersons for public health and safe driving. The spiritual basis and self-help methods of Alcoholics Anonymous had the same effect, and conflict erupted between the paraprofessionals—often AA members—who staffed treatment centers and the new alcohol professionals.[53]

In addition, sharply rising per capita consumption rates after 1960 gave impetus to the search for new directions in alcohol theory and policy. All three types of alcoholic beverage benefited. Wine consumption per capita reached unprecedented heights. Beer nearly matched its pre-Prohibition level, and spirits regained the level of consumption reached during the post–Civil War years. By the mid-1970s total consumption of absolute alcohol per capita stood at about two gallons, the highest level since the 1830s.[54]

The level of consumption was driven up by new drinkers (abstainers dropped from 45 percent of the adult population in 1959 to 29 percent by 1977) and by increases in intake on the part of veteran drinkers. The prosperity of the sixties facilitated the actions of both groups. Death rates from cirrhosis of the liver and from motor vehicle accidents also rose during the sixties. Debate flourished over the nature and extent of alcohol's role in these developments, but general acceptance of the presence of some causal link undergirded attempts to construct new and more coercive social policies toward drinking.[55]

By the beginning of the 1980s the latest cycle of temperance reform produced diverse results. A vastly expanded treatment system for people with drinking problems and a burgeoning network of occupational alcoholism programs were the principal institutional legacies of the alcoholism advocates, although the treatment system (upon which the occupational programs depended) was threatened by the funding cuts of the Reagan administration. The needs of institutional survival led treatment agencies to broaden the definition of their client populations, accepting referrals from the criminal justice system even when the client's primary problem was not drinking; through this process coercion became mixed with treatment in yet another way.[56]

The Yale Center of Alcohol Studies moved to Rutgers University in 1962, but the death or retirement of leading figures from its early days, attacks on the disease concept, and establishment of other academic alcohol research institutions eroded its unique leading role in alcohol studies. The disease concept of alcoholism remained the governing paradigm in alcohol studies. Allegiance to the disease concept varied, however, among professionals. It commanded more support among medical than among social researchers and held the loyalty of more treatment professionals than researchers. Difficulties in obtaining definitional consensus continued, and even the strongest defenders of the disease concept rested their case upon the utility of a medical model in bringing social resources to bear upon drinking problems and in bringing problem drinkers under professional care. When in its 1978 report the National Institute of Alcohol Abuse and Alcoholism adopted a public health model in advocating preventive measures to control drinking, the new model was simply overlaid on the old. In public opinion the disease concept coexisted with a lingering unwillingness to excuse drunkards for their behavior. Because both drinking problems and the drunkard's stigma remained, Alcoholics Anonymous continued to flourish.[57]

Government policies began to include specific coercive measures aimed at particular groups. Many states tightened or toughened laws against drunken driving, in some cases in response to campaigns waged by new citizens' organizations such as Mothers Against Drunk Driving (founded in 1980). The federal government briefly turned coercion against the states by threatening to withhold a portion of highway construction funds unless a legal drinking age of twenty-one years was enacted. Meanwhile, per capita consumption declined slightly from its high peak in the late 1970s.

News reports on the new preventive and punitive measures and the decline in per capita consumption applied the label "neo-temperance" as if temperance reform, having died at Repeal, were now experiencing a rebirth. As this chapter has shown, efforts to control drinking did not die with Repeal. They lived on in the old temperance organizations, whose popular support caused the liquor industry to tread wearily for at least a decade after Repeal and conditioned the forming of new alcohol control systems as well as the strategies of a new generation of reformers. The founders of Alcoholics Anonymous sought to help those most injured by drink, and the alcoholism professionals added to this goal a desire to help moderate drinkers remain that way. To accomplish their goals both groups felt compelled to distance themselves from the politics of wet versus dry. The new reformers therefore obscured their inheritance from previous generations of temperance folk. That legacy included an appreciation of drink's capacity for damage, a respect for science, and a concept of chronic drunkenness as addictive behavior. The new reformers presented their concept of addiction in such a way as to leave the implication that only habitual drunkards risked damage, however, and the alcoholism professionals portrayed their devotion to science as unique in public discussion of the liquor issue. Their links with earlier reformers were further obscured when both AA and the alcoholism professionals described their concern for those most injured as something new, as if previous reformers' care for the social effects of drink necessarily implied blaming the drinker.

The new approach attracted considerable support from official and semiofficial agencies and even managed to change the ways in which ordinary people thought about drinking. Its successes were aided by the relatively low and stable level of per capita consumption during the third of a century following Repeal. When consumption began to rise sharply during the 1960s, however—in a society in which the automobile had become inextricably interwoven with daily life—the new approach lost some of its luster as alcohol's effects were perceived in traffic accidents and cirrhosis and other health problems. These developments placed coercive measures once more upon the public-policy agenda. Meanwhile, coercion in the treatment of alcohol problems had already appeared in occupational programs and became more widely employed as such programs spread. Coercion appeared in a third form as other treatment institutions spawned by the new approach took on control as well as treatment functions.

Whether the current cycle of temperance reform will continue past the end point of this study is of course impossible to tell. The early 1980s was chosen as a terminus for the narrative not to indicate the end of the cycle but rather to mark a point at which a historical perspective begins to lose its utility. Viewed historically, the latest cycle of temperance re- · form reveals continuing themes found in previous cycles: debates over moderation versus abstinence, over whose behavior was to be changed, and over moral suasion versus coercion. Its most notable feature was the revival and dissemination of a disease concept of chronic drunkenness whose origins lay in the late eighteenth century.

Although the old debates continued, their context changed dramatically. In its heyday the temperance cause attracted mass participation as have few issues in American history. This changed with the emergence of the bureaucratic Anti-Saloon League, but still during national Prohibition drink remained an issue that gripped the emotions and defined the politics of millions. During the period since Repeal, however, the significant debates over liquor policy have occurred among elites in business, government, and the professions. The liquor issue has been largely removed from the public arena. Although the number of Americans who drink has increased, fewer than before participate in the decisions that affect the conditions governing their drinking. In this respect as in so many others during its history, temperance reform mirrored the society in which it appeared.

A Look Backward

Seen in comparative perspective, temperance reform in the United States has been both powerful and durable relative to most other countries. A thorough comparative analysis, beyond the scope of this study, will be necessary to identify reasons for the intensity and persistence of American temperance reform. Possibilities include the prominent place of spirits in American drinking patterns, the strength of evangelical Protestantism, and America's relatively early capitalist development, which generated tributary concerns that flowed into the temperance stream. No answer to this question can be complete, however, that does not take into account the experience of temperance reformers themselves.

Temperance reform in America was created by successive generations of reformers, each of which acted according to a set of motives and perceptions that differed in important ways from those of their predecessors. If any of these successive groups had failed to enter the fray, the history of American temperance reform would have been shorter and the legacy to later reformers would have been different. As we have seen, the cumulative experience of temperance reformers shaped each new generation's choice of methods. Each set of reformers came to grips with the legacy of its predecessors, however, in a new historical environment that impelled them to act, channeled their perceptions, and limited their choices. Together, the basic characteristics of American society and drinking patterns, temperance reformers' understanding of their history, and a series of changing historical environments shaped the long and often successful course of American temperance reform.

The path of temperance reform in the United States suggests the difficulties faced by a liberal capitalist society in dealing with a form of individual behavior that persistently brings into question its basic assumptions. Liberal ideology assumes free and autonomous individuals, but the social effects of drinking reveal human interdependence while the inability or unwillingness of some drinkers to stop acting in a self-destructive manner raises the possibility that individuals are not free. Temperance reformers' sensitivity to alcoholic damage has therefore led them again and again to advocate measures that, although supported as means of restoring individual freedom, actually result in augmenting social controls instead. The most conspicuous example, is, of course, national Prohibition, with which temperance reformers helped galvanize into existence a competing strain of liberalism (now known as "conservatism") dedicated to reducing some forms of centralized power.

Still, temperance reformers have generally remained good liberals, willing to advocate only piecemeal change rather than to push their insights into interdependence and the social nature of humankind to a collectivist conclusion. The tension thus created made the issue of moral suasion versus coercion more than a debate over means. As successive generations of temperance reformers came to grips with increasing social complexity and the intractability of some drinking behavior, their choice of means became a recurrent test of their attachment to the liberal dream. From this point of view temperance reformers appear not as quaint exponents of an archaic morality but rather as citizens who have grappled with basic dilemmas of their society and as sometime pioneers exploring new responses.

Events of 1975–87

1976

The U.S. Supreme Court declared unconstitutional an Oklahoma law allowing women to buy beer of 3.2 percent alcohol content at age eighteen while men were prevented from buying the beer until age twenty-one.

1977

As a result of investigations by the federal Bureau of Alcohol, Tobacco, and Firearms, various spirits and beer producers and wholesalers admitted paying kickbacks to retailers.

Secretary of Health, Education and Welfare Joseph Califano signed regulations implementing a 1973 law that banned discrimination against handicapped persons in programs receiving federal funds. Rehabilitated alcoholics were covered by the regulations.

1978

Anheuser-Busch, Inc., agreed to pay a $750,000 penalty to settle charges that it had paid illegal rebates to retailers. The Jos. Schlitz Brewing Co. settled a complaint that it had paid illegal kickbacks to retailers by agreeing not to violate federal securities laws in the future. The Seagram Co., Ltd., similarly settled a complaint that it had made secret cash payments to retailers and politicians. In a separate case involving alleged illegal kickbacks, the Schlitz Co. pleaded no contest and paid a $750,000 fine.

The U.S. Supreme Court divided 4–4, thereby technically affirming a Massachusetts court decision that a drunk man cannot validly waive his rights to remain silent and to consult a lawyer upon arrest.

1979

The Securities and Exchange Commission entered into a consent decree with Schenley Industries, Inc., concerning Schenley's pricing and discount policies. An SEC complaint had charged that Schenley had granted illegal discounts to selected customers and that its pricing practices violated the liquor regulations of thirty-five states.

The U.S. Supreme Court upheld a Massachusetts law allowing the state to suspend for up to ninety days the license of a driver who refused to take a police breath-analysis test.

1980

Mothers Against Drunk Driving was founded.

The U.S. Supreme Court overturned a California law that allowed wine producers and wholesalers to set uniform minimum prices.

The U.S. Supreme Court ruled that an agreement by five California beer wholesalers to eliminate the interest-free credit they had offered their retail customers violated federal laws against price fixing.

The U.S. Treasury Department issued new regulations requiring producers and importers of alcoholic beverages to list the ingredients of their products. Producers and importers could either list the ingredients on the label or provide an address where the list could be obtained.

1981

Students Against Driving Drunk was founded.

The U.S. Treasury Department dropped the rule requiring manufacturers of liquor, wine, and beer to list the ingredients in their products.

The U.S. Supreme Court upheld a New York State law giving the State Liquor Authority power to prohibit topless entertainment in bars serving alcoholic beverages.

1982

The U.S. Supreme Court ruled that a California law that restricted distribution of liquor produced out-of-state was not automatically in contravention of federal antitrust law.

The National Transportation Safety Board recommended that states raise the legal drinking age to twenty-one so as to reduce traffic deaths involving drunken teenagers.

The U.S. Supreme Court held unconstitutional a Massachusetts law that allowed churches to prevent clubs and restaurants within a 150-meter radius from obtaining liquor licenses.

1983

The U.S. Supreme Court upheld a South Dakota law (similar to those in many other states) permitting a motorist's refusal to take a blood alcohol test to be used as evidence in a drunken-driving case.

The U.S. Supreme Court affirmed a ruling that a Connecticut law regulating the sale of beer was unconstitutional. The law required Connecticut brewers to sell beer in the state at prices lower than those charged in neighboring states.

A Presidential Commission on Drunk Driving recommended that Congress deny federal highway funds to states whose minimum drinking ages were below twenty-one years.

During the year forty states toughened their laws against driving while intoxicated, and eleven states raised their minimum legal drinking ages.

1984

Congress increased the excise tax on liquor.

The New Jersey Supreme Court ruled that a host who personally served liquor to a guest and then allowed the guest to drive away intoxicated could be held liable for injuries caused by the drunken driver.

The U.S. Supreme Court struck down Hawaii's liquor sales tax law because it exempted two locally produced alcoholic beverages.

In July President Reagan signed legislation that would cut federal highway funding (by 5 percent in fiscal 1987, 10 percent in 1988) to states whose minimum drinking age remained below twenty-one years. Twenty-seven states were affected. In addition, the legislation provided for increased federal highway safety funding for states that passed mandatory sentencing laws for persons convicted of drunken driving.

1985

The federal Department of Transportation announced rules designed to reduce alcohol and drug abuse by railroad employees. Drug and alcohol use was prohibited during working hours; employees involved in major accidents would be subjected to alcohol and drug testing; applications for "safety-related" jobs would be routinely screened for drug use before hiring; and employees showing alcohol or drug dependence would be referred in the first instance to an employee-assistance program.

Congress eliminated from the final version of the government's omnibus spending bill a clause cutting highway aid for states that refused to increase their minimum drinking age.

1986

The U.S. Supreme Court ruled unconstitutional a New York State law requiring distillers to pledge that the prices they charged wholesalers in the state would not be higher than those charged in other states. Thirty-eight other states had similar laws.

The U.S. Supreme Court, in a majority opinion in a case dealing with government power to curb advertising of casino gambling, held that government had authority to ban or restrict advertising "of products or activities deemed harmful, such as cigarettes, alcoholic beverages and prostitution."

A study prepared for the American Federation of State, County and Municipal Employees concluded that federal spending on alcohol, mental health, and drug abuse programs had decreased during the first five years of the Reagan administration by $1.7 billion below what it would have been under the rules and service levels in effect before Reagan.

1987

The U.S. Supreme Court invalidated New York State's law requiring retailers to sell at 12 percent above bottle prices posted with the state by wholesalers. The New York law was held to be contrary to federal antitrust legislation.

Notes and References

Chapter One

1. David W. Robson, "'My Unhappy Son': A Narrative of Drinking in Federalist Pennsylvania," *Pennsylvania History* 52 (January 1985): 24.
2. Ibid., 24–25.
3. Ibid., 22–35.
4. Mark Edward Lender and James Kirby Martin, *Drinking in America: A History,* 2d ed. (New York: Free Press, 1987), chap. 1; W. J. Rorabaugh, *The Alcoholic Republic: An American Tradition* (New York: Oxford University Press, 1979), 23–57, 232; Dean Albertson, "Puritan Liquor in the Planting of New England," *New England Quarterly* 23 (December 1950): 479; Edmund S. Morgan, *American Slavery, American Freedom: The Ordeal of Colonial Virginia* (New York: W. W. Norton, 1975), 111, 113.
5. Stanley Baron, *Brewed in American: A History of Beer and Ale in the United States* (Boston: Little, Brown, 1962), 56, 58; Margaret K. Bacon, "Cross-Cultural Studies of Drinking: Integrated Drinking and Sex Differences in the Use of Alcoholic Beverages," in Michael W. Everett, Jack O. Waddell, and Dwight B. Heath, eds., *Cross-Cultural Approaches to the Study of Alcohol: An Interdisciplinary Perspective* (Paris and the Hague: Mouton, 1976), 27–29; Robert Popham, "The Social History of the Tavern," in Yedy Israel et al., eds., *Research Advances in Alcohol and Drug Problems,* vol. 4 (New York: Plenum Press, 1978), 225–302; Ian R. Tyrrell, *Sobering Up: From Temperance to Prohibition in Antebellum America* (Westport, Conn.: Greenwood Press, 1979), 16–25; Mary E. Saracino, "Household Production of Alcoholic Beverages in Early-Eighteenth-Century Connecticut," *Journal of Studies on Alcohol* 46 (May 1985): 244–52; Rorabaugh, *Alcoholic Republic,* chap. 2; Lender and Martin, *Drinking in America,* chap. 1.
6. Carol Steinsapir, "The Ante-Bellum Total Abstinence Movement at the Local Level: A Case Study of Schenectady, New York" (Ph.D. diss., Rutgers University, 1983), 71; Macell D. Ezell, "Early Attitudes toward Alcoholic Beverages in the South," *Red River Valley Historical Review* 7 (Winter 1982): 69.
7. Rorabaugh, *Alcoholic Republic,* 249; Pauline Maier, "Popular Uprisings and Civil Authority in Eighteenth-Century America," *William and Mary Quar-*

terly, 3d ser. 27 (January 1970): 3–35; Gary Nash, *The Urban Crucible: Social Change, Political Consciousness, and the Origins of the American Revolution* (Cambridge, Mass., and London: Harvard University Press, 1979).

8. Edward G. Baird, "The Alcohol Problem and the Law: II, The Common-Law Bases of Modern Liquor Controls," *Quarterly Journal of Studies on Alcohol* 5 (June 1944): 143–48; Edward G. Baird, "The Alcohol Problem and the Law: III, The Beginnings of the Alcoholic Beverage Control Laws in America," *Quarterly Journal of Studies on Alcohol* 6 (December 1945): 335–83; 7 (June 1946): 110–62; 7 (September 1946): 271–96; Karen R. Stubaus, "'The Good Creatures': Drinking Law and Custom in Seventeenth-Century Massachusetts and Virginia" (Ph.D. Diss., Rutgers University, 1984), chap. 2; Harry Gene Levine, "The Good Creature of God and the Demon Rum: Colonial American and 19th Century Ideas about Alcohol, Crime, and Accidents," in Robin Room and Gary Collins, eds., *Alcohol and Disinhibition: Nature and Meaning of the Link* (Rockville, Md.: National Institute on Alcohol Abuse and Alcoholism, 1983), 111–71; Harry Gene Levine, "The Discovery of Addiction: Changing Conceptions of Drunkenness in America," *Journal of Studies on Alcohol* 39 (January 1978): 143–74; Mark Lender, "Drunkenness as an Offense in Early New England: A Study of 'Puritan' Attitudes," *Quarterly Journal of Studies on Alcohol* 34 (1973): 353–66.

9. Baird, "Alcohol Problem and the Law: II," 126–61; Baird, "Alcohol Problem and the Law: III," 335–83, 110–62, 271–96; Popham, "Social History of the Tavern," 265; Stubaus, "'Good Creatures,'" chap. 2; Peter Clark, *The English Alehouse: A Social History, 1200–1830* (London and New York: Longman, 1983), 166–72; Frederick R. Johnson and Ruth Kessler, "The Liquor License System—Its Origins and Constitutional Development," *New York University Law Quarterly Review* 15 (January 1938): 210–51; 15 (March 1938): 380–424; W. W. Woollen and W. W. Thornton, *Intoxicating Liquors: The Law Relating to the Traffic in Intoxicating Liquors and Drunkenness,* 2 vols. (Cincinnati, Ohio: W. H. Anderson, 1910), 1:103; Paton Yoder, "Tavern Regulation in Virginia: Rationale and Reality," *Virginia Magazine of History and Biography* 87 (July 1979): 259–78.

10. Yoder, "Tavern Regulation in Virginia," 261; Stubaus, "'Good Creatures,'" 65–66, 166; Steinsapir, "Ante-Bellum Total Abstinence Movement," 33.

11. Steinsapir, "Ante-Bellum Total Abstinence Movement," 78–80; Joan M. Jensen, *Loosening the Bonds: Mid-Atlantic Farm Women, 1750–1850* (New Haven and London: Yale University Press, 1986), 186.

12. Rorabaugh, *Alcoholic Republic,* 76–82.

13. Quoted in Steinsapir, "Ante-Bellum Total Abstinence Movement," 266–67.

14. Rorabaugh, *Alcoholic Republic,* 95–100, 232.

15. Popham, "Social History of the Tavern," 246–47; Tyrrell, *Sobering Up,* 26–28; Steinsapir, "Ante-Bellum Total Abstinence Movement," 71.

16. Tyrrell, *Sobering Up*, chap. 2; Steinsapir, "Ante-Bellum Total Abstinence Movement," 83; Robert L. Hampel, *Temperance and Prohibition in Massachusetts, 1813–1852* (Ann Arbor, Mich.: UMI Research Press, 1982), chap. 2.

17. Tyrrell, *Sobering Up*, chap. 2; Hampel, *Temperance and Prohibition in Mass.*, chap. 2.

18. Tyrrell, *Sobering Up*, 54–55, 61–65.

19. Steinsapir, "Ante-Bellum Total Abstinence Movement," chap. 5; Emil C. Vigilante, "The Temperance Reform in New York State, 1829–1851" (Ph.D. diss., New York University, 1964), 15; Tyrrell, *Sobering Up*, 87.

20. Tyrrell, *Sobering Up*, 65–67; Steinsapir, "Ante-Bellum Total Abstinence Movement," 162; Vigilante, "Temperance Reform in N.Y.," 40–42.

21. Tyrrell, *Sobering Up*, 88–89; Mark Edward Lender, *Dictionary of American Temperance Biography: From Temperance Reform to Alcohol Research, the 1600s to the 1980s* (Westport, Conn.: Greenwood Press, 1984), 131–32.

22. Tyrrell, *Sobering Up*, 66.

23. Steinsapir, "Ante-Bellum Total Abstinence Movement," 119, 144, 266; Hampel, *Temperance and Prohibition in Mass.*, 29–30, 92; Vigilante, "Temperance Reform in N.Y.," 40–42; John S. Gilkeson, Jr., *Middle-Class Providence, 1820–1940* (Princeton, N.J.: Princeton University Press, 1986), 28; Tyrrell, *Sobering Up*, 87; Brian Harrison, *Drink and the Victorians: The Temperance Question in England, 1815–1872* (London: Faber & Faber, 1971), 150.

24. Tyrrell, *Sobering Up*, chaps. 3–5; Bruce Laurie, *Working People of Philadelphia, 1800–1850* (Philadelphia: Temple University Press, 1980), 40; Thomas L. Haskell, "Capitalism and the Origins of the Humanitarian Sensibility, Part I," *American Historical Review* 90 (April 1985): 339–61, "Part II," 90 (June 1985): 547–66.

25. Steinsapir, "Ante-Bellum Total Abstinence Movement," 108–109, 111.

26. Ibid.

27. Levine, "Discovery of Addiction," 156; Steinsapir, "Ante-Bellum Total Abstinence Movement," 51, 72, 106, 322; Gilkeson, *Middle-Class Providence,* 28; Hampel, *Temperance and Prohibition in Mass.*, 53; Patricia A. Dean, "The Meek Get in Their Licks: Temperance Literature of the Early Nineteenth Century as an Expression of Private Feminism" (Ph.D. diss., University of Minnesota, 1981), 64.

28. Quoted in Steinsapir, "Ante-Bellum Total Abstinence Movement," 63.

29. Ibid., 3.

30. Paul E. Johnson, *A Shopkeeper's Millennium: Society and Revivals in Rochester, New York, 1815–1837* (New York: Hill & Wang, 1978), 79–83; Laurie, *Working People of Philadelphia*, 42–51; Gilkeson, *Middle-Class Providence,* 29; Steinsapir, "Ante-Bellum Total Abstinence Movement," 6; Hampel, *Temperance and Prohibition in Mass.*, chap. 3.

31. Steinsapir, "Ante-Bellum Total Abstinence Movement," 6, 197–98; Hampel, *Temperance and Prohibition in Mass.*, 31; Gilkeson, *Middle-Class Providence,* 27.

32. David R. Huehner, "'Water Is Indeed Best': Temperance and the Pre–Civil War New England College," in Jack S. Blocker Jr., ed., *Alcohol, Reform and Society: The Liquor Issue in Social Context* (Westport, Conn.: Greenwood Press, 1979), 69–100; Douglas Wiley Carlson, "Temperance Reform in the Cotton Kingdom" (Ph.D. diss., University of Illinois, 1982), 145–46.

33. Tyrrell, *Sobering Up*, 89–90; Sarah E. Williams, "The Use of Beverage Alcohol as Medicine, 1790–1860," *Journal of Studies on Alcohol* 41 (May 1980): 543–66.

34. Ian R. Tyrrell, "Women and Temperance in Antebellum America, 1830–1860," *Civil War History* 28 (June 1982); 128–52; Paul R. Meyer, Jr., "The Transformation of American Temperance: The Popularization and Radicalization of a Reform Movement" (Ph.D. diss., University of Iowa, 1976), 87–89; Hampel, *Temperance and Prohibition in Mass.*, 28; Gilkeson, *Middle-Class Providence*, 28–29; Steinsapir, "Ante-Bellum Total Abstinence Movement," 196–97; Charles H. Bohner, "Rum and Reform: Temperance in Delaware Politics," *Delaware History* 5 (September 1953): 247–48; Frank L. Byrne, *Prophet of Prohibition: Neal Dow and His Crusade* (Madison: State Historical Society of Wisconsin, 1961), 26.

35. Nancy A. Hewitt, *Women's Activism and Social Change: Rochester, New York, 1822–1872* (Ithaca and London: Cornell University Press, 1984), 160.

36. Tyrrell, "Women and Temperance," 130–34, 142; Hampel, *Temperance and Prohibition in Mass.*, 28; Dean, "The Meek Get in Their Licks," chap. 5; Harry Gene Levine, "Temperance and Women in 19th-Century United States," in O. Kalant, ed., *Research Advances in Alcohol and Drug Problems*, vol. 5 (New York: Plenum Press, 1980), 45.

37. Jensen, *Loosening the Bonds*, 161–62, 186, 196; Steinsapir, "Ante-Bellum Total Abstinence Movement," 71.

38. Gilkeson, *Middle-Class Providence*, 24–25; Vigilante, "Temperance Reform in N.Y.," 22, 33–34, 44–45; Tyrrell, *Sobering Up*, 74; Steinsapir, "Ante-Bellum Total Abstinence Movement," 117–18.

39. Steinsapir, "Ante-Bellum Total Abstinence Movement," 125; Carlson, "Temperance Reform in the Cotton Kingdom," 197; Hampel, *Temperance and Prohibition in Mass.*, 90; Marc L. Harris, "The Process of Voluntary Association: Organizing the Ravenna Temperance Society, 1830," *Ohio History* 94 (Summer-Autumn 1985): 158–70.

40. Tyrrell, *Sobering Up*, 139–40; Steinsapir, "Ante-Bellum Total Abstinence Movement," 225–26.

41. Tyrrell, *Sobering Up*, 138–39; Vigilante, "Temperance Reform in N.Y.," 20; Steinsapir, "Ante-Bellum Total Abstinence Movement," 7–8.

42. Steinsapir, "Ante-Bellum Total Abstinence Movement," 102; Rorabaugh, *Alcoholic Republic*, 101–02.

43. Tyrrell, *Sobering Up*, 148; John J. Coffey, "A Political History of the Temperance Movement in New York State, 1808–1920" (Ph.D., diss., Pennsylvania State University, 1976), 26.

44. Tyrrell, *Sobering Up,* 149–50.

45. Harrison, *Drink and the Victorians,* 185–87.

46. Tyrrell, *Sobering Up,* 145–48.

47. Vigilante, "Temperance Reform in N.Y.," passim; Steinsapir, "Ante-Bellum Total Abstinence Movement," 263.

48. Tyrrell, *Sobering Up,* 227–37.

49. Ibid., 237–39; Hampel, *Temperance and Prohibition in Mass.,* 90.

50. Carlson, "Temperance Reform in the Cotton Kingdom," 165, 171–93; Lloyd L. Sponholtz, "Pittsburgh and Temperance, 1830–1854," *Western Pennsylvania Historical Magazine* 46 (October 1963): 369; Vigilante, "Temperance Reform in N.Y.," 141–42; Gilkeson, *Middle-Class Providence,* 33; Henry A. Scomp, *King Alcohol in the Realm of King Cotton, or, a History of the Liquor Traffic and of the Temperance Movement in Georgia from 1733 to 1887* (Chicago: Blakely Printing, 1888), 325–39; Ian R. Tyrrell, "Drink and Temperance in the Antebellum South: An Overview and Interpretation," *Journal of Southern History* 48 (November 1982): 488–89.

51. Tyrrell, "Drink and Temperance in the Antebellum South," 485–510; Carlson, "Temperance Reform in the Cotton Kingdom," 13, 86–88, 118–19, 149–50, 193–205; Scomp, *King Alcohol,* 236, 325–39; John A. Krout, *The Origins of Prohibition* (New York: Alfred A. Knopf, 1925), 157; William Graham Davis, "Attacking 'The Matchless Evil': Temperance and Prohibition in Mississippi, 1817–1908" (Ph.D. diss., Mississippi State University, 1975), 10–15; James B. Sellers, *The Prohibition Movement in Alabama, 1702 to 1943* (Chapel Hill: University of North Carolina Press, 1943), 19–21; Daniel J. Whitener, *Prohibition in North Carolina, 1715–1945* (Chapel Hill: University of North Carolina Press, 1945), 26–27; C. C. Pearson and J. Edwin Hendricks, *Liquor and Anti-Liquor in Virginia, 1619–1919* (Durham, N.C.: Duke University Press, 1967), 55, 59–62, 73, 75, 85, 88.

52. Compare Levine, "Discovery of Addiction"; Levine, "The Good Creature of God and the Demon Rum."

53. Rorabaugh, *Alcoholic Republic,* 232.

Chapter Two

1. Byrne, *Prophet of Prohibition, 45.*

2. Ibid., 62.

3. Ibid., chaps. 1–8; Neal Dow, *The Reminiscences of Neal Dow: Recollections of Eighty Years* (Portland, Maine: Evening Express Publishing, 1898).

4. Steinsapir, "Ante-Bellum Total Abstinence Movement," chap. 8; Williams, "Use of Beverage Alcohol as Medicine," 560-62; Coffey, "Political History," 58; Susan G. Davis, "'Making Night Hideous': Christmas Revelry and Public Disorder in Nineteenth Century Philadelphia," *American Quarterly* 34

(Summer 1982): 185–99; Gilkeson, *Middle-Class Providence,* 26; Carlson, "Temperance Reform in the Cotton Kingdom," 73.

5. Gretchen A. Condran and Eileen Crimmins-Gardner, "Public Health Measures and Mortality in U.S. Cities in the Late Nineteenth Century," *Human Ecology* 6 (March 1978): 27–54; Coffey, "Political History," 19–20; Rorabaugh, *Alcoholic Republic,* 100.

6. Steinsapir, "Ante-Bellum Total Abstinence Movement," 311.

7. Allan M. Winkler, "Drinking on the American Frontier," *Quarterly Journal of Studies on Alcohol* 29 (March 1968): 413–45; Popham, "Social History of the Tavern," 246–47, 270–71; Elliott West, *The Saloon on the Rocky Mountain Mining Frontier* (Lincoln and London: University of Nebraska Press, 1979); Perry R. Duis, *The Saloon: Public Drinking in Chicago and Boston, 1880–1920* (Urbana and Chicago: University of Illinois Press, 1983).

8. Laurie, *Working People of Philadelphia,* chap. 2; Jill Siegel Dodd, "The Working Classes and the Temperance Movement in Ante-Bellum Boston," *Labor History* 19 (Fall 1978): 522–23.

9. Hasia R. Diner, *Erin's Daughters in America: Irish Immigrant Women in the Nineteenth Century* (Baltimore and London: Johns Hopkins University Press, 1983), 112–14.

10. Laurie, *Working People of Philadelphia,* 71–72; Sean Wilentz, *Chants Democratic: New York City and the Rise of the American Working Class, 1788–1850* (New York and Oxford: Oxford University Press, 1984), 255; Richard Stivers, *A Hair of the Dog: Irish Drinking and American Stereotype* (University Park: Pennsylvania State University Press, 1976); James R. Barrett, "Why Paddy Drank: The Social Importance of Whiskey in Pre-Famine Ireland," *Journal of Popular Culture* 11 (Summer 1977): 155–66; Tyrrell, *Sobering Up,* 275.

11. Rorabaugh, *Alcoholic Republic,* 232; William L. Downard, *Dictionary of the History of the American Brewing and Distilling Industries* (Westport, Conn.: Greenwood Press, 1980).

12. Tyrrell, *Sobering Up,* 168–69; Laurie, *Working People of Philadelphia,* 120-22; Wilentz, *Chants Democratic,* 306–07; Nancy Ray Siegel, "A Matter of the Public Welfare: The Temperance Movement in Ante-Bellum Cincinnati" (M.A. thesis, University of Cincinnati, 1971), 11.

13. Quoted in Milton A. Maxwell, "The Washingtonian Movement," *Quarterly Journal of Studies on Alcohol* 11 (September 1950): 417–18.

14. Vigilante, "Temperance Reform in N.Y.," 166–67; Sponholtz, "Pittsburgh and Temperance," 355; Tyrrell, *Sobering Up,* 160; Hampel, *Temperance and Prohibition in Mass.,* 104; Maxwell, "Washingtonian Movement," 422–23.

15. Tyrrell, *Sobering Up,* 164–67; Wilentz, *Chants Democratic,* 308; Hampel, *Temperance and Prohibition in Mass.,* 112.

16. Wilentz, *Chants Democratic,* 308; Tyrrell, *Sobering Up,* 167; Hampel, *Temperance and Prohibition in Mass.,* 113.

17. Pearson and Hendricks, *Liquor and Anti-Liquor in Virginia,* 91–96; Whitener, *Prohibition in North Carolina,* 28–29; Sellers, *Prohibition Movement*

in Alabama, 22; Krout, *Origins of Prohibition*, 189–90; Carlson, "Temperance Reform in the Cotton Kingdom," 223–24; Scomp, *King Alcohol in the Realm of King Cotton*, 367, 393, 398.

18. Maxwell, "Washington Movement," 413.

19. Tyrrell, *Sobering Up*, 174.

20. Ibid., 176–79.

21. Hampel, *Temperance and Prohibition in Mass.*, 107; Tyrrell, *Sobering Up*, 179–82; Siegel, "A Matter of the Public Welfare," 72; Mary P. Ryan, *Cradle of the Middle Class: The Family in Oneida County, New York, 1790–1865* (Cambridge: Cambridge University Press, 1981), 135.

22. Quoted in Donald Weldon Beattie, "Sons of Temperance: Pioneers in Total Abstinence and 'Constitutional' Prohibition" (Ph.D. diss., Boston University, 1966), 20.

23. Tyrrell, *Sobering Up*, 194–96; Dodd, "Working Classes and the Temperance Movement," 512; Ryan, *Cradle of the Middle Class*; Hampel, *Temperance and Prohibition in Mass.*, 120–21.

24. Tyrrell, *Sobering Up*, 196–99; Hampel, *Temperance and Prohibition in Mass.*, 113, 117–20; Maxwell, "Washingtonian Movement," 438–39.

25. Tyrrell, *Sobering Up*, 199–201; Hampel, *Temperance and Prohibition in Mass.*, 122–26; Vigilante, "Temperance Reform in N.Y.," 187; Leonard U. Blumberg, "The Significance of the Alcohol Prohibitionists for the Washington Temperance Societies; with Special Reference to Paterson and Newark, New Jersey," *Journal of Studies on Alcohol* 41 (January 1980): 37–77.

26. Tyrrell, *Sobering Up*, 206–08; Wilentz, *Chants Democratic*, 312–14.

27. Quoted in Beattie, "Sons of Temperance," 140.

28. Ibid., 349–56, 435–39.

29. Hampel, *Temperance and Prohibition in Mass.*, 130–31.

30. Beattie, "Sons of Temperance," 398–99, 410–11.

31. Tyrrell, "Women and Temperance," 128–52; Siegel, "A Matter of the Public Welfare." 73.

32. Tyrrell, "Drink and Temperance in the Antebellum South," 485–510; Hampel, *Temperance and Prohibition in Mass.*, 131–33, 144–45; W. J. Rorabaugh, "The Sons of Temperance in Antebellum Jasper County," *Georgia Historical Quarterly* 64 (Fall 1980): 263–79.

33. Carlson, "Temperance Reform in the Cotton Kingdom," 30; Sellers, *Prohibition Movement in Alabama*, 23*n*; Whitener, *Prohibition in North Carolina*, 31.

34. Tyrrell, *Sobering Up*, 212–18; Hampel, *Temperance and Prohibition in Mass.*, 134–43.

35. Davis, "'Making Night Hideous.'"

36. Jed Dannenbaum, *Drink and Disorder: Temperance Reform in Cincinnati from the Washingtonian Revival to the WCTU* (Urbana and Chicago: University of Illinois Press, 1984), 88–90.

37. Tyrrell, *Sobering Up*, 228; Daniel J. Ryan, "History of Liquor Legisla-

tion in Ohio," in Emilius O. Randall and Daniel J. Ryan, eds., *History of Ohio,* 4 vols. (New York: Century History, 1912), 4:519; Hampel, *Temperance and Prohibition in Mass.,* 170; Davis, "Attacking 'The Matchless Evil,'" 36–37, 40; Steinsapir, "Ante-Bellum Total Abstinence Movement," 277–78.

38. Joseph R. Gusfield, *Symbolic Crusade: Status Politics and the American Temperance Movement* (Urbana and London: University of Illinois Press, 1963); Tyrrell, *Sobering Up,* 254–59; Hampel, *Temperance and Prohibition in Mass.,* 148–53; Vigilante, "Temperance Reform in N.Y.," 239.

39. Bohner, "Rum and Reform"; Carlson, "Temperance Reform in the Cotton Kingdom," 234–48, 257–85; Dannenbaum, *Drink and Disorder,* 144; Asa Earl Martin, "The Temperance Movement in Pennsylvania Prior to the Civil War," *Pennsylvania Magazine of History and Biography* 49 (1925): 221–23.

40. Tyrrell, *Sobering Up,* 243–44; Dannenbaum, *Drink and Disorder,* 135; Peter Weisensel, "The Wisconsin Temperance Crusade to 1919" (M.S. thesis, University of Wisconsin, 1965), 27; Steven J. Ross, *Workers on the Edge: Work, Leisure, and Politics in Industrializing Cincinnati, 1788–1890* (New York: Columbia University Press, 1985), 170–71.

41. Bohner, "Rum and Reform," 256, 262–69; Pearson and Hendricks, *Liquor and Anti-Liquor in Virginia,* 125–40; Martin, "Temperance Movement in Pa.," 226; Sponholtz, "Pittsburgh and Temperance," 379; W. J. Rorabaugh, "Prohibition as Progress: New York State's License Elections, 1846," *Journal of Social History* 14 (Spring 1981): 427–28.

42. Hampel, *Temperance and Prohibition in Mass.,* 144–45.

43. Michael F. Holt, *The Political Crisis of the 1850s* (New York: Wiley, 1978); Tyrrell, *Sobering Up,* 260–69; Hampel, *Temperance and Prohibition in Mass.,* 162; Bohner, "Rum and Reform," 262–69; William John Jackson, "Prohibition as an Issue in New York State Politics, 1836–1933" (Ed.D. diss., Columbia University, 1974), 18–19; Dannenbaum, *Drink and Disorder,* 141–42, 156–57; Frank L. Byrne, "Maine Law versus Lager Beer: A Dilemma of Wisconsin's Young Republican Party," *Wisconsin Magazine of History* 52 (Winter 1958–59): 115–20; William E. Gienapp, "Nativism and the Creation of a Republican Majority in the North before the Civil War," *Journal of American History* 72 (December 1985): 529–59.

44. Gilkeson, *Middle-Class Providence,* 13; Stuart M. Blumin, "The Hypothesis of Middle-Class Formation in Nineteenth-Century America; A Critique and Some Proposals," *American Historical Review* 90 (April 1985): 299–338.

45. Martin, "Temperance Movement in Pennsylvania," 225; Carlson, "Temperance Reform in the Cotton Kingdom," 272.

46. Hampel, *Temperance and Prohibition in Mass.,* 154; Ernest H. Cherrington et al., *Standard Encyclopedia of the Alcohol Problem,* 6 vols. (Westerville, Ohio: American Issue Publishing, 1924–30), 2:525.

47. Coffey, "Political History," 99, 112–13; Tyrrell, *Sobering Up,* 296–97; Martin, "Temperance Movement in Pa.," 225.

48. Tyrrell, *Sobering Up,* chap. 11; Paul O. Weinbaum, "Temperance,

Politics, and the New York City Riots of 1857," *New York Historical Society Quarterly* 59 (July 1975): 246–70.

49. Tyrrell, "Women and Temperance"; Jed Dannenbaum, "The Origins of Temperance Activism and Militancy among American Women," *Journal of Social History* 15 (Winter 1981): 235–52; Carlson, "Temperance Reform in the Cotton Kingdom," 72–73; Siegel, "A Matter of the Public Welfare," 73–74; Jensen, *Loosening the Bonds,* 196, 198; Meyer, "Transformation of American Temperance," 183, 197.

Chapter Three

1. Matilda Gilruth Carpenter, *The Crusade: Its Origin and Development at Washington Court House and its Results* (Columbus, Ohio: W. G. Hubbard, 1893), 35–36.

2. Ibid., 43.

3. Ibid., 45.

4. Ibid., 32–101; Jack S. Blocker Jr., *"Give to the Winds Thy Fears": The Women's Temperance Crusade, 1873–1874* (Westport, Conn.: Greenwood Press, 1985); Blocker, "Market Integration, Urban Growth and Economic Change in an Ohio County, 1850–1880." *Ohio History* 90 (Autumn 1981): 298–316.

5. Rorabaugh, *Alcoholic Republic,* 232; Blocker, *"Give to the Winds,"* 97–99, 221.

6. Thomas C. Cochran, *The Pabst Brewing Company: The History of an American Business* (New York: New York University Press, 1948), 59–60, 86, 102, 143, 146; Baron, *Brewed in America,* 257, 268–70; Downard, *Dictionary of the History of the American Brewing and Distilling Industries,* 229, 242–43; Duis, *The Saloon,* chap. 1.

7. Blocker, *"Give to the Winds,"* 98.

8. Baron, *Brewed in America,* 213–16; Cochran, *Pabst Brewing Company,* 51, 307; Amy Helaine Mittelman, "The Politics of Alcohol Production: The Liquor Industry and the Federal Government, 1862–1900" (Ph.D. diss., Columbia University, 1986); Andrew Sinclair, *Era of Excess: A Social History of the Prohibition Movement* (New York: Harper & Row, 1964), 101.

9. Robin Room, "Cultural Contingencies of Alcoholism: Variations between and within Nineteenth-Century Urban Ethnic Groups in Alcohol-Related Death Rates," *Journal of Health and Social Behavior* 9 (June 1968): 99–113; Blocker, *"Give to the Winds,"* 101–07; Duane R. Lindberg, "Pastors, Prohibition and Politics: The Role of Norwegian Clergy in the North Dakota Abstinence Movement, 1880–1920," *North Dakota Quarterly* 49 (Autumn 1981): 21–38.

10. John C. Schneider, *Detroit and the Problem of Order, 1850–1880: A Geography of Crime, Riot, and Policing* (Lincoln: University of Nebraska Press, 1980), 16–19; Blocker, *"Give to the Winds,"* 101; Thomas J. Noel, *The City and the Saloon: Denver, 1858–1916* (Lincoln and London: University of Nebraska

Press, 1982), chap. 7; Leonard Harry Ellis, "Men among Men: An Exploration of All-Male Relationships in Victorian America" (Ph.D. diss., Columbia University, 1982), 127–28; Duis, *The Saloon,* chap. 7.

11. Blocker, *"Give to the Winds,"* 101–07.

12. Ellis, "Men among Men," 149–56, 174–92; Larry Engelmann, "Old Saloon Days in Michigan," *Michigan History* 61 (Summer 1977): 103–04.

13. John Modell, "Patterns of Consumption, Acculturation, and Family Income Strategies in Late Nineteenth-Century America," in Tamara K. Hareven and Maris A. Vinovskis, eds., *Family and Population in Nineteenth-Century America* (Princeton: Princeton University Press, 1978), 206–40; Ronald Morris Benson, "American Workers and Temperance Reform, 1866–1933" (Ph.D. diss., University of Notre Dame, 1974), 130, 134.

14. Quoted in Benson, "American Workers," 89.

15. Benson, "American Workers," chaps. 1–5; Samuel Walker, "Terence V. Powderly, the Knights of Labor, and the Temperance Issue," *Societas* 5 (Autumn 1975): 279–93; David Brundage, "The Producing Classes and the Saloon: Denver in the 1880s," *Labor History* 26 (Winter 1985): 29–52; Francis G. Couvares, *The Remaking of Pittsburgh: Class and Culture in an Industrializing City, 1877–1919* (Albany: State University of New York Press, 1984), 51–52; James R. Green, "The 'Salesmen-Soldiers' of the '*Appeal* Army': A Profile of Rank-and-File Socialist Agitators," in Bruce Stave, ed., *Socialism and the Cities* (Port Washington, N.Y. and London: Kennikat Press, 1975), 29.

16. Lender, *Dictionary of Temp. Biography,* 354–56, 418–19; Couvares, *Remaking Pittsburgh,* 51–52; Engelmann, "Old Saloon Days," 121; Earl C. Kaylor, Jr., "The Prohibition Movement in Pennsylvania, 1865–1920" (Ph.D., diss., Pennsylvania State University, 1963), chap. 7; Robert Smith Bader, *Prohibition in Kansas: A History* (Lawrence: University Press of Kansas, 1986), 34–35; Gerald Vanwoerkom, "They 'Dared to Do Right': Prohibition in Muskegon," *Michigan History* 55 (Spring 1971): 41–60; Sister Joan Bland, *Hibernian Crusade: The Story of the Catholic Total Abstinence Union of America* (Washington, D.C.: Catholic University of America Press, 1951); Martin G. Towey and Margaret LoPiccolo Sullivan, "The Knights of Father Matthew: Parallel Ethnic Reform," *Missouri Historical Review* 75 (January 1981): 168–83.

17. Ellis, "Men among Men."

18. William H. Robinson, Jr., "Prohibition in the Confederacy," *American Historical Review* 37 (October 1931): 50–58; Davis, "Attacking 'The Matchless Evil,'" 43–45.

19. James R. Turner, "The American Prohibition Movement, 1865–1897" (Ph.D. diss., University of Wisconsin, 1972), 208; Benson, "American Workers," 51–52; Arnold Jaffe, *Addiction Reform in the Progressive Age: Scientific and Social Responses to Drug Dependence in the United States, 1870–1930* (New York: Arno Press, 1981), chaps. 1–2; Edward M. Brown, "'What Shall We Do with the Inebriate?': Asylum Treatment and the Disease Concept of Alcoholism in the Late Nineteenth Century," *Journal of the History of the Behavioral Sciences* 21 (January

1985): 48–59; Lender and Martin, *Drinking in America,* 119–22; Jim Baumohl and Robin Room, "Inebriety, Doctors, and the State: Alcoholism Treatment Institutions before 1940," in Marc Galanter, ed., *Recent Developments in Alcoholism,* vol. 5 (New York: Plenum Press, 1987), 135–74.

20. Blocker, *"Give to the Winds,"* 69; Annual Reports, Grand Lodge of North America, IOGT, Edward C. Sturges Papers, Olin Library, Cornell University; Kaylor, "Prohibition Movement," 89–96, 152; Lender, *Dictionary of Temp. Biography,* 49–50.

21. Journal of the Massachusetts Grand Lodge, IOGT, 1859–73, Mudd Learning Center, Oberlin College; Blocker, *"Give to the Winds,"* 68–69; Dannenbaum, *Drink and Disorder,* 200–202; Annual Reports, Grand Lodge of North America, IOGT, Sturges Papers.

22. Blocker, *"Give to the Winds,"* 96, 110.

23. Ibid., 112–13.

24. Ibid., 124–33, 172.

25. Ibid., chaps. 1–3.

26. Ibid., 17–26.

27. Ibid., chaps. 1, 4.

28. Ibid., 48, 118–23, 139–40.

29. Ibid., 67–72; Turner, "American Prohibition Movement," 93–94.

30. Blocker, *"Give to the Winds."* 227–29; Theodore L. Agnew, "Jennie Fowler Willing," in Edward T. James, Janet Wilson James, and Paul S. Boyer, eds. *Notable American Women,* 3 vols. (Cambridge, Mass.: Harvard University Press, 1971), 3:623–25.

31. Ruth Bordin, *Frances Willard: A Biography* (Chapel Hill and London: University of North Carolina Press, 1986), chaps. 1–7.

32. Paul Boyer, *Urban Masses and Moral Order in America, 1820–1920* (Cambridge, Mass., and London: Harvard University Press, 1978), 125–29; Jack S. Blocker Jr., *Retreat from Reform: The Prohibition Movement in the United States, 1890–1913* (Westport, Conn.: Greenwood Press, 1976), chap. 1.

33. Norton Mezvinsky, "The White-Ribbon Reform, 1874–1920" (Ph.D. diss., University of Wisconsin, 1959), 73–74; Gusfield, *Symbolic Crusade,* 80–81; Robert A. Hohner, "The Prohibitionists: Who Were They?" *South Atlantic Quarterly* 68 (Autumn 1969): 499–500; Ruth Bordin, *Woman and Temperance: The Quest for Power and Liberty, 1873–1900* (Philadelphia: Temple University Press, 1981), 163–75; Deborah P. Clifford, "The Women's War against Rum," *Vermont History* 52 (Summer 1984): 141–60.

34. Benson, "American Workers," 194–215; Bordin, *Woman and Temperance,* chap. 6; Vigilante, "Temperance Reform in N.Y.," 43, 151.

35. Bordin, *Woman and Temperance,* chaps. 6–7; Norton Mezvinsky, "Scientific Temperance Education in the Schools," *History of Education Quarterly* 1 (March 1961): 48–56; Mezvinsky, "White-Ribbon Reform," 154.

36. Ian Tyrrell, "Women and Temperance in International Perspective: The

World's WCTU, 1880s–1920s." Paper presented at the International Conference on the Social History of Alcohol, Berkeley, California, 4 January 1984.

37. Bordin, *Woman and Temperance,* chaps. 6–7; Mari Jo Buhle, *Women and American Socialism, 1870-1920* (Urbana, Chicago, and London: University of Illinois Press, 1981), chaps. 1–2.

38. Barbara Leslie Epstein, *The Politics of Domesticity: Women, Evangelism, and Temperance in Nineteenth-Century America* (Middletown, Conn.: Wesleyan University Press, 1981), chap. 5; Ellen Dubois, "The Radicalism of the Woman Suffrage Movement: Notes toward the Reconstruction of Nineteenth-Century Feminism," *Feminist Studies* 3 (Fall 1975):63–71; Linda Gordon, *Woman's Body, Woman's Right: A Social History of Birth Control in America* (New York: Grossman, 1976), chap. 5.

39. Bordin, *Woman and Temperance,* chap. 5; Turner, "American Prohibition Movement," 260. Compare Naomi Rosenthal, Meryl Fingrutd, Michele Ethier, Roberta Karant, and David McDonald, "Social Movements and Network Analysis: A Case Study of Nineteenth-Century Women's Reform in New York State," *American Journal of Sociology* 90 (March 1985): 1022–54.

40. Bordin, *Woman and Temperance,* chap. 7; Marian J. Morton, "Temperance, Benevolence, and the City: The Cleveland Non-Partisan Woman's Christian Temperance Union, 1874–1900," *Ohio History* 91 (1982): 58–73; Jane L. McKeever, "The Woman's Temperance Publishing Association," *Library Quarterly* 55 (October 1985): 365–97.

41. Lee Benson, "Research Problems in American Political Historiography," in Mirra Komarovsky, ed., *Common Frontiers of the Social Sciences* (Glencoe, Ill.: Free Press, 1957), 113–83; Emil Pocock, "Wet or Dry? The Presidential Election of 1884 in Upstate New York," *New York History* 54 (April 1973): 174–90; Coffey, "Political History," 189–90; Kaylor, "Prohibition Movement," 182–87.

42. Paul Kleppner, *The Third Electoral System, 1853–1892: Parties, Voters, and Political Cultures* (Chapel Hill: University of North Carolina Press, 1979), 240–57; Turner, "American Prohibition Movement," 91–94; Gilman M. Ostrander, *The Prohibition Movement in California, 1848–1933* (Berkeley and Los Angeles: University of California Press, 1957), 26, 34–37; Blocker, *Retreat from Reform,* 83–84.

43. Blocker, *Retreat from Reform,* 39–43.

44. Ibid., 8–13, 44–46; Kleppner, *Third Electoral System,* 240–57; Dale Baum, "Teetotalers Enter Politics: The Massachusetts Prohibitionist Party in the Early 1870s," *Mid-America* 65 (October 1983): 137–54; Coffey, "Political History," 189, 199; Brundage, "Producing Classes"; Leon Fink, *Workingmen's Democracy: The Knights of Labor and American Politics* (Urbana, Chicago, and London: University of Illinois Press, 1983), 47.

45. Kleppner, *Third Electoral System;* Kleppner, *The Cross of Culture: A Social Analysis of Midwestern Politics, 1850–1900* (New York: Free Press,

1970); Richard Jensen, *The Winning of the Midwest: Social and Political Conflict, 1888–1896* (Chicago: University of Chicago Press, 1971); Robert E. Wenger, "The Anti-Saloon League in Nebraska Politics," *Nebraska History* 52 (Fall 1971): 268.

46. *Cyclopædia of Temperance and Prohibition* (New York, London, and Toronto: Funk & Wagnalls, 1891), 97–128; Bader, *Prohibition in Kansas,* chap. 3; Kaylor, "Prohibition Movement," chap. 8; F. M. Whitaker, "Ohio WCTU and the Prohibition Amendment Campaign of 1883," *Ohio History* 83 (Spring 1974): 83–102; Jerry Harrington, "Bottled Conflict: Keokuk and the Prohibition Question, 1888–1889," *Annals of Iowa* 46 (Spring 1983): 595; Ballard C. Campbell, "Did Democracy Work? Prohibition in Late Nineteenth-Century Iowa: A Test Case," *Journal of Interdisciplinary History* 8 (Summer 1977): 99–100.

47. Pearson and Hendricks, *Liquor and Anti-Liquor,* chap. 9; Davis, "Attacking 'The Matchless Evil,'" 213; Sellers, *Prohibition Movement in Alabama,* 74–94; Whitener, *Prohibition in North Carolina,* 86; E. M. Coulter, "The Athens Dispensary," *Georgia Historical Quarterly* 50 (March 1966): 14–36; Grace Leab, "Tennessee Temperance Activities, 1870–1899," *East Tennessee Historical Society Publications,* no. 21 (1949): 52–68; Paul E. Isaac, *Prohibition and Politics: Turbulent Decades in Tennessee, 1885–1920* (Knoxville: University of Tennessee Press, 1965).

48. Tyrrell, "Drink and Temperance in the Antebellum South," 509–10; Pearson and Hendricks, *Liquor and Anti-Liquor,* chap. 9; John Hammond Moore, "The Negro and Prohibition in Atlanta, 1885–1887," *South Atlantic Quarterly* 69 (Winter 1970): 38–57; Isaac, *Prohibition and Politics,* 57; Davis, "Attacking 'The Matchless Evil,'" 151; T. F. Parker, *History of the Independent Order of Good Templars* (New York: Phillips & Hunt, 1882), 142–264.

49. George C. Wittet, "Concerned Citizens: The Prohibitionists of 1883 Ohio," in Blocker, ed., *Alcohol, Reform and Society,* 111–47; Thomas G. Ryan, "Supporters and Opponents of Prohibition: Iowa in 1917," *Annals of Iowa* 46 (Winter 1983): 510–22; Bader, *Prohibition in Kansas,* chap. 3; *National Temperance Advocate,* April 1873; Edison K. Putnam, "The Prohibition Movement in Idaho, 1863–1934" (Ph.D. diss., University of Idaho, 1979), 127*n*; Eric H. Monkkonen, "A Disorderly People? Urban Order in the Nineteenth and Twentieth Centuries," *Journal of American History* 68 (December 1981): 539–59; Kaylor, "Prohibition Movement," 275–76; Lindberg, "Pastors, Prohibition and Politics"; Norman H. Clark, *The Dry Years: Prohibition and Social Change in Washington* (Seattle: University of Washington Press, 1965), chap. 4.

50. *Cyclopædia of Temperance and Prohibition,* 102–28; Kaylor, "Prohibition Movement," 283–94; Duis, *The Saloon,* 31.

51. Kleppner, *Third Electoral System,* chap. 8; Blocker, *Retreat from Reform,* 39–49.

52. Lawrence Goodwyn, *Democratic Promise: The Populist Moment in America* (New York: Oxford University Press, 1976); Jack S. Blocker Jr., "The

Politics of Reform: Populists, Prohibition, and Woman Suffrage, 1891–1892," *Historian* 34 (August 1972): 614–32; Bordin, *Willard,* chaps. 12–14.

Chapter Four

1. Quoted in Justin Steuart, *Wayne Wheeler, Dry Boss: An Uncensored Biography of Wayne B. Wheeler* (New York: Fleming H. Revell, 1928), 211–12.

2. Lincoln Steffens, *The Autobiography of Lincoln Steffens* (New York: Harcourt, Brace, 1931), 859–60.

3. Steuart, *Wheeler,* 214–16; K. Austin Kerr, *Organized for Prohibition: A New History of the Anti-Saloon League* (New Haven and London: Yale University Press, 1985), 231–35.

4. Bader, *Prohibition in Kansas,* 191.

5. Jack S. Blocker Jr., "The Modernity of Prohibitionists: An Analysis of Leadership Structure and Background," in Blocker, ed., *Alcohol, Reform and Society,* 152–54.

6. Blocker, *Retreat from Reform,* chaps. 2–4.

7. Ibid., 165–66; Kerr, *Organized for Prohibition,* 93–95; Blocker, "Modernity of Prohibitionists," 155, 158.

8. Ostrander, *Prohibition Movement in California,* 85; William Elliott West, "Dry Crusade: The Prohibition Movement in Colorado, 1858–1933" (Ph.D. diss., University of Colorado, 1971), 364; Robert A. Hohner, "Bishop Cannon's Apprenticeship in Temperance Politics, 1900–1918," *Journal of Southern History* 34 (February 1968): 33–49.

9. Blocker, *Retreat from Reform,* chaps. 5, 7.

10. Quoted in Kerr, *Organized for Prohibition,* 95.

11. Marian J. Morton, "Temperance Reform in the 'Providential Environment,' Cleveland, 1830–1934," in David D. Van Tassel and John J. Grabowski, eds., *Cleveland: A Tradition of Reform* (Kent, Ohio: Kent State University Press, 1986), 61; Coffey, "Political History," 299; Blocker, *Retreat from Reform,* 217.

12. Quoted in Blocker, *Retreat from Reform,* 162.

13. Kerr, *Organized for Prohibition,* 99–114, 168–70; Lloyd Sponholtz, "The Politics of Temperance in Ohio, 1880–1912," *Ohio History* 85 (Winter 1976): 4–27.

14. Kerr, *Organized for Prohibition,* 154, 244–45; Blocker, "Modernity of Prohibitionists," 152–56; Blocker, *Retreat from Reform,* 161, 203–04.

15. Kerr, *Organized for Prohibition,* 81; Blocker, *Retreat from Reform,* 166.

16. Blocker, *Retreat from Reform,* chaps. 6–8; Francis Myron Whitaker, "A History of the Ohio Woman's Christian Temperance Union, 1874–1920" (Ph.D. diss., Ohio State University, 1971), 431, 433; Wenger, "Anti-Saloon League in Nebraska Politics," 287–88.

17. Blocker, *Retreat from Reform*, 201; Isaac, *Prohibition and Politics*, chap. 11; Davis, "Attacking 'The Matchless Evil,'" chap. 8; C. Vann Woodward, *Origins of the New South, 1877–1913* (Baton Rouge: Louisiana State University Press, 1951), 389–90; Thomas H. Appleton, "'Like Banquo's Ghost': The Emergence of the Prohibition Issue in Kentucky Politics" (Ph.D. diss., University of Kentucky, 1981).

18. Sinclair, *Era of Excess*, 29–32; Denise A. Herd, "Prohibition, Racism and Class Politics in the Post-Reconstruction South," *Journal of Drug Issues* 13 (Winter 1983):77–94; Lewis L. Gould, *Progressives and Prohibitionists: Texas Democrats in the Wilson Era* (Austin and London: University of Texas Press, 1973), 24; Davis, "Attacking 'The Matchless Evil,'" 225, 241, 254; Woodward, *Origins of the New South*, 390; Frederick Heath and Harriet H. Kinnard, "Prohibition in South Carolina, 1880–1940: An Overview," *Proceedings of the South Carolina Historical Association* (1980): 125.

19. Woodward, *Origins of the New South*, 140, 291–320, 406–16; Pearson and Hendricks, *Liquor and Anti-Liquor*, 210; Hohner, "The Prohibitionists: Who Were They?"; Gould, *Progressives and Prohibitionists*, 289.

20. West, *Saloon on the Rocky Mountain Mining Frontier;* West, "Dry Crusade," 285, 334, 389–90; Putnam, "Prohibition Movement in Idaho," 189, 265, 268–69.

21. James H. Timberlake, *Prohibition and the Progressive Movement, 1900–1920* (Cambridge, Mass.: Harvard University Press, 1963); Hohner, "The Prohibitionists: Who Were They?"; G. K. Renner, "Prohibition Comes to Missouri, 1910–1919," *Missouri Historical Review* 62 (July 1968): 387–88; Jackson, "Prohibition as an Issue in N.Y. Politics," 47, 51–52; Kaylor, "Prohibition Movement in Pennsylvania," 387–88; Larry D. Engelmann, "O Whiskey: The History of Prohibition in Michigan" (Ph.D. diss., University of Michigan, 1971), 248, 249, 250, 283; Benson, "American Workers," 252–53, 274; West, "Dry Crusade," chap. 6.

22. Floyd Streeter, "History of Prohibition Legislation in Michigan," *Michigan History Magazine* 2 (1918): 306–08; Engelmann, "O Whiskey," 110, 119–24; Leslie J. Stegh, "Wet and Dry Battles in the Cradle State of Prohibition: Robert J. Bulkley and the Repeal of Prohibition in Ohio" (Ph.D. diss., Kent State University, 1975), 516–21; Peter Roberts, *Anthracite Coal Communities* (New York: Macmillan, 1904), 205; Clark Warburton, *The Economic Results of Prohibition* (New York: Columbia University Press, 1932), 123–27; Robert Coit Chapin, *The Standard of Living Among Workingmen's Families in New York City* (New York: Russell Sage Foundation, 1909), 134–35.

23. Quoted in T. J. Jackson Lears, *No Place of Grace: Antimodernism and the Transformation of American Culture, 1880–1920* (New York: Pantheon Books, 1981), 54.

24. Quoted in West, "Dry Crusade," 353; Lears, *No Place of Grace*, 11, 28, 37; Couvares, *Remaking Pittsburgh*, 125; Daniel Horowitz, *The Morality of Spending: Attitudes toward the Consumer Society in America, 1875–1940* (Balti-

more: Johns Hopkins University Press, 1985), xxvi–xxvii; Lewis A. Erenberg, *Steppin' Out: New York Nightlife and the Transformation of American Culture, 1890–1930* (Westport, Conn.: Greenwood Press, 1981).

25. Katherine Harris, "A Study of Feminine and Class Identity in the Woman's Christian Temperance Union, 1920–1979: A Case Study," *Historicus* 2 (Fall-Winter 1981): 62; Daniel T. Rodgers, *The Work Ethic in Industrial America, 1850–1920* (Chicago and London: University of Chicago Press, 1978).

26. Mezvinsky, "White-Ribbon Reform," 108–09; Joan L. Silverman, "'I'll Never Touch Another Drop': Images of Alcohol and Temperance in American Popular Culture, 1874–1919" (Ph.D. diss., New York University, 1979), 338–40; Silverman, "*The Birth of a Nation:* Prohibition Propaganda," *Southern Quarterly* 19 (Spring-Summer 1981): 23–30.

27. Renner, "Prohibition Comes to Missouri," 393–94.

28. Whitaker, "History of the Ohio WCTU," 434–35; Sponholtz, "Politics of Temperance," 18; Coffey, "Political History," 298; Jackson, "Prohibition as an Issue in N.Y. Politics," 74; West, "Dry Crusade," 212; Putnam, "Prohibition Movement," 265; John E. Caswell, "The Prohibition Movement in Oregon, Part 2, 1904–1915," *Oregon Historical Quarterly* 40 (1939): 73–74; Blocker, *Retreat from Reform,* 216.

29. Renner, "Prohibition Comes to Missouri," 393–94; Clement E. Vose, *Constitutional Change: Amendment Politics and Supreme Court Litigation since 1900* (Lexington, Mass.: D. C. Heath, 1972), 84.

30. Kerr, *Organized for Prohibition,* chap. 7; Sponholtz, "Politics of Temperance."

31. Blocker, *Retreat from Reform,* 220–27.

32. Charles Merz, *The Dry Decade* (New York: Doubleday, Doran, 1931), 307–08.

33. Kerr, *Organized for Prohibition,* 148, 185–210; Jackson, "Prohibition as an Issue in N.Y. Politics," 120; Kaylor, "Prohibition Movement," 354.

34. Kerr, *Organized for Prohibition,* 180–84; Engelmann, "Old Saloon Days," 133–34.

35. *Annual Report of the Commissioner of Internal Revenue* (Washington, D.C.: U.S. Government Printing Office, 1900–1913); Rorabaugh, *Alcoholic Republic,* 232; Warburton, *Economic Results of Prohibition,* 114–15, 121–22; Benson Y. Landis, "Estimated Consumer Expenditures for Alcoholic Beverages in the United States, 1890–1943," *Quarterly Journal of Studies on Alcohol* 6 (June 1945): 93.

36. Warburton, *Economic Results of Prohibition,* 90; E. M. Jellinek, "Recent Trends in Alcoholism and in Alcohol Consumption," *Quarterly Journal of Studies on Alcohol* 8 (June 1947): 1–42.

37. Blocker, *Retreat from Reform,* 192–94, 205–10, 240–41; Benson, "American Workers," 254, 263–64; Benson, "'Sober Workmen': Late Nineteenth Century Enthusiasm for Temperance Reform among American Workers," paper presented at the annual meeting of the Organization of American Historians, New

Orleans, April 11–14, 1979; Green, "'Salesmen-Soldiers,'" 29; Lindberg, "Pastors, Prohibition and Politics"; Michael Karni, "Finnish Temperance and Its Clash with Emerging Socialism in Minnesota," in Michael Karni, ed., *Finnish Diaspora*, vol. 2, *United States* (Toronto: Multicultural History Society of Ontario, 1981), 169–72; Landis, "Estimated Consumer Expenditures," 93; Warburton, *Economic Results of Prohibition*, chap. 6.

38. Sinclair, *Age of Excess*, 119–21; Merz, *Dry Decade*, 25–42; Blocker, *Retreat from Reform*, 239–40.

39. Merz, *Dry Decade*, 307–08, 334; Kaylor, "Prohibition Movement," 325, 354; Kerr, *Organized for Prohibition*, 209n; Larry Engelmann, *Intemperance: The Lost War Against Liquor* (New York: Free Press, 1979), chap. 1; Whitaker, "History of the Ohio WCTU," 475, 478.

40. Blocker, *Retreat from Reform*, 239.

41. Warburton, *Economic Results of Prohibition*, 107, 142.

42. Ibid.; Rorabaugh, *Alcoholic Republic*, 232; John R. Meers, "The California Wine and Grape Industry and Prohibition," *California Historical Society Quarterly* 46 (1967): 19–32.

43. Warburton, *Economic Results of Prohibition*, 235, 237, 240–41, 255–56.

44. Quoted in David E. Kyvig, *Repealing National Prohibition* (Chicago and London: University of Chicago Press, 1979), 50.

45. Ibid., chaps. 3–5.

46. Quoted in ibid., 84.

47. Ibid., chap. 5.

48. Kerr, *Organized for Prohibition*, 213, 242–48; Steuart, *Wheeler*, 168; Norman H. Dohn, "The History of the Anti-Saloon League" (Ph.D. diss., Ohio State University, 1959), 233, 259; Stegh, "Wet and Dry Battles," 152; Kaylor, "Prohibition Movement," 5; Bader, *Prohibition in Kansas*, 209; Putnam, "Prohibition Movement," 349.

49. Harris, "Feminine and Class Identity," 72.

50. David E. Kyvig, "Women against Prohibition," *American Quarterly* 28 (1976): 465–82.

51. Kerr, *Organized for Prohibition*, 216, 226–31; Steuart, *Wheeler*; Ostrander, *Prohibition Movement in California*, 169.

52. Kerr, *Organized for Prohibition*, 215–20.

53. Ostrander, *Prohibition Movement in California*, 151.

54. Quoted in Engelmann, "O Whiskey," 627.

55. Ostrander, *Prohibition Movement in California*, 168.

56. Jellinek, "Recent Trends," 20; Warburton, *Economic Results*, 216–17; Milton Terris, "Epidemiology of Cirrhosis of the Liver: National Mortality Data," *American Journal of Public Health* 57 (December 1967): 2076–88; Carney Landis and Jane F. Cushman, "The Relation of National Prohibition to the Incidence of Mental Disease," *Quarterly Journal of Studies on Alcohol* 5 (March 1945): 527–34; J. C. Burnham, "New Perspectives on the Prohibition 'Experiment' of the

1920's," *Journal of Social History* 2 (Fall 1968): 60; E. H. L. Corwin and E. V. Cunningham, "History of Special Institutions for the Treatment of Alcohol Addiction," in *Institutional Facilities for the Treatment of Alcoholism*, Research report no. 7 (New York: Research Council on Problems of Alcohol, 1944), 19.

57. Quoted in Kyvig, *Repealing National Prohibition*, 114.

58. Ostrander, *Prohibition Movement in California*, 193; Kyvig, *Repealing National Prohibition*, 111–15.

59. Virginius Dabney, *Dry Messiah: The Life of Bishop Cannon* (New York: Alfred A. Knopf, 1949), chaps. 15–18; James Cannon, Jr., *Bishop Cannon's Own Story: Life as I Have Seen It*, ed. Richard L. Watson, Jr. (Durham: Duke University Press, 1955); Michael S. Patterson, "The Fall of a Bishop: James Cannon, Jr., *versus* Carter Glass, 1909–34," *Journal of Southern History* 39 (November 1973): 493–518.

60. Kyvig, *Repealing National Prohibition*, 147–68; Alan P. Grimes, *Democracy and the Amendments to the Constitution* (Lexington, Mass.: Lexington Books, 1978), 109–12.

61. Kyvig, *Repealing National Prohibition*, 171–74; Vose, *Constitutional Change*, chap. 5; Clement Vose, "Repeal as a Political Achievement," in David E. Kyvig, ed., *Law, Alcohol, and Order: Perspectives on National Prohibition* (Westport, Conn.: Greenwood Press, 1985), 97–121.

62. Kyvig, *Repealing National Prohibition*, chap. 9; Robert F. Zeidel, "Beer Returns to Cream City," *Milwaukee History* 4 (Spring 1981): 20–32.

63. Robin Room, "'A Reverence for Strong Drink': The Lost Generation and the Elevation of Alcohol in American Culture," *Journal of Studies on Alcohol* 45 (November 1984): 540–46.

Chapter Five

1. *Alcoholics Anonymous: The Story of How Many Thousands of Men and Women Have Recovered from Alcoholism*, 3d ed. (New York: Alcoholics Anonymous World Services, 1976), 180. Emphasis in original.

2. Ernest Kurtz, *Not-God: A History of Alcoholics Anonymous* (Center City, Minn.: Hazelden Educational Services, 1979), chap. 1; Robert Thomsen, *Bill W.* (New York, Evanston, Ill., San Francisco, and London: Harper & Row, 1975).

3. David Fogarty, "From Saloon to Supermarket: Packaged Beer and the Reshaping of the U.S. Brewing Industry," *Contemporary Drug Problems* 12 (Winter 1985): 541–92.

4. Quoted in Harry Gene Levine, "The Birth of American Alcohol Control: Prohibition, the Power Elite, and the Problem of Lawlessness," *Contemporary Drug Problems* 12 (Spring 1985): 87.

5. Ibid.

6. Ibid.; Fogarty, "From Saloon to Supermarket"; Kyvig, *Repealing*

National Prohibition, 187–89; Leonard V. Harrison and Elizabeth Laine, *After Repeal: A Study of Liquor Control Administration* (New York and London: Harper & Bros., 1936), 231–48; Monkkonen, "A Disorderly People?"; Landis, "Estimated Consumer Expenditures," 93; U.S. Bureau of the Census, *Historical Statistics of the United States, Colonial Times to 1970* (Washington, D.C.: U.S. Government Printing Office, 1975), 317, 1107, 1129.

7. Levine, "Birth of American Alcohol Control"; Fogarty, "From Saloon to Supermarket"; Downard, *Dictionary of the History of the American Brewing and Distilling Industries,* 234–35, 243; Cochran, *Pabst Brewing Company,* 369.

8. Cochran, *Pabst Brewing Company,* 386; Rorabaugh, *Alcoholic Republic,* 232; Joseph R. Gusfield, "Prohibition: The Impact of Political Utopianism," in John Braeman, Robert Bremner, and David Brody, eds., *Change and Continuity in Twentieth Century America* (Columbus: Ohio State University Press, 1968), 286.

9. Dean R. Gerstein, "Alcohol Use and Consequences," in Mark H. Moore and Dean R. Gerstein, eds., *Alcohol and Public Policy: Beyond the Shadow of Prohibition* (Washington, D.C.: National Academy Press, 1981), 194, 202; Robin Room, "Region and Urbanization as Factors in Drinking Practices and Problems," in Benjamin Kissin and Henry Begleiter, eds., *The Biology of Alcoholism, vol. 6, The Pathogenesis of Alcoholism: Psychosocial Factors* (New York: Plenum Press, 1983), 579.

10. Jay L. Rubin, "The Wet War: American Liquor Control, 1941–45," in Blocker, ed., *Alcohol, Reform and Society,* 235–58.

11. Kurtz, *Not-God,* 48.

12. Ibid., 48–50.

13. Quoted in Ernest Kurtz, "Why A.A. Works: The Intellectual Significance of Alcoholics Anonymous," *Journal of Studies on Alcohol* 43 (January 1982): 45–46.

14. Kurtz, *Not-God,* 43–52.

15. Quoted in Leonard U. Blumberg, "The Ideology of a Therapeutic Social Movement: Alcoholics Anonymous," *Journal of Studies on Alcohol* 38 (November 1977): 2125.

16. Kurtz, *Not-God,* 15–20; Blumberg, "Ideology of a Therapeutic Social Movement," 2122–30; Barry Leach and John L. Norris, "Factors in the Development of Alcoholics Anonymous (A.A.)," in Benjamin Kissin and Henry Begleiter, eds., *The Biology of Alcoholism,* vol. 5, *Treatment and Rehabilitation of the Chronic Alcoholic* (New York: Plenum Press, 1977), 458–59.

17. Bruce H. Johnson, "The Alcoholism Movement in America: A Study in Cultural Innovation" (Ph.D. diss., University of Illinois at Urbana-Champaign, 1973), 287; Kurtz, *Not-God,* 67–77; Leach and Norris, "Factors," 510–11.

18. Leach and Norris, "Factors," 510–11; Kurtz, *Not-God,* 85-87, chap. 5; Johnson, "Alcoholism Movement," 287.

19. Kurtz, *Not-God,* 86–88, 95–96; Leach and Norris, "Factors," 467 (quotation).

20. Quoted in Leach and Norris, "Factors," 466.

21. Ibid., 466–67, 469, 515.

22. Ibid., 471–79; Walter B. Clark and Lorraine Midanik, "Alcohol Use and Alcohol Problems among U.S. Adults: Results of the 1979 National Survey," in *Alcohol Consumption and Related Problems,* Alcohol and Health Monograph no. 1 (Washington, D.C.: U.S. Government Printing Office, 1982), 3–52; Peter Park, "Social-Class Factors in Alcoholism," in Kissin and Begleiter, eds., *The Biology of Alcoholism,* 6:365–404.

23. Dan E. Beauchamp, *Beyond Alcoholism: Alcohol and Public Health Policy* (Philadelphia: Temple University Press, 1980), 56; Leach and Norris, "Factors," 451, 459, 497–99.

24. See chapter 3 above; Mark Edward Lender, "Jellinek's Typology of Alcoholism: Some Historical Antecedents," *Journal of Studies on Alcohol* 40 (May 1979): 361–75.

25. Johnson, "Alcoholism Movement," 223–38.

26. Ibid., 378–79; Lender, *Dictionary of Temp. Biography,* 257–59.

27. Lender, "Jellinek's Typology."

28. Lender, *Dictionary of Temp. Biography,* 258.

29. Johnson, "Alcoholism Movement," 232–33, 240, 252; Lender, *Dictionary of Temp. Biography,* 207–08.

30. Quoted in Herbert Fingarettc, "Philosophical and Legal Aspects of the Disease Concept of Alcoholism," in Reginald G. Smart et al., eds., *Research Advances in Alcohol and Drug Problems,* vol. 7 (New York and London: Plenum Press, 1983), 4.

31. Johnson, "Alcoholism Movement," 257–58; Robin Room, "Sociological Aspects of the Disease Concept of Alcoholism," in Smart et al., eds., *Research Advances in Alcohol and Drug Problems,* 7:47–91; Fingarette, "Philosophical and Legal Aspects," 1–45; Thomas D. Watts, "The Uneasy Triumph of a Concept: The 'Disease' Conception of Alcoholism," *Journal of Drug Issues* 11 (Fall 1981): 451–60.

32. Johnson, "Alcoholism Movement," 239–58.

33. Quoted in Kurtz, *Not-God,* 118.

34. Johnson, "Alcoholism Movement," 259–73, 285–99; Kurtz, *Not-God,* 117–18; Lender, *Dictionary of Temp. Biography,* 322–23.

35. Johnson, "Alcoholism Movement," 419; Jay L. Rubin, "Shifting Perspectives on the Alcoholism Treatment Movement, 1940–1955," *Journal of Studies on Alcohol* 40 (May 1979): 376–86; Patricia Morgan, "The State as Mediator: Alcohol Problem Management in the Postwar Period," *Contemporary Drug Problems* 9 (Spring 1980): 115–16.

36. Johnson, "Alcoholism Movement," 127–35, 336–49.

37. Quoted in ibid., 91.

38. Rubin, "Wet War"; Johnson, "Alcoholism Movement," 90–92, 283–85, 324–34.

39. Steven Goldberg, "Putting Science in the Constitution: The Prohibition Experience," in Kyvig, ed., *Law, Alcohol, and Order,* 21–34.

40. Timberlake, *Prohibition and the Progressive Movement,* 47; Kyvig,

pealing National Prohibition, 33–34; Johnson, "Alcoholism Movement," 94–99, 314–22.

41. Room, "Sociological Aspects," 69–70.

42. Johnson, "Alcoholism Movement," 99–103, 276–81, 308–09; Morgan, "State as Mediator," 115–16; Constance M. Weisner, "The Alcohol Treatment System and Social Control: A Study in Institutional Change," *Journal of Drug Issues* 13 (Winter 1983): 119–20.

43. Quoted in Johnson, "Alcoholism Movement," 104.

44. Ibid., 103–04, 229–30.

45. Ibid., 103–12, 349–76; Gerstein, "Alcohol Use and Consequences," 218.

46. Weisner, "Alcohol Treatment System," 119–20; Norman R. Kurtz and Marilyn Regier, "The Uniform Alcoholism and Intoxication Treatment Act: The Compromising Process of Social Policy Formation," *Journal of Studies on Alcohol* 36 (November 1975): 1421–41.

47. Carol D. S. Surles, "Historical Development of Alcoholism Control Programs in Industry from 1940–1978" (D. Ed. diss., University of Michigan, 1978), 23, 57–58, 79; Harrison M. Trice and Mona Schonbrunn, "A History of Job-Based Alcoholism Programs: 1900–1955," *Journal of Drug Issues* 11 (Spring 1981): 171–98.

48. NIAAA, *Third Special Report to the U.S. Congress on Alcohol and Health* (Washington, D.C.: U.S. Government Printing Office, 1978), 78–79; Surles, "Historical Development," 28, 65.

49. Richard Edwards, *Contested Terrain: The Transformation of the Workplace in the Twentieth Century* (New York: Basic Books, 1979); NIAAA, *Third Special Report,* 79.

50. Johnson, "Alcoholism Movement," 310–13, 323–24, 327–28.

51. Ibid., 336–49; Beauchamp, *Beyond Alcoholism,* chap. 2; Robin Room, "Ambivalence as a Sociological Explanation: The Case of Cultural Explanations of Alcohol Problems," *American Sociological Review* 41 (December 1976): 1047–65; Harry Gene Levine, "What Is an Alcohol-Related Problem? (Or, What Are People Talking about When They Refer to Alcohol Problems?)," *Journal of Drug Issues* 14 (Winter 1984): 49–54.

52. Beauchamp, *Beyond Alcoholism,* chap. 7; Room, "Sociological Aspects," 62; Levine, "What Is an Alcohol-Related Problem?"; Benjamin Kissin, "The Disease Concept of Alcoholism," in Smart et al., eds., *Research Advances in Alcohol and Drug Problems,* 7:94; Carolyn Wiener, *The Politics of Alcoholism: Building an Arena around a Social Problem* (New Brunswick, N.J., and London: Transaction Books, 1981), chap. 7; Thomas D. Watts, "Three Traditions in Social Thought on Alcoholism," *International Journal of the Addictions* 17 (1982): 1231–39; Paul C. Whitehead and Jan Simpkins, "Occupational Factors in Alcoholism," in Kissin and Begleiter, eds., *The Biology of Alcoholism,* 6:486; NIAAA, *Third Special Report,* chap. 12; "Report of the Panel," in Moore and Gerstein, eds., *Alcohol and Public Policy,* 3–124.

53. Albert E. Wilkerson, Jr., "A History of the Concept of Alcoholism as a Disease" (D.S.W. diss., University of Pennsylvania, 1966), 2; Wiener, *Politics of Alcoholism,* 222; Weisner, "Alcohol Treatment System," 119–20; Beauchamp, *Beyond Alcoholism,* chap. 13; Melvyn Kalb and Morton S. Propper, "The Future of Alcohology: Craft or Science?" *American Journal of Psychiatry* 133 (June 1976): 641–45; R. E. Tournier, "Alcoholics Anonymous as Treatment and as Ideology," *Journal of Studies on Alcohol* 40 (March 1979): 230–39; Ernest Kurtz and Linda Farris Kurtz, "The Social Thought of Alcoholics," *Journal of Drug Issues* 15 (Winter 1985): 119–34.

54. Rorabaugh, *Alcoholic Republic,* 232–33.

55. Gerstein, "Alcohol Use and Consequences."

56. Weisner, "Alcohol Treatment System"; Room, "Sociological Aspects," 79.

57. Room, "Sociological Aspects,"; Kissin, "Disease Concept"; Lender and Martin, *Drinking in America,* chap. 5.

Bibliographic Essay

Temperance reform in the United States is the subject of a large and growing literature. Two previous synoptic works have given this scholarship much of its direction. Historians of temperance have reason to be grateful that one of the first sustained treatments of their topic attained the theoretical clarity found in *Symbolic Crusade* (Urbana: University of Illinois Press, 1963) by sociologist Joseph Gusfield. Gusfield's argument that temperance reform provided a channel for expression of class, ethnic, religious, and urban-rural conflicts was challenged by Norman Clark, *Deliver Us from Evil* (New York: W.W. Norton, 1976), which eloquently set forth the view that temperance reform grew out of the impact of drinking problems upon an emerging bourgeois sensibility. Clark also pointed to the actual rather than symbolic success of national Prohibition in reducing consumption and alcoholic damage, a point put forward by John Burnham, "New Perspectives on the Prohibition 'Experiment' of the 1920s," *Journal of Social History* (1968). The findings of much recent research are reflected in a very helpful reference tool, Mark Lender's *Dictionary of American Temperance Biography* (Westport, Conn.: Greenwood Press, 1984).

Norman Clark's emphasis on variations in drinking behavior in explaining temperance reform points to the importance of understanding the history of the alcoholic beverage industry. Two books—one old, one new—are indispensable to that task: Thomas Cochran, *The Pabst Brewing Company* (New York: New York University Press, 1948), and Perry Duis, *The Saloon: Public Drinking in Chicago and Boston, 1880–1920* (Urbana: University of Illinois Press, 1983). Stanley Baron, *Brewed in America* (Boston: Little, Brown, 1962) is useful for the brewing industry, but unfortunately no counterpart study is available for either distilling or wine making. Until the distilling industry receives sustained scholarly treatment, much information may be found in William Downard, *Dictionary of the History of the American Brewing and Distilling Industries* (Westport, Conn.: Greenwood Press, 1980). The Western saloon is treated capably in Thomas Noel, *The City and the Saloon: Denver, 1858–1916* (Lincoln: University of Nebraska Press, 1982), and in Elliott West, *The Saloon on the Rocky Mountain*

Mining Frontier (Lincoln: University of Nebraska Press, 1979); the saloon in a midwestern state is examined in Larry Engelmann, "Old Saloon Days in Michigan," *Michigan History* (1977). A pioneering and very suggestive study of the brewing industry since Repeal is David Fogarty, "From Saloon to Supermarket," *Contemporary Drug Problems* (1985). The neglected topic of relations between the liquor industry and government is treated at the federal level for the late nineteenth century in Amy Mittelman, "The Politics of Alcohol Production" (Ph.D. diss., Columbia University, 1986).

In *Drinking in America,* rev. ed. (New York: Free Press, 1987), Mark Lender and James Martin present an overview of the history of drinking preferences and behavior. Much work remains to be done in understanding variations in drinking behavior between groups and over time. A good starting point and benchmark for research into drinking has been provided by W. J. Rorabaugh, *The Alcoholic Republic* (New York: Oxford University Press, 1979), a study of aggregate consumption and drinking practices before 1840. A most insightful analysis of drinking patterns among working-class and upper-class men is in Leonard Ellis, "Men among Men: An Exploration of All-Male Relationships in Victorian America" (Ph.D. diss., Columbia University, 1982). Robin Room, "Cultural Contingencies of Alcoholism," *Journal of Health and Social Behavior* (1968) is one of the very few historical studies of drinking patterns among subgroups of the American population.

Basic to understanding the origins and early years of temperance reform is Ian Tyrrell, *Sobering Up: From Temperance to Prohibition in Antebellum America, 1800–1860* (Westport, Conn.: Greenwood Press, 1979). This rich and subtle work rewards close scrutiny of its arguments. Abundant additional information on drinking, drinkers, law enforcement, temperance reform, and reformers may be found in a careful state study, Robert Hampel, *Temperance and Prohibition in Massachusetts, 1813–1852* (Ann Arbor, Mich.: UMI Research Press, 1982). Tyrrell's interpretation has been challenged at some points and supplemented at others by an excellent local case study of temperance reform in Schenectady, New York, during the 1820s and 1830s: Carol Steinsapir, "The Ante-Bellum Total Abstinence Movement at the Local Level" (Ph.D. diss., Rutgers University, 1983). The arguments of *Sobering Up* have been extended across the gender line and across the Mason-Dixon line in two important articles by Ian Tyrrell, "Women and Temperance in Antebellum American, 1830–1860," *Civil War History* (1982), and "Drink and Temperance in the Antebellum South," *Journal of Southern History* (1982). Jed Dannenbaum, *Drink and Disorder* (Urbana: University of Illinois Press, 1984), a case study of temperance reform in Cincinnati during the middle of the nineteenth century, provides a good analysis of local conflict over prohibition in the 1850s.

No traveler in the country of temperance studies should miss the imaginative and forcefully argued work of sociologist Harry Levine, which has been presented thus far in a large number of articles. A good place to start is the widely cited essay, "The Discovery of Addiction," *Journal of Studies on Alcohol* (1978). Other stimulating essays include "Temperance and Women in 19th Century United States," in O. Kalant, ed., *Research Advances in Alcohol and Drug Problems,* vol. 5 (New York: Plenum Press, 1980), and "The Birth of American Alcohol Control," *Contemporary Drug Problems* (1985). For an attempt to deflate bureaucratic rhetoric, see Levine's "What Is an Alcohol-Related Problem?" *Journal of Drug Issues* (1984).

Frances Willard and her Woman's Christian Temperance Union are described in Ruth Bordin, *Woman and Temperance* (Philadelphia: Temple University Press, 1981) and, by the same author, *Frances Willard* (Chapel Hill: University of North Carolina Press, 1986), and in the latter chapters of Barbara Epstein, *The Politics of Domesticity* (Middletown, Conn.: Wesleyan University Press, 1981). Jack Blocker, *"Give to the Winds Thy Fears"* (Westport, Conn.: Greenwood Press, 1985), describes and analyzes the Women's Temperance Crusade of 1873–74 at the national, state (Ohio), and local (Washington Court House, Ohio) levels. A major lack in temperance history is studies of the WCTU after Willard's death in 1898.

Although not all states have been treated, many studies have been written of temperance movements or conflicts over prohibition in individual states, most commonly for the period from the Civil War to the repeal of national Prohibition. Among the best are Gilman Ostrander, *The Prohibition Movement in California* (Berkeley: University of California Press, 1957); Norman Clark, *The Dry Years: Prohibition and Social Change in Washington* (Seattle: University of Washington Press, 1965); Larry Engelmann, "O Whiskey: The History of Prohibition in Michigan" (Ph.D. diss., University of Michigan, 1971); and Robert Bader, *Prohibition in Kansas* (Lawrence: University Press of Kansas, 1986). Local studies, however, are few for this period. At the national level, Jack Blocker treats the leadership transition from the Prohibition party to the Anti-Saloon League in *Retreat from Reform* (Westport, Conn.: Greenwood Press, 1976); Ronald Benson examines the attitudes of workers and their leaders in "American Workers and Temperance Reform" (Ph.D. diss., University of Notre Dame, 1974); James Timberlake discusses links between two sets of reforms and reformers in *Prohibition and the Progressive Movement* (Cambridge: Harvard University Press, 1963); Austin Kerr traces the evolution of the Anti-Saloon League and its liquor-industry opposition in *Organized for Prohibition* (New Haven: Yale University Press, 1985); and Andrew Sinclair describes the conflict over national Prohibition in a much criticized but still useful work, *Prohibition: The Era of Excess* (New York: Harper and Row, 1962). David Kyvig presents a history of the organized opposition to the Eighteenth Amendment in *Repealing National Prohibition* (Chicago: University of Chicago Press, 1979), and Leslie Stegh provides a useful case study of wet politics in "Wet and Dry Battles in the Cradle State of Prohibition" (Ph.D. diss., Kent State University, 1975). Clark Warburton, *The Economic Results of Prohibition* (New York: Columbia University Press, 1932), is still invaluable on the effects of the Eighteenth Amendment and the Volstead Act.

The best place to begin a study of Alcoholics Anonymous is Ernest Kurtz, *Not-God* (Center City, Minn.: Hazelden, 1979), a strong defense of the AA approach. Also useful is a long article, Barry Leach and John Norris, "Factors in the Development of Alcoholics Anonymous (A.A.)," in Benjamin Kissin and Henry Begleiter, eds., *The Biology of Alcoholism,* vol. 5, *Treatment and Rehabilitation of the Chronic Alcoholic* (New York: Plenum Press, 1977), which is also favorable to AA. The most complete history of the alcoholism coalition may be found in a dissertation in sociology, Bruce Johnson, "The Alcoholism Movement in America" (University of Illinois at Urbana-Champaign, 1973).

Index